The Theory and Practice of Grading Writing

Edited by
FRANCES ZAK
CHRISTOPHER C. WEAVER

The Theory and Practice of Grading Writing

Problems and Possibilities

STATE UNIVERSITY OF NEW YORK PRESS

Published by
State University of New York Press, Albany

Printed in the United States of America

For information, address State University of New York Press,
State University Plaza, Albany, NY 12246

Production design by David Ford
Marketing by Anne M. Valentine

Library of Congress Cataloging-in-Publication Data

The theory and practice of grading writing : problems and
possibilities / edited by Frances Zak, Christopher C. Weaver.
p. cm.
Includes bibliographical references and index.
ISBN 0-7914-3669-1 (hardcover : alk. paper). — ISBN 0-7914-3670-5
(pbk. : alk. paper)
1. English language—Rhetoric—Study and teaching. 2. English language—Rhetoric—Study and teaching—Theory, etc. 3. English language—Rhetoric—Ability testing. 4. Grading and marking (Students) I. Zak, Frances, 1939– . II. Weaver, Christopher C., 1962–
PE1404.T478 1998
808′.042′07—dc21

97–20416
CIP

10 9 8 7 6 5 4 3 2 1

to Pat Belanoff

Contents

Pat Belanoff

Foreword

Grading is the bottom line. As teachers, we can talk about what we do, why we do what we do, how we assign and respond to writing, how we can collaborate better with others, whether we should have program and department guidelines and syllabi, what might be the value of new designs for assessment—but, at the end, almost all of us have to put letters on grade sheets, "pass" and "fail" or assigned letter grades on portfolios, or conclude our responses with that all-powerful grade. And regardless of how much we may deplore the weight students give to those letters, we cannot get around their power.

The paradox here is that, in comparison to the plethora of words about assessment, we do not write much about actual grading. An abundance of articles addressing assessment from a variety of positions have been written over the past years (I myself have contributed to that stream), but grading itself remains (to quote myself) the dirty little thing we do in our closets.

I see two reasons for this situation. First, the subject itself is difficult. Is there really a right way to do it? Is it possible to uncover, discover, invent, a grading system which all can accept as flawless? I suspect there are many within the profession who believe there can be such a system and who seek it. I am not one of those. Still, I see no harm (and possibly some good) in such a search provided its proponents do not dictatorially enforce whatever they devise. I recall a graduate-student discussion of grading at a pre-semester meeting in graduate school when one of the participants announced that she knew what an "A" was and did not need to collaborate with others in grading. I marveled at the time, but thought that perhaps it was my inexperience that dictated my need for such talk, that I would in time outgrow that need. But I recognize now that both of us were inexperienced; continued experience has taught me—and continues to teach me—how very complex the whole subject is. What I have discovered is that the more experienced a teacher is, the more likely she or he is to acknowledge puzzlement and the way in which it implicates all aspects of the teaching of writing. Let me be even more generalizing and say that thoughtful, committed discussions about grading inevitably encompass all aspects of literacy.

The second reason I see for the lack of direct address of grading is that grading represents the most unquestioned power any of us have as teachers. We reserve this space for ourselves. The discipline of English Studies (or whatever name one gives to what used to be called "English") is fragmenting. Interpretive acts are viewed as culturally constructed; we are told that our culture writes us and our interpretations. Our authority as readers of canonical texts is thus undermined, and many of us are not familiar with the marginalized texts our own graduate students study. Our departments control our curriculum, the size of our classes, when we retire, whom we work with, what kinds of external assessment both we and our students are subject to, how much of a raise we get, and who is in our classes. But, unless harassment of some sort can be proven, no one questions our semester grades or our grades on student papers. Do we avoid writing about this area because it represents our final bastion? Our final area of self-determination?

Our myopia on the subject of grading allows us not to see the relevance of current theory. Many of our fellow practitioners and theorists (I too am guilty here in my unguarded moments) are more than willing to posit the difficulties of text interpretation, the ways in which our cultural environment conditions such interpretations, and—in a larger sense—the ways in which our culture writes us. But, ironically, we hold onto our right to assign student grades as totally self-determined creators of text—for, after all, a grade is a text. In truth, I find the discipline a bit hypocritical here—our theories of interpretation are lauded when applied to "high" literary texts and ignored when grading "low" student texts. We no longer believe in the inspired creative writer who waits for the touch of the muse, but we do seem to believe in a muse of grading who inspires us to inscribe the "right" letter on student papers and portfolios and on semester grade sheets. We cannot continue to enact this split—particularly as our student bodies become more and more diverse and culturally differentiated.

The editors of this collection and those who have contributed to it are breaking new ground—devoting themselves to not avoiding the pragmatic aspects of grading and the ways in which those interact with theory. I applaud them all. We need to find ways to validate our doubts about grading, to acknowledge those doubts to the public, and to our colleagues in other fields. And we need to find ways to make it work better for us and for our students since it is not likely to go away.

But I applaud this collection for another reason. The increasing growth of the push for standardized testing in this country at all levels of education reflects a deep distrust of local educational systems and teachers. Floating in the air among parents, legislators, educators, and administrators is some largely unexamined faith that if only our nation could create the perfect testing system, learning would improve and the problems of our schools would evaporate. Our faith encourages us to seek a new Eden, a new paradise, in which all students achieve up to and even beyond their potential—and many advocate a national testing system as the path to this Eden. The individual classroom teacher would become a mere supplement to the process.

Our discipline cannot claim innocence in this outcome. For too long, we have not been open about the truths uncovered in our research, which include the following fairly unpleasant ideas: all As are not equal, teachers do not agree on grades, teachers do not even agree on what is good writing. We have not shared these ideas with those outside our classrooms largely because we are defensive about them. We must open up channels of communication with all segments of the public and with our colleagues in other disciplines and share with them what we know about grading and assessment—and we must do that without relying on what my grandmother called "high-falutin' language." If we do not begin this conversation, we may well find that standardized assessment has taken over our classroom and made what we do there valuable only as it helps to prepare students for the important judgments which occur outside those classrooms. The longer we refuse to acknowledge to everyone that absolute standards are a myth and timidly avoid acknowledging the variability of our grades, the stronger the push will be for creating a national test.

Am I saying that the topic of grading is a complete morass? That we can never agree on anything? Not exactly. But I am saying that the conversation on grading, once entered into, will never end. And this is a good thing for all of us because it guarantees that we will never be content to retreat into our closet and commune with our inner selves as we inscribe those powerful letters on our students' work. The ongoing conversation will keep us all honest, for it is the conversation which is most likely to result in grades useful to our students. We can agree on the purpose served by such conversations and the purposes and value of grades, and we can share that agreement with the public at large.

This book opens a discussion, an honest discussion on actual grading—one which all of us involved hope will continue as long as teachers have to make judgments about students' work.

Frances Zak
Christopher C. Weaver

Preface

The two of us spent most of the last two years working on this book on different coasts: Chris in Juneau, Alaska and Fran in Port Jefferson, New York. We communicated by fax, phone, and e-mail, all the while negotiating a four hour time difference. But when we came together in July of 1996 at Fran's kitchen table to put the finishing touches on the manuscript and to write this introduction, we realized something for the first time: when family, friends or colleagues had asked either of us what our book was about, we both found ourselves vaguely embarrassed to tell them we were working on a book about the grading of writing. It was the word "grading" which felt embarrassingly unprofessional, unacademic, unscholarly, and we found ourselves saying the book was about assessment or evaluation of writing—concepts that sounded somehow more academically respectable. Sitting at the kitchen table later and laughing about our common experience, we realized it was important to acknowledge that the reticence we felt personally was also part of the professional landscape in which we work; that the deep ambivalence we were feeling was part of a larger schizophrenia in the field of composition and rhetoric, and about the subject of grading and its connection to the teaching of writing.

We think it is worthwhile, then, at the outset, to point out why it is that we have deliberately chosen to use the word "grading" in our title. If this word does not sound "academic" enough for the title of a serious scholarly book, then we hope this fact emphasizes a point we wish to make here: in the scholarly writing of our discipline, we often deliberately avoid this term.

This is not to say that we are, as a profession, unconcerned with our own evaluative practices, and a large body of literature on "evaluation" will attest to that. However, whether dealing with writing as "product" or "process," none of the assessment strategies we know of addresses the grading of individual student papers in the writing classroom, the focus of this book; these strategies mandate our thinking in different ways. Most of the conversation and literature on evaluation is theoretical and centers on the problems of what constitutes good writing or writing improvement and how to demonstrate, describe, and measure it. The conversation and the literature stops short before it reaches the problem of how to connect evaluation theory to the classroom practice of grading.

What makes our lack of academic interest in grading even stranger is that it is set against an abundance of informal discussion of the subject in the everyday lives of writing teachers. Nick Carbone and Margaret Daisley begin their chapter, "Grading as a Rhetorical Construct" by noting how talk about grading "percolates at the end of every semester." "Such talk," they write, "permeates the air of our hallways and offices, hangs in the glances and questions of students in our classrooms, and becomes a long and sustained conversational thread in our electronic discussion groups." How is it possible that grading, so much a part of our institutional lives, plays such a slight role in our scholarship? In our avoidance of the term "grading," have we created a split between the two roles most of us play in our professional lives?

In their chapter on the literature of grading, Bruce Speck and Tammy Jones take compositionists to task for using terms such as assessment, evaluation, and grading interchangeably. Speck and Jones maintain that these terms have been conflated and misused to the point where they have virtually no meaning. It is significant, we think, that while "evaluation" and "assessment" might be used to apply to almost any enterprise, "grading" is exclusively connected to "schooling." Evaluation and assessment can easily be connected with the idea of scholarship, as bold, rigorous, and probing, while grading connotes a system of reward and punishment, even remediation, perhaps more associated with the roles of secondary school teachers than college professors. Does this conflation of terms suggest that the profession itself is self-conscious or uncomfortable talking about the grading of writing?

Perhaps the answer resides in our profound uneasiness with the various aspects of our professional identities and with a reluctance to confront the disjunction between them. Viewed in this light, the absence of grading from our professional discussions makes it seem very much as though we are trying to use our scholarly pursuits to escape from the conflicts of our institutional lives. We may be reticent to write about grading because it seems so untheoretical and pedestrian, unworthy of our professional time and energy. In a discipline that has only recently elevated itself to academic respectability and has yet to earn the respect of many of our literature colleagues, such a possibility is not easily dismissed.

Another conflict may lie between our roles as classroom teachers and our obligations as institutional record-keepers. We may identify with the voice in the dialogue between Kathleen Blake Yancey and Brian Huot that is repelled by grading "because it has so little to do with my ideas about teaching and the theory of language which informs my teaching." Or, we may feel that grading puts us in the uncomfortable position of having to reconcile our authority over students with our desire to empower them. In a discipline where many of us are striving to create more egalitarian, student-centered classrooms, the need to grade students—foregrounding whatever differences grades may imply to their multiple readers—may be something of an embarrassment.

Part of this project, we realized, was to confront our uneasiness, both professional and personal. The goal of this book is to face these conflicts and discomforts and to open a discussion aimed at integrating scholarly concern with pragmatic necessity: bringing our hallway and on-line discussions into our academic writing and giving the former the power and authority of theory and scholarship.

Whatever our conflicts, compositionists cannot for much longer afford ourselves the luxury of avoiding the grading issue. For while grading has been absent from our professional conversations, it has become an important topic in the culture at large. We live in a society that already distrusts academics—which complains about our tenure protection and claims we are havens for liberals and "cultural elites." If compositionists do not make the case for systems of grading that support our "liberal" process-based pedagogies, we are likely to see them undermined by social conservatives, a process that has, to some extent, already begun.

Witness, for example, the language of an editorial in the usually liberal *New York Times* ("Making the Grades," June 5, 1994), attacking grade inflation in American colleges and universities.[1] The editors equate our systems of grading with moral laxity. The language is steeped in moral outrage and righteous indignation: teachers and administrators are accused of having "promiscuous" grading systems, with "permissive" grading practices. The editors claim that "rampant grade inflation" has "destroyed the idea of merit" and undermined the value of "honest toil." They conclude by asserting that we have neglected our responsibilities as "guardians" of "traditional values." Our tendency within the discipline of composition and rhetoric may be to dismiss or even to ridicule such attacks. We believe that we do so at our peril.

If we do not demonstrate concern and if we do not foster conversations about the grading of writing among ourselves and in the larger culture, we may see our pedagogies undermined by legislators' demands for standardization in the name of "accountability." We hope this book will further the conversations which have only recently begun in the profession.

The writers in this collection often disagree with each other about how we should address these problems and about what pedagogies to follow; however, their work rests on a common theoretical assumption: the movement of our discipline to a process model of language. None of the essays here argues for the justification of this model; instead, the authors explore the issues and problems that have emerged as our ideas about grading have lagged behind and have been challenged by our beliefs about writing as a process.

Our agreement about our need to view writing as a process rather than a product is particularly remarkable because it holds up in the face of intense disagreement over the nature of that process—whether, for instance, it is best understood as an author's internal process of discovery or as a community's external process of establishing discourse conventions. Both sides of this debate (as well as many who claim positions in between) agree on the need to establish teaching practices which foster students' awareness of the process through which writing is produced rather than solely on the features of that writing. However, after all the definition, description, and discussion, none of the ideologies which have proliferated in the last thirty years—from expressivism to social construction—have explored the real world of grading papers. It is the position of the authors in this collection and of the editors that such pedagogies are worth little unless we are certain that our systems of grading support them.

Each of the book's five sections considers grading within a particular context of our professional lives. We begin Part I with a reexamination of the discipline's attitudes and assumptions about grading and close, in Part V, with a call for new grading strategies. The intervening sections consider how grades shape and are shaped by teachers, students, and the institutions in which we interact.

The authors in Part I reveal our disciplinary ambivalence about grading and examine some of the contradictions which make the subject problematic. Richard Boyd's chapter provides a historical context for understanding the formation and agendas of grading systems established in the nineteenth century, which exist in comparable forms today. Bruce Speck and Tammy Jones focus their chapter on the literature of grading and find that compositionists have sidestepped the issue almost entirely. The claims in Bruce Maylath's chapter follow the conclusions drawn by Boyd, Speck, and Jones. Maylath points to a growing body of research that foregrounds the contradictions between what writing instructors say they do and what they actually do.

In Part II, the writers explore how grades determine our roles and our identities as teachers in ways that are often at odds with our goals. In a multi-vocal email dialogue, Kathleen Blake Yancey and Brian Huot examine how grades construct us and our authority as teachers, and propose sharing that authority by involving students in discussions about grading. Michael Bernard-Donals reconsiders a seminal article in the literature of grading, Peter Elbow's "Ranking, Evaluating, and Liking," and questions Elbow's contention that a teacher can ever escape from his authority as a grader into the haven of "evaluation-free zones." His chapter is followed by an exchange of letters in which he and Elbow elaborate on their positions.

The writers in Part III question the assumptions we make about the ways in which students understand and misunderstand the meaning of grades. These chapters reach some unsettling conclusions about our tendency to misjudge students' responses to grades and about their tendency to reject the role certain strategies play in "liberating and empowering" them, suggesting that students are both more and less sophisticated at interpreting grades than we think. Nick Carbone and Margaret Daisley examine the concept of letter grades as signifiers and find that the message sent is rarely the message received. Stephen VanderStaay attempts to employ grades as facilitators rather than evaluators, only to reach the disturbing conclusion that students do not want grades to play this role.

Part IV considers how the institutions in which we teach exert subtle and sometimes unacknowledged pressures on the ways we grade students' writing. The writers in this section use the discrepancy between traditional grading practices and current theory as a point of departure from which to open a discussion about the tensions inherent in our instructional and institutional roles. Pauline Uchmanowicz discusses her inability to avoid the influence that institutional contexts exert on her identity as a grader and examines the political and social significance of these influences. Maureen Neal considers institutional pressures on writing programs that may lead to the misuse of portfolios as evaluative tools and to a backlash against the entire portfolio movement.

Finally, in Part V, several contributors attempt to resolve in their classroom practices some of the conflicting roles and impulses examined in the previous sections. These following chapters suggest alternative grading strategies that are more consistent with modern discourse theory and give voice to the teachers who have begun to articulate the dissonance and to analyze and describe the problem as well as to suggest solutions. Christopher Weaver proposes a system which shifts the authority of the teacher from students' papers to their process writing. In Irene Papoulis' discussion of the influences of gender on grading, she shifts the usual focus on the gender of the grader to a consideration of the gendered "method." Cherryl

Smith and Angus Dunstan explore ways to avoid grading altogether, or at least to avoid attaching grades to writing. And finally, Peter Elbow asserts that "grading" and "not grading" are false choices and that teachers have more power than we think to make small but important changes within conventional grading systems.

Our intent in this section is not to provide readers with some formula for classroom success, but to add to the book's conversation about our theoretical assumptions about grading and the practices that grow out of them. Although we hope these essays end the book on a hopeful note, the writers in this section present their accounts not as universal solutions but as carefully contextualized responses to theoretical concerns.

We conclude the collection with a dialogue among several of our contributors on the volatile and timely issue of grade inflation. And finally, we believe this volume would not be complete without the voices of our students, talking about their feelings and experiences with grades and grading. Excerpts from comments made by students in composition classes at the State University of New York at Stony Brook, the University of Alaska Southeast, the University of Massachusetts at Amherst, and the University of Louisville precede each of the book's five sections.

We hope that readers not only become involved with the ideas in these chapters, but hear the voices of our contributors and extend those voices into conversations of their own: in the hallways with colleagues, in sessions at professional conferences, in classrooms with students, and in research and written scholarship. Finally, we hope the voices of teachers find a way to connect to conversations already taking place within the public sector and find a way to be heard by administrators, politicians, the parents and families of our students, and by the public at large.

As grades are read and interpreted by multiple readers in multiple ways and factor into decisions being made in the real world as well as on campus—about everything from scholarships to the workplace—teachers need to actively participate in the articulation of the issues. We hope *The Theory and Practice of Grading Writing* helps to make this happen.

Note

1. A contributor's dialogue on grade inflation can be found in chapter 15, at the end of this book.

Acknowledgments

We are grateful to the many people who helped make this book possible and extend our thanks to:

Clare Frost, without whose initial work on the prospectus, the project would not have been launched.

The composition students who submitted their stories about grading: Victoria Savalei, Yana Polyakova, Russell Gilchrist, Daniel Paknia, Will Boberg, Julie Parrino, Rachelle Whitfield, Hans Stevenson Go, Karen Koprivnik, Jennifer Foster, Sonal Patel, Andrea Pekovich, Craig Banger, Stacy Taylor.

Victoria Savalei, a remarkable undergraduate, who read the entire manuscript and provided insight far beyond her years and experience.

The staff at the University of Alaska Southeast Computer Center, who helped us devise solutions when we thought none were possible: Jason Bourgoin, Michael Ceri, LeeAnn Dickson, Joe Nell, Mona Yarnall, and especially Barney Norwick, who helped set up a web forum on the Internet for our contributors.

Colleagues and friends whose encouragement and good advice helped move us forward: Doris Alkon, Dianne Belle, Don Cecil, Sheryl Fontaine, Carolyn McGrath, and Charles Schuster.

Our editors, David Ford, Judy Spevack, Anne Valentine, and especially Priscilla Ross and her assistant, Jennie Doling at the State University of New York Press, for helping us produce the best book possible.

David Z. Cohen, for his generous contribution of the cover design.

Our families, for their love and support: Minette Weaver, Dylan Weaver, David Z. Cohen, Lekha Menon, and Ida Zak.

Peter Elbow, where it all began.

And finally, Pat Belanoff: our mentor, colleague, and friend, whom we hold in the highest esteem.

I

Directions and Misdirections

Student Voices

I can remember flunking my first course ever in my whole life. It happened my junior year in college and it was a statistics course. It was a such a terrible feeling, as if the F stood for f—kg stupid." I did not want my parents to find out about it. I thought they would absolutely kill me, or even worse . . . give me some tiring lecture about how they were not paying my way through college for me to flunk courses. They eventually found out about it and were naturally disturbed by it. But, they also realized that I had been a good student all my life and would not say that one F would destroy my hopes of graduating from school and getting a good job. I must admit that it did give me some sort of a wake-up call. — *Will Boberg*

Most professors seem more comfortable putting a grade on everything for their own sake (less work) as well as the students. — *Julie Parrino*

I remember in grade 10 when I received an A+ on an English paper—the highest mark in the class. I was so happy because I never received these high grades in high school. My teacher sent me to a young authors conference where "real" authors viewed your paper and told you and everyone else their comments about it. The author totally tore up my paper and humiliated me in front of twenty other students. I was so upset that at the break I left and never came back for the rest of the conference. My teacher had to convince me that I did a really good job and it was worth the A+. But I wondered what grade my paper was really worth. — *Rachelle Whitfield*

If I were to get a grade of, say a B, I would feel I was in a B range and how do I get out of it? How many more points do I need to get that A? By not having a grade, I feel a freedom to play with my drafts, to add things or to take things out without being penalized. I enjoy revising. — *Jennifer Foster*

I think that by not having a grade, students tend to take the class less seriously. — *Sonal Patel*

1

Richard Boyd

The Origins and Evolution of Grading Student Writing

Pedagogical Imperatives and Cultural Anxieties

Grading, as it is commonly understood today, has not always been a feature of American higher education. During colonial times, college students did not typically receive grades of any sort. Rather, the formal evaluation of their scholastic achievement seems to have been restricted to an examination given near the end of their collegiate matriculation which was intended to certify that a level of intellectual competency and moral rectitude deemed appropriate for the college graduate had been attained. As Harvard College would declare in 1646: "Every scholar that on proof is found able to read the original of the old and new testament into the Latin tongue, and to resolve them logically[;] withall being of honest life and conversation and at any public act hath the approbation of the overseers, and Master of the College may be invested with his first degree" (quoted in Smallwood, 8).

This "proof" was primarily attained through an oral examination, borrowed in large part from European practice, that soon evolved into a more formalized system of public and private recitations. These recitations, which chiefly measured a student's proficiency in rote memorization, constituted the primary means of evaluating student achievement by the middle of the eighteenth century (Rudolph 1981, 146). Under this system, colleges designated several days at the conclusion of each academic year when students would come before their professors and a trustee committee to be examined on the year's work. It was left to the trustees—who had the right to participate actively in the examination—to determine the success or failure of each student (Rudolph 1981, 146). However, as Frederick Rudolph points out, these examinations tended to be more "gestures in public relations" than rigorous interrogations, and "there [were] no surprises in these performances, [with] . . . no searching questions, no stimulation to the imagination, and no real testing of the student or of the teacher's effectiveness" (145–46).

A certain dissatisfaction with this method of evaluation thus quickly manifested itself, and by the 1830s, leading colleges like Harvard and Yale had initiated the more rigorous system of biennial *written* examinations to be taken at the end of the sophomore and senior years (Rudolph 146; Smallwood 15).[1] Many colleges across the nation imitated this grading reform, for while these new examinations were still quite restrictive of student initiative and creativity in thinking, the fact that they were in writing did have the attractive benefit of enhancing the possibility of comparatively ranking individual student performances (Rudolph 146). They also had the effect of elevating the instructor to the principal position in the measurement of student achievement, with college trustees no longer the final arbiters and the more "public" qualities of the old examination procedure allowed to wither away.

The change to an emphasis on scored writing provided impetus to the growing use of grades as definitive markers of a student's academic merit and worth. To be sure, prior to the Revolutionary War, an *implied* grading system had begun to take shape in colleges, seen chiefly in the designation and ranking of graduating seniors for parts in commencement exercises (i.e., the selection of valedictorian, salutatorian, etc.), but it was not until 1785 that an American college developed and employed a clearly defined scale of measurement to differentiate and rank its students. In that year, Yale adopted the four tiered system of *Optimi*, *Second Optimi*, *Inferiores*, and *Pejores*, most probably borrowing the terminology from the English system of "Honor Men," "Pass Men," "Charity Passes," and "the Unnamed" (students whose names were not published in university records [Smallwood 107–8]). By 1813, Yale had modified their ranking system to one based on a numerical scale of 1–4, a change that permitted much more discrimination among individual students (Yale used both whole numbers and decimals), and, when coupled with the advent of the graded written examination, helped to stimulate a growing interest in elaborate and intricate marking systems. Harvard, for example, soon adopted a 20-point grading scale that was even more quickly replaced by a 100-point scale, as the quest for even greater exactness in measurement continued to spur innovations in grading (Smallwood 108).

The new, quantified method of evaluation was generally applied across the board in academic courses. Each recitation, and indeed nearly every part of the student's work, was graded and averaged into an overall number representing the relative ranking of the student's performance in college (Rudolph 147). As Ezekiel Belden would note in his account of undergraduate life at Yale, in the early 1840s: "A mark is recorded of each recitation denoting its merit. These marks range from 0 to 4. Two is considered as the average; and a student not receiving this average in all the studies of a term, is obliged to leave his class, and not allowed to re-enter it, until he can pass an examination in all branches to which his class has attended" (quoted in Smallwood 47). Grades had thus, by the antebellum period, become definitive markers of student achievement and of the worthiness of individual students to remain within the academic community.

The fascination with the ranking and discriminating potentialities, inherent within the grading system, intensified through the collapse of the classical curriculum and the advent, in the years following the Civil War, of higher education's developing commitment to training the nation's emerging professional elite. As colleges moved away from the recitation model, with its concentration on the classical languages and the tenets of faculty psychology, and toward a Harvard-inspired philosophy of education that would foreground, in the words of President Charles W. Eliot, "the systematic study of the English language" (59) in a new elective system of undergraduate study, they did not abandon the old grading procedures. Rather they sought to adapt the grades ever more perfectly to pedagogical and institutional imperatives. Thus, Freshman Composition became a fundamental part of the general education curriculum at Harvard during the 1880s, the very same decade that the school moved to replace its numerical scale of grading with one based on a five letter grade (A through E) system (Smallwood 51). Obviously, one academic innovation did not necessarily imply or produce the other, but it is worth noting their relative contiguity in time. And just as Harvard's way of teaching writing "swept over the land" (Lounsbury 866) through the powerful influence of its English A course (established in 1885), so too did Harvard's new marking system serve as an influential model widely imitated across the landscape of American higher education.

To be sure, the essential configurations of the system for grading student writing, which emerged during the latter stages of the nineteenth century, look exceedingly familiar from a late twentieth century perspective; few today, for instance, would be astonished by Professor Charles Copeland's explanation of the grading scales in Harvard's freshman writing program:

> One may, however, explain A (a mark rarely given) as signifying that a man's work not only is correct, but has some maturity of thought, some distinction of style, some originality; B (90 to 78), that the work, though less distinguished, still shows more individual qualities than the average; C (78 to 60), that it is in the main sound and intelligent—that the writer need not take any further course in composition unless he wishes to do so; D (60 to 40), that it is faulty or irregular, and that in his Sophomore year the writer must take a half-course in composition; and E, that he must take English A again (76).

However, it is also important to recognize that Copeland's easy confidence about grades and grading conceals a certain anxiety over methods of evaluation even as colleges moved inexorably toward the kind of scale developing at Harvard. Copeland himself admitted that "of course, grades that stand for an instructor's impression of a piece of writing cannot be mathematically precise" (76), thereby giving voice to the perceived problems in objectivity and standardization in the grading of composition that would plague writing instructors and administrators for a number of years. No perfect solution to the problem of reliability in grading ever emerged; even the early twentieth century efforts of behaviorist reformers like Edward C. Thorndike of Columbia Teacher's College, who proposed "scientific" measurement scales to replace the dependency upon personal judgment in the marking of compositions, soon succumbed to critiques assailing their essential validity (Younglove).

All of these twists and turns in the evolution of grading are important, and, taken as a whole, they suggest a variety of pedagogical, institutional, and social pressures shaping the methods by which student writing came to be evaluated in the current-traditional classroom. But, I wish to focus the remainder of this essay on one particular element in the evolution of grading: an imperative shaping the modes of discriminating among student writers, which I believe can be labelled as something of a constant in this long history, for its origins can be seen to extend as far back as the earliest days of higher education on the new continent and to be present throughout the various incarnations of grades and grading systems so far discussed in this essay.

In his magisterial study, *The Emergence of the American University* (1965), Laurence Veysey remarks that "the university in the United States had become [by the early twentieth century] largely an agency for social control" (440), a conclusion that the last thirty years of historical inquiry have done little to undermine. And the grading system, with its obvious ties to the disciplinary function of education, must be regarded as an important component of the quest to exercise and impart "social control." Indeed, Veysey himself has argued that much of the impetus for reforming the grading system in the early twentieth century, and especially for demanding "tougher" standards in grading (e.g., the end to the time-honored tradition of the "gentleman's C"), can be traced to "a protest against moral laxity and student dissipation, rooted in the conscience of the Progressive Era" (254). Just as attacks on hedonism and moral laxity among the general citizenry animated the reformist political rhetoric of the day, so too were "lazy" students condemned and stricter grading standards imposed to remedy the situation (254).

Grading has always been turned outward toward the community-at-large as much as it has inwardly focussed on student performance in the classroom; the political state and the state of education were and are inextricably linked, and grades, because they involve degrees, rank, and difference, are at the heart of the matter. Thus, this "social history" of grading is an essential constant in the evolution of grades and grading in the writing classroom. It is also the principal issue that I wish to explore in the remaining pages of this essay.

From the very beginnings of American higher education, a scholastic grade or ranking meant more than a simple measure of academic achievement; in point of fact, colonial colleges most probably classified students not on the basis of scholarly merit but "according to the social position of their families" (Smallwood 41). Once grading came to be driven explicitly by academic performance, this conflation of scholastic success and social behavior did not disappear, but merely re-surfaced under the form of a grading calculus that linked scholarship and character. As a 1770 College of William and Mary faculty report would declare, graduation examinations (and the class-rankings which derived from them) had the particular merit of inducing students "to use their best Endeavors to render their whole Conduct acceptable and approved by the President and Masters, . . . [thus encouraging them] to persevere in the same Good Conduct afterwards [after graduation]" (quoted in Smallwood 24).

During the antebellum era, grades and class rankings were most generally determined by an average of academic marks; what the historian Charles Smallwood terms the "personality factor"; and what Samuel Osgood described in 1861 as "considerations of personal character" that would modify undergraduate rankings should a student's "faults" be "so strong as to show [him to be] in open indolence or vice" (Smallwood 66; quoted in Smallwood 66).

Only in 1869 did Harvard begin the de-linking of such formal ties between grades and social character when its faculty voted to separate matters of scholarship and conduct in grading (Smallwood 74). But as the required writing course began to take shape in the new world of academic merit earned in a non-classical, elective curriculum, the social function of grading did not fade away, nor did it even slip very far below the surface. Indeed, President Eliot of Harvard decided to give voice to just this continuing concern in his 1869 inaugural address, justifying the ranking of students on the grounds that it "reinforces higher motives. In the campaign for character, no auxiliaries are to be refused," even if those means carry with them the acknowledged danger of inciting an excessive "self-reference" in those "aspirants" to high rank (67).

To be sure, Eliot's interest in waging this "campaign for character" was motivated by more than a simple institutional desire for a more virtuous student population. Eliot's claim that Harvard's scholarly environs provide society's best "safeguards against sloth, vulgarity, and depravity" (67) resonated far beyond the walls of the college. The years between 1870 and 1920 were, in fact, dominated by quite broadly based fears among the professional class concerning its place in an uncertain world and its own hedonistic impulses set free in an emerging consumerist culture (Ehrenreich 248). College-trained professionals of this era inhabited an increasingly urbanized nation, where they were free of the traditional restraints upon consumption that had obtained in an earlier time's closely knit small-town settings. But in this age of relative material excess, professionals were also besieged by the need to prove their worth (both financial and social) through hard work and a self-evident dedication to their profession.[2] Not coincidently, professional literature from the new field of composition (a part of the curriculum which President Eliot enthusiastically supported) was exhorting writing instructors to correct with enthusiasm those students whose composing practices seemed "careless" (Hill, *Foundations* 105) and "lax" (Copeland 41). To instill "discipline" was among the primary imperatives in grading, since "[l]azy and careless students appear everywhere" (Tieje, et al. 590) and "a slovenly disregard for good form" (Slater 3) were said to dominate student writing. As John Rothwell Slater would complain in his *Freshman Rhetoric* (1913, revised 1922), "No professional salary could pay a teacher with any literary sense for reading some of the rubbish that lazy freshmen write" (150). Or listen to the "model" instructor's comments Charles Copeland of Harvard provides on a failing theme produced in his freshman writing course: "This is discreditable work. Your spelling is weak, your sentences are a mere slop of 'and' and 'but,' and your paragraphs are bunches of words without any organic relation to the whole composition. The progress of the whole theme is careless and erratic" (93). Can one not locate within this way of reading and marking student discourse the anxieties of an age and cultural ethos much influenced by Progressivist reforms, Spenserian Social Darwinism, the "survival of the fittest," and by what Josiah Strong described, in his immensely popular 1889 text, *Our Country*, as the need to train up a "race of unequalled energy, with all the majesty of numbers and the might of wealth behind it . . . [and] having developed peculiarly aggressive traits calculated to impress its institutions upon mankind" (214)? Certainly Copeland knew something of Strong's refrain when he explained how, with "[a] few slashes of the pen," the composition instructor could "show a beginner how to transform loose, shambling sentences into firm ones that march with confidence" (40). Grades were a primary tool for instilling this kind of "vigor" (Copeland 40) in student writing (and, by implication, in their character); among the composition course's most primary tasks was to be, as A. S. Hill—the originator of English A at Harvard College—would put it, the development of a "self-control [in a student] which a young man old enough to be in college should exercise in the matter of writing, as in other things (*Principles* 100–1).

These "other things" evoked by Hill thus figure large in the evolution of grading scales and procedures in the current-traditional writing classroom. Grading practices, in fact, reproduced social practices, and in more than just the pursuit of personal and cultural "vigor." The historian Robert Wiebe has characterized the years between 1877 and 1920 in the United States as ones marked by a nearly all-consuming "search for order" as the nation struggled to overcome the dislocations of the Civil War and a rapid urbanization that initiated the collapse of most antebellum structures of social control. Arising in its place was an emergent technology of discipline, including most certainly the much larger and more culturally influential post-war system of higher education.[3]

Grades clearly had a role to play in this regard, particularly as they were deployed in the new required writing courses. Despite Copeland's suggestion that grades reflect an essay's relative degree of "individual qualities" and "distinction of style," the current-traditional system of grading was far more powerfully driven by an obsession with mechanical correctness at the sentence level.[4] As R. E. Tieje and his colleagues at the University of Illinois would insist in their 1915 discussion of "systemizing grading in Freshman Composition at the large university:" "the student is graded according as he misses the ideal of correct, well-punctuated, idiomatic, and fluent English which the staff feels it may reasonably expect" (588). The mania for marking and scoring the student's derivations from "the ideal," for covering a paper with red ink and then tabulating the errors (at the University of Illinois, an essay received a failing grade of "E" if it contained two misspelled words or one grammatical error [594]), suggests the desire to mark student writing so as to render it easily observed, classified, and subject to correction in the manner deemed most appropriate. This methodology was indeed "objective," as Tieje et al. maintain, but only in a starkly disciplinary fashion. Susan Miller has argued that "the practice of attending to mechanical errors allowed written texts to become instruments for examining the 'body' of *a* student, not just *the* student body. This attention allows a teacher (an 'auditor' in both aural and accounting senses) to examine the student's language with the same attitude that controls a clinical medical examination" (57).

And with the medical examiner at hand, the penal warden could not be far behind. In numerous explanations and justifications of grading and the enforcement of grading standards in student writing, the tropes of legal punishment and penal incarceration were employed with considerable fervor. Tieje et al. describe, for example, "principles which may be violated in a theme" (those principles being chiefly of the sentence level variety) and how students are "charged" with these "sins"[5] against their academic records (588). Should students persist in such errors as "the comma fault, or the half-sentence fault," Tieje and his co-authors recommend that "the teacher is at liberty to inflict as severe a penalty as to him seems desirable. First offenses usually receive notice in the comment on the outside of the theme. Later ones are met with firm and increasing reductions of grades until the error disappears. Upon reoccurrence the offence is again punished by a failing-grade" (591).

This turn to the language and methods of the prison system was common in the composition literature of the day, but perhaps nowhere in more extreme form than in a 1916 University of California attempt to institutionalize the criminalization of certain kinds of student writing. In that year, the University of California Academic Senate adopted the following guidelines for the grading and policing of essays written for various departments in the university. I will quote these guidelines at length and with little comment, for in the context of this discussion, they would seem to provide sufficient commentary in and of themselves. The university faculty were informed that:

> In correcting papers instructors commonly find that the English expression of certain students is, without a doubt, unsatisfactory. Papers of such students shall be stamped in some way that will warn each student that his expression is unsatisfactory. A list of students so warned shall be kept by the instructor. If at any time after such a warning has been given a student, the instructor finds the written work of that student again unsatisfactory, the instructor shall report the student for delinquency in English. . . . The instructor shall report delinquencies to a central committee to be known as the Committee on Students' English. . . . This Com-

> mittee shall pass upon all reports of delinquency. After examining the papers of students who have been reported, it shall decide whether or not the English of such students is below the proper standard. Every student whose English is unsatisfactory shall then be required to present himself to the Secretary of this Committee for instruction in English Composition. (343–44) [6]

While the University of California's experiment with such methods of (re)education may seem rather extraordinary eighty years after the fact, the nexus between grades and the disciplinary project of colleges should not appear all that remarkable. After all, the contemporary practice of academic probation, with all its suggestion of deviant student behavior, continues to be driven almost exclusively by the offender's GPA. And the history of the deployment of these tropes of punishment and incarceration is certainly worth considering for those of us in the contemporary university. Yet, I believe that one can also detect within the grading systems of the current-traditional era of writing instruction a less obvious, and perhaps less recognizable, imperative driving the institutionalized desire to bestow marks on student writing. The "social history" of grading in fact runs deeper and is more complex than the relatively simple story I have so far told.

I therefore return briefly to that 1916 University of California document because it offers as the ultimate justification for the plan the prospect that "the students themselves will come to respect good English more than they have hitherto" (345). By foregrounding the problem of "respect," University of California faculty revealed something of their own concerns over the stability of those hierarchies of difference that would make any language practice an object of "respect." This move, of course, returns us to grades which derive, at least etymologically, from the Latin word *gradus,* meaning "rank, distinction, discrimination, hierarchy, *difference*" (Girard 161). Thus, as the cultural theorist Rene Girard points out, grades have always had a social meaning far beyond the confines of the classroom walls because the capacity to mark conclusively and thus differentiate clearly the most fundamental distinctions (e.g., just vs. unjust, truth vs. falsehood, inside vs. outside) defines the very possibility of the cultural order in human society (161–62).[7] To establish grades, to teach "respect" for the "ideal of correct . . . English" (Tieje 588) and a desire to shun the "irregular" (Copeland 76), is to seek to re-establish fixed boundaries and restore the order inherent in stable cultural hierarchies. And in an era of labor unrest, class conflict, and the hope of many in a new meritocracy led by college educated professionals, these were not inconsiderable, nor easily attained, ends (Ehrenreich 241–44).

Girard argues that "degree" (his word for culturally sanctioned scales of grading and gradation)[8] is in reality a most fragile social construct, "highly vulnerable" to collapse and the ravages of human conflict. "It [degree] has no other reality than the respect it inspires. If this respect turns to disrespect, . . . contagion is sure to follow and Degree will quickly dissolve in the undifferentiation of mimetic rivalry" and social chaos (164). Interestingly enough, R. E. Tieje and his co-authors at the University of Illinois invoke just such a picture of paralyzing chaos at the opening of their proposal "to secure uniformity in grading" (586). They present their readers with the specter of the "chaos [which] would result if each instructor graded themes entirely according to his own notion" (586), that is to say, as if there were no universally respected grading system. Such a situation would give rise, the authors claim, to "[o]dious comparisons" among instructors, leading to generalized "strife, not only without, but within—*esprit de corps* would be impossible," social unity destroyed: "There would be no health in us" (586).

These images of violent upheaval and the collapse of all order function to impress the reader that a non-standardized method of grading can only issue in the "complication of diseases" which threaten all (586). To forestall such a grim future, Tieje et al. propose a "fixed standard" of grading that can restore transcendence to an otherwise fragile order.[9] They define their new system chiefly by its capacity to withstand the vagaries of whim or disrespect. It is, first and foremost, a "definite and fair system" (587). Its aim is "to afford grounds on which a firm stand may [be] taken against illiteracy, and a means by which the standard of the course may be raised as high as possible" (587), as if "illiteracy" were some sort of invasive, alien entity whose defeat no reasonable person could question. The system is worthy of respect in the modern and practical world of professionalism because it has been *proven* to work and has been fully accepted by all the instructors at the University of Illinois. It is, in essence, the re-appearance of the transcendent and imperishable in a world of grading that had seemed only moments earlier perched on the brink of "chaos."

For the purposes of this essay, the precise outlines of this proposed grading schema are less important than what the new system promised to bring to beleaguered writing instructors everywhere. The success of the University of Illinois's system is evident, so its authors report, in the renewed capacity of instructors to clearly and confidently mark student performance. Grades can, in this system, measure absolutely and they can conclusively differentiate among students, especially at that crucial line between failure and passing, or what the authors term the "exceptionally bad" and the "positive" (591–92). Tieje et al. characterize the grade of "C–" as "the strip between the desert and the sown ground" (592), a trope implying an almost biblical division between the lost and the saved,[10] yet one perfectly in keeping with the essay's representation of restored boundaries and unchallenged markers of difference. The "chaos" of the opening page has been conclusively vanquished.

But that victory is not easily earned, as the violence in the texts makes plainly evident. The punitive language of "sanctions" and "penalty" against students "afflicted" with error, of teachers "at liberty to inflict as severe a penalty as . . . seems desirable" suggests an anxious and violent effort to suppress and "eradicate" disorder as it appears under the form of sentence level error and other resistance to the grading standards (591). Tropes of condemnation and violent expulsion abound in the essay, sometimes in rather whimsical references to assigning certain perhaps "excusable violations" in stylistics to an "*index expurgatorius*," but more often and more powerfully in such bold declarations as "the aim of the first semester's work in composition, then, must be to remove such traces of illiteracy as still remain" (588, 590), as if the student were a carrier of disease who might infect all. Of course, that is precisely the student's situation in this world of systematized grading, which at least partially explains why the University of Illinois would adopt and recommend the policy of failing a student paper, "[r]egardless of merit in thought and style," if that essay contained "one grammatical error" (594). No hint of these signs of disorder could be allowed to remain, for they have the power to blur distinctions and erase boundaries and thus to undermine the entire grading system. If an "A" paper contained a comma splice and so did one receiving an "E," what would happen to those "fixed standard[s]" and clear degrees of difference? The University of Illinois apparently decided it did not want to find out, and thus chose to suppress these "errors" through rather draconian methods and secure its systemized grading by means of distinctly violent measures.

I believe the "crisis of degree" (Girard 160) evident in Tieje et al.'s evocation of pedagogical "chaos" helps to explain not only the severity of their disciplinary project against "error," but also that of the University of California and so many other institutions and classrooms of the current-traditional era. Much more was at stake in grading than the simple ranking of students or even the attempt to secure a particular kind of performance in student writing. Grades made concrete a renewed world of order and difference, of what Tieje and his co-authors called a "unified and coherent" (590) site of student writing (and thus, by implication, student behaviors and lives) that had as much to do with sociocultural exigencies as it did with rhetorical elements in an essay. A fixed—and respected—method of grading could mark the return of the transcendent to a troubled universe beset by the "complication of diseases" (Tieje et al. 586), but only if its own violence were concealed and its disciplinary project unchallenged. Thus, the fixation on both the legitimacy of grades and the sternness of their administration. And just as grades in the colonial college had once measured character and the degree to which a student's "whole conduct" could be found to be "acceptable and approved by the President and the Masters," a very similar kind of "social history" of grades weighed equally heavy upon their particular incarnations in current-traditional classrooms.

Living at the conclusion of the second millennium, it might seem that writing instructors and the composition programs in which they teach have moved a considerable distance from this earlier era's version of the current-traditional rhetoric, and that the motives driving our grading practices are vastly different from those obtaining a century or so ago. True enough, for the rigid and overtly disciplinary tactics employed by the Universities of California and Illinois have largely been abandoned by a profession that has lately struggled to deal honestly with issues of authority and power in the writing classroom. We are now witness to distinctly different visions of the grading process, and we listen closely when people like Richard Bullock urge that instructors surrender "complete autonomy over their students' grades" and instead grade collaboratively as a way to "lessen—or, indeed, eliminate—the tensions between our beliefs about writing, its teaching and evaluation, and the demands our culture places upon us" (191, 190). Robert Schwegler has even traced a notable current among recent composition theorists who attack the old "formalist strategies of reading and response" to student writing and instead urge the acknowledgement of grading's ideological and political contexts (207–11).[11] One might even argue that the door has been opened to a radically new vision of grading student writing, one that would resist the old models and in their place offer a more democratic process that included space for "difference, struggle, and student criticism" (Schwegler 222).[12]

Yet, as the prior pages of this essay have tried to document, grading has long been an intensely ideological activity that has worked consistently to promote socially conservative values. The legacy of one's institutional history is perhaps not all that easily overcome. The cultural power of grades has certainly *not* disappeared from contemporary university life; if anything, today's students are more "grade conscious" than their turn of the century predecessors. So, at least, the potential to use grades in a normative and punitive fashion lives on, even if the current-traditional rhetoric's obsession with hunting down "errors" has been superseded by an emphasis on process and revision. But even more to the point, can not one hear something of that earlier era's "crisis of degree" in today's rhetoric about "grade inflation" and the "loss of standards" that emerges as much—if not more—from perceived sociocultural imperatives as from institutional and pedagogical concerns?[13] The practice of grading always has had, and always will have, a "social history," and it inevitably inserts the writing instructor into the very real world of conflict and cultural praxis, where the teacher's role as a cultural worker is very much on display. The contemporary instructor would be well advised to consider seriously the cultural legacy of his or her professional life as an evaluator of student writing. The marking of that student essay with a grade is not an insignificant, nor apolitical, gesture.

Notes

1. This is not to say that the oral examination had disappeared completely from the collegiate scene. Harvard, for example, would maintain the option of an oral examination until 1870 (Smallwood 16).

2. For two interesting perspectives on these kinds of dynamics within the professional class of this era, see Erenberg and Ehrenreich.

3. Of course, Michel Foucault is the essential theorist in respect to this "technology of discipline." In *Discipline and Punish*, for example, "educationalists" play a primary role in the new "army of technicians" mustered to defend the state against the "criminal" (11).

4. Indeed, Copeland offers a number of sentence level "faults" (e.g., poor spelling and punctuation, an inappropriate use of words) as among the "chief" defects in student writing that would warrant a failing grade (11). The best overview of the "current-traditional" rhetoric's obsession with mechanical correctness can be found in Connors.

5. Of course, such a trope also evokes the realm of religion and the sacred and implies a moral failing on the part of the student and a need for his conversion.

6. This University of California policy was roughly contemporaneous with Harvard's "Committee on the Use of English" which also employed a "Secretary" to supervise those students reported by their teachers as delinquent in their writing. However, in Harvard's case, these students were said to be only dealt a dose of "fatherly advice" (Grandgent 70).

7. Girard's theory is more subtle than this rather bold statement would indicate, and it is particularly important not to read a necessary endorsement of these cultural behaviors within Girard's—or my—analysis.

8. The link between "degree" in this sense and an academic "degree" is one that Girard himself makes available, since both depend on difference and, in fact, serve as markers of difference (162).

9. Tieje, et al. actually use the term "fixed standard" to describe a system of grading "almost absolutely" (588), that is to say, with no allowance for the student's improvement over the course of the term. However, in the context of the author's obvious anxiety about a collapsing "uniformity" and stability in grading (586), it seems fair to assume that an adjective like "fixed" carried more than a purely technical function.

10. Metaphors of salvation and "sin" (588) are, in fact, frequent in the essay.

11. Schwegler has, in fact, criticized these thinkers for not going far enough in adopting "social, interactive perspectives" on grading, and he thus offers his own proposals for responding to make evident "the extent to which the process is grounded in personal, social, and cultural ideology and experience" (211, 212).

12. Schwegler points out, however, that these new proposals (including his own) are not necessarily ideal and "may in turn prove to contain [their] own repressions, though in ways different from [their] predecessors" (223).

13. For a most interesting historical overview of this sense of crisis as it has pertained to the state of student writing in general, see Trimbur.

2

Bruce W. Speck
Tammy R. Jones

Direction in the Grading of Writing?

What the Literature on the Grading of Writing Does and Doesn't Tell Us

A long, hard look into the literature of grading reveals the conflict and confusion that surrounds this subject. While many compositionists claim to offer readers advice on how to grade student writing, their work actually makes us aware that in this troubled field, there are more problems than solutions—problems of inter-grader reliability, single-grader consistency, and ultimate accountability for the grades we assign. Moreover, while much of the literature addresses grading-related issues, almost none confronts the task of actually deciding how to assign a grade.

The problem of grader reliability has been well-documented. What one teacher thinks is good writing, another teacher considers substandard. In fact, the same teacher may grade the same paper twice and give it two different grades (Branthwaite, Trueman, and Berrisford; Edwards). The problem we are citing is not new. Twenty-five years ago, McColly said, "There is a dramatic disagreement among the hundreds of thousands of English teachers as to what good writing is and is not" (148). What the literature seems to be saying is that grading is subjective, so subjective, in fact, that the same teacher cannot be relied upon to use his or her grading "standards" uniformly.

The problem of reliability leads to another question: what does a grade mean? Weeks says that the meaning for a grade is imputed and that different people impute different meanings to the same grade (164). Using Weeks' logic, we ask, if a grade means what the teacher says it means, why do institutions say that an A means excellent as though every A the institution awards is within a range of excellence that can be clearly defined? Problems with accountability follow. If an A is not an A is not an A, then what is an A?[1] A legislator might well wonder, and in wondering, might determine that teachers must justify their grades. The literature takes accountability seriously and suggests ways to justify grades before legislators decide to impose standards. But the literature on grading recommends local standards as the basis for justifying grades. Can we, then, link local standards with national standards? What is the relationship between an A at our university and an A at your university? Answers to these questions have direct impact on policies associated with transfer of credit from one institution to another.

However, even if we could find common assumptions for our standard and common interpretations for what a grade means, we would find very little in the literature on grading to help us decide how to assign grades to writing. Instead, the literature reveals a gap between the teaching of writing and assigning grades—a gap that has been made particularly evident by the emergence of process approaches to composition. On one side of the gap, process theorists provide all kinds of advice about how to help students write: how to generate ideas, how to work collaboratively, how to revise, even how to participate in "grading" their own or their peers' papers. The task of assigning a grade to this writing falls on the other side of the gap. Readers looking for advice about getting from one side to the other may find many articles providing scoring categories or grading rubrics. This literature does not bridge the gap, but rather, finesses the grading problem. The critical juncture is located between the teaching of writing and the grading of writing; no one seems able to describe how to choose the numbers for the categories or what grades to assign. While most of us would agree that the teaching and grading of writing should be inextricably linked, it seems we don't know how to link them.

In this chapter we review the literature about grading to untangle the strands that link teaching to grading. In order to do that, we will (1) present an example of the problem, (2) sort out the terms that are used interchangeably with grading, and (3) examine procedures that purport to explain how to grade students' writing but that are techniques for using the process approach to writing.

Example of the Problem

One indication of the grading gap is the title that misleads the reader about an article's content. Many articles that use the word "grading" in their title are actually not about grading at all, but about responding. For example, in "Praiseworthy Grading," Dragga devotes the entire article to the premise that teachers should comment positively on students' writing and stop "calling the attention of students to their communicative failures" (266). The only thing Dragga says in the article about grading is "the more praiseworthy things discovered in a student's essay, the higher the grade that is awarded" (266). He does not explain what letter grade or number a student should receive. We have singled out Dragga's article because it has been widely cited in the literature on grading and not because we disagree with his thesis. His argument about the value of praiseworthy responding is, indeed, praiseworthy. However, this misadvertisement of his subject is by no means an isolated case (Carson and McTasney; Freeman and Hatch).

Part of the problem with grading is that it is a "conflict laden process" (Bogart and Kistler 39), and a familiar entanglement in the literature on grading is the irresolution between instructors' roles as coaches and graders. Indeed, after wholeheartedly supporting the observations of those who find the task of assigning grades an arbitrary (and, therefore, meaningless) endeavor, McDonald goes on to say: "The inherent failure of the grading process . . . [occurs when] we are forced to reduce a complex of observations and responses and assessments to a single symbol, the letter grade, a manifest impossibility for a composition course" (155). Lynch even argues that the current emphasis on the final grade as the marker of achievement might not be appropriate for the process approach. She writes that throughout the stages of the writing process, "students face different problems, and that their successes in solving these problems need to be measured separately if they are to develop as writers" (310). Duke agrees, adding that the focus on product undermines the entire process model (3).

While we are sympathetic to the conflict laden task of assigning a letter grade or number to a student's writing, we believe that grading is a normal outcome of the writing process. We liken grading to the acceptance or rejection of an article for a journal. In both cases, at least one professional makes a judgment about the worth of a particular piece of writing for a particular context. Certainly, the impulses for writing in both cases may differ from each other, and the negotiations that attend publishing may have different dynamics than those that attend classroom negotiations. Indeed, the status of writers in both cases may differ markedly. But in both cases, someone makes a judgment about the writing. In most public displays of writing, judgments are part and parcel of the context, whether those judgments are realized in terms of money, prestige, or some other form of award or negative criticism—such as an unfavorable review of a book or a deluge of letters to an editor expressing acrimonious disagreement with a particular columnist's viewpoint. The writing classroom is a public forum for writing, and the teacher has the responsibility to make judgments about student writing because the teacher is assumed to be a professional. The students are paying for credit hours and the marker that determines whether they receive those credit hours is a grade.[2]

Those teachers who want to relinquish their role as professional graders because they see conflict between their roles as mentors of the writing process and graders of their students' writing should recognize that their students' writing will be evaluated nonetheless. The central question is by whom? Later, we recommend techniques cited in the literature on grading that teachers can employ to lessen the strain between the dual role of mentor and grader, but we insist that grading is a normal and natural outcome of the writing process. Indeed, grading is a professional responsibility that teachers should see as a necessary part of the writing process.

Untangling the Terms

One of the problems in the literature on grading is an indiscriminate use of terminology. Many different terms are used interchangeably: evaluation, assessment, commenting, responding, and feedback. These terms have discrete meanings, and that they are all used to mean grading is a source of confusion. When we became interested in this subject, for instance, we collected articles and books we thought would address the issue of grading. However, our final collection of materials included scholarship on a variety of topics, from feedback to assessment, and made it clear to us that a number of terms were being used interchangeably to refer to grading, obscuring the pertinent issues. As a result, our initial task was to make distinctions and clarify meanings among these terms.

Evaluation implies measurement, resulting in a grade or a score. However, problems arise when we consider the two main uses of the term *evaluation*—summative and formative evaluation—in the literature on grading. Summative evaluation does indeed measure something, usually a final product or a summary of previous activities, such as performance on a test or in a course. Formative evaluation, on the other hand, helps students achieve the goals they must meet to get a satisfactory summative evaluation. Formative evaluation often consists of *comments* or *feedback*. No measurement is involved, however, and the term is misleading when it is used in the context of grading. For instance, when Elbow distinguishes between ranking and evaluating, he is really talking about the difference between summative and formative evaluation ("Ranking"). When we use the term *grading* in this chapter we are referring to summative evaluation, "an external, terminal judgment," not formative evaluation, "internal continual feedback to the performer-in-action" (Lucas 1).

Grading should also refer to the process teachers use to arrive at those grades students will receive. However, this meaning of the word is seldom used correctly in the literature. When teachers report on a successful grading technique, what they usually mean is they have found a strategy that saves time, involves students, or takes a set of criteria into account. They generally do not describe the process used to calculate, measure, or determine a grade. The one consistent use of the term grading, however, is its reference to where grading takes place. *Grading* is specific to the classroom situation and measures individual performance on a particular assignment or in a particular course.

Assessment, on the other hand, typically means large-scale measurement for institutional purposes (i.e., placement, exit exams, ranking). Instruments used for assessment vary from institution to institution, but the most common techniques are analytic scales, holistic scoring, and primary trait scoring (Diederich; Odell and Cooper). All three of these commonly used assessment techniques are noted for their ability to produce reliable scores, but they have been severely criticized for the absence of validity. For example, Brian Huot has pointed out problems of validity on several grounds including the fact that a number of variables cause bias in raters and that "holistic ratings cannot be used beyond the population which generated them" (201–2).

Commenting does not involve measurement. For example, Lees explains seven types of comments teachers might use in response to a student's work: correcting, emoting, describing, suggesting, questioning, reminding, and assigning (370). Notice that in spite of the title of her article, "Evaluating Student Writing," only one of the categories she mentions—correcting—is clearly evaluative. While most of us would certainly agree that comments can convey a judgment (Larson), a comment, in itself, is not a measurement. Although comments do not measure, they do serve two primary purposes: they can give advice about how to revise for improvement or they can be used to justify a grade. *Feedback*, although used as a substitute for the term *commenting*, is generally used to provide suggestions or instructions for revision. Feedback, however, is not usually a comment made to justify a grade.

Responding, in the literature, is also interchangeable with the idea of commenting, and in fact, the two terms are often synonymous. Indeed, in earlier literature on commenting and responding, the two terms were used a fairly even number of times. For example, Ziv discusses "comments" aimed at various levels of discourse, and Knoblauch and Brannon's review of empirical work on the subject likewise addresses "teacher commentary." However, in a subsequent article, Brannon and Knoblauch, in describing several guidelines for commenting on students' texts, adopt the term *response* in place of *commentary*. In fact, as scholarship has increased on the topic, *response* seems to be gaining ground as the privileged term. Chris Anson's *Writing and Response*, an entire volume devoted to the subject of responding to writing, is a recent example of the disappearance of the use of the term *comments*. Researchers seem to prefer the term *responding* over *commenting* even though the two have historically been used interchangeably. Perhaps a *response* seems to indicate a more serious or formal approach to feedback whereas a comment may imply a less thoughtful, even a passing, remark. Perhaps response conveys a more interactive, humanistic approach than comment does.

Returning to the umbrella term of evaluation, we can see that commenting, responding, and giving feedback fall under the heading of formative evaluation. Assessment and grading come under summative evaluation. The problem with all of this vocabulary is that the ideas these terms stand for are all related, and the relationships are often blurred because of the way the terms are used in the literature. Why don't authors use the terms consistently? We can only speculate, but perhaps one reason for overlapping terminology has to do with authors' unfamiliarity with the extensive body of literature on grading. Perhaps authors have not critically analyzed the terms they use, assuming that a word like *grading* has a transparent meaning. To provide further evidence of the problem of terminology, in the following section we analyze several current evaluation techniques which are usually labeled "grading" but which are actually techniques for responding.

Techniques for Evaluating Students' Writing

We have grouped the various techniques for evaluating students' writing into the following categories: computer "grading"; minimalist "grading"; cassette "grading"; and collaborative "grading." We found that authors often justify the techniques because they fit with the intentions of the process approach or because they are pragmatically useful. For instance, they save time. The thrust of the literature is an attempt to reduce a messy and contentious issue to a practical matter. Thus, to finesse slippery issues related to grading, authors provide seemingly effective techniques for arriving at a grade. In our review of these techniques, we begin with the one that offers the most pragmatic justification and move to those that support the intentions of the process approach.

Computer "Grading"

A critical issue in the grading of student papers is the time spent in commenting on those papers. Providing students with comments on their papers so that they can revise them or to justify a grade is a time-consuming task. Either way, the literature about computer "grading" offers teachers a means of cutting the time required to respond to student papers, but it does not tell us how to assign grades to those papers. For instance, Rushing focuses on cutting down grading time by creating a "paperless" classroom. He does not use a hard copy of students' writing but comments on and grades their work on disk. He also uses a glossary of stock comments that he can insert in students' papers.

Others, however, question the time-saving benefits of using a computer to "grade" students' writing. For Marling, commenting on students' papers on a computer takes longer than writing them. He programmed a computer to make standard comments for frequent errors, but found that the need to comment marginally did not decrease. Furthermore, scrolling the papers up and down on the computer consumed a great deal of time and was not as convenient as flipping pages of a hard copy. He also found his initial readings of papers were not sufficient since the computer makes text look correct. As a result, he had to read papers several times to get a real sense of their problems and errors. He concludes, "While computers are of obvious advantage to writers, their benefits to graders are still up in the air" (808). Jobs reaches a similar conclusion based on his experience using a computer program to comment on student papers. However, neither of these authors describe how they assign a grade to a paper.

While the time savings of using computers to comment on papers appears to be a matter of ongoing argument, a more important concern is whether using computers to grade papers is theoretically sound. For instance, most computer programs for evaluating writing rely on error analysis to compute a score and deliver an "individualized" report to the student about his or her weaknesses and strengths based on that score. But as Sirc points out, "Taken as a whole, computer response programs announce an unfortunate return to a pre-process paradigm, emphasizing form and surface correctness, at the possible expense of our students' own writing processes" (197).

We believe that computer evaluation is not going to go away. Computers are becoming stock-in-trade for the academic culture and the society as a whole. The real question is how the computer will be used to grade students' writing. If students' writing is graded by means of a packaged software program that does not take into account local requirements for writing assignments, students will be graded on criteria that are not applicable to the writing context in which they are learning to write. In addition, as Sirc says, data derived from computer software designed to evaluate writing do not give adequate attention to rhetorical issues. If grades are based on progress in writing, especially if progress is measured in the development of rhetorical sophistication, then grading via computer software assumes the existence of software that can measure such development. If the software is programmed based on local standards, this could be quite helpful in saving teachers time in calculating grades. However, such a program should not supplant professional judgment; we are concerned that the writing teacher would be put in a position of conforming to a prepackaged notion of what constitutes good writing instead of inputting variables that would require the computer to adjust its way of thinking.

Minimalist "Grading"

Those who advocate various minimalist "grading" techniques—codes, checkmarks, or minimal marking—also appeal to time savings as a reason for using their methods. A teacher's use of marginal symbols—like those found in grammar handbooks—can alert students to errors, but the students must locate the actual errors and fix them. For instance, Borja and Spader developed a series of three letter codes that are shorthand for particular writing problems. The code BIB means brief answer/inadequately developed/lacks breadth. The authors contend that the time saved in using codes allows a teacher to write "short notes" (114) to explain how to fix problems.

Another method, the checkmark system, is even sparser. In this system the teacher uses an exclamation point ("!") to show approval of what a student writes and a question mark ("?") to show passages where meaning is unclear. When the instructors want to indicate a problem that should be eliminated, they simply annotate "No!" (Freeman and Hatch 2). Students' final grade for a course is based on the number of papers they revise successfully—if they need to revise at all—using the checkmarks as a guide for revision. Others support the checkmark system while offering suggestions for improving it (Buchholz; Ceccio; Throop and Jameson). However, the checkmark system has been criticized because it is time consuming (Bowman, Branchaw, and Welsh), does not provide specific feedback (Sorenson, Savage, and Hartman), assumes students understand the meaning of codes or checkmarks (Carson and McTasney; Hays), bases grades on perseverance (Bowman, Branchaw, and Welsh), and fails to promote excellence (Rentz).

In keeping with the austere spirit of checkmark grading, Haswell literally places checkmarks in the margins of students' papers to indicate errors. Appropriately, he calls his system minimal marking. Students correct errors in class, and, according to Haswell, during one term, students' error rates dropped by about 52 percent while fluency increased by 23 percent (603). While the purposes of these techniques for minimalist "grading"—to motivate students to find their errors and correct them, to encourage students to take responsibility for their work, to use the teacher's time efficiently—are worthy, the relationship between using the techniques and assigning grades is not clear.

Codes, checkmarks, and minimal marking do not provide answers for how to assign grades to students' writing, partly because all three "grading" systems do not really deal with the problem of grading. What they do deal with is the problem of responding to students' writing so that students can revise, eliminating errors and gaining fluency. All three "grading" systems are pragmatic attempts to finesse the complex problem of assigning grades.

Cassette "Grading"

Supporters of cassette "grading" also appeal to time efficiency as well as the presence of personal contact as the reasons for using a cassette to "grade" students' papers (Carson and McTasney; Klammer). These researchers argue that once the task of using a cassette is mastered, talking into a cassette to comment on students' papers is faster than writing comments. Not only the amount of information, but the quality of information, is at issue. As Carson and McTasney note, "difficult and particular problems of organization, style, and syntax (which were almost impossible to handle adequately with written comments) could be explained quickly on a cassette tape" (141).

The second virtue of cassette "grading" is personal contact, the sound of the human voice. For instance, teachers can use their voices to express empathy (Clark) and can mention the students' names to develop rapport (Rubens). Hays uses the cassette recorder to let students hear how a reader struggles for meaning when reading. Hays, however, says nothing about actually grading students' writing, nor do other advocates of responding on tape (Rubens).

In an empirical study comparing cassette "grading" with traditional grading, Yarbro and Angevine did not find that either method of grading made a difference in student performance. At the same time, they found that students and teachers were enthusiastic about teachers' use of cassettes to provide feedback to students. However, this study, like the others, is silent on the topic of how to assign grades.

Two things can be said about cassette "grading" in relationship to the process approach to writing. One, cassette "grading" is valuable, not as a method of grading, but as a method of responding to writing because the teacher can give support more easily than by using written comments solely. Two, students can use the comments to revise, and, in fact, the role of the human voice—as a way to humanize and substantiate the teacher's presence—may be one reason students like taped response and may be a motivation for them to revise their writing.

Collaborative "Grading"

The methods of "grading" we have examined thus far are often explicitly justified upon the pragmatic principle of saving time in *commenting* on students' papers, with implicit concerns for supporting the process approach to composition. Collaborative "grading" methods, however, are often justified on principles of collaboration and of the teacher's role as a coach, not a judge. Indeed, writers are not solitary figures but members of discourse communities; therefore, in an attempt to integrate theoretical concerns about collaboration, discourse communities, and either the social constructivist or expressivist point of view, teachers recognize the need to foster collaboration in the composing process, even collaborative "grading."

Literature about collaborative "grading" can be divided into two types. The first type is in-class collaboration, which takes place among the participants in the classroom, the teacher and students. In-class collaboration includes student self-evaluation (Bishop), group evaluation, contract "grading" (Beale and King; Duke; Proffitt), peer evaluation (Christenbury; "Involving"; Pasternack) and some combination of student and teacher evaluation (Bishop). The second type of collaborative "grading" is external collaboration, collaboration with those external to the classroom. External collaboration can be divided into two categories: collaborators external to the classroom grade student papers (Burnette; Cazort; Grogan and Daiker; Peek; Raymond; Sawyer; Tritt) and the classroom teacher and an external evaluator grade student papers (Lotto and Smith). While these authors may focus on a particular aspect of collaborative evaluation—i.e., self-evaluation—the authors are really discussing some combination of student and teacher evaluation. Furthermore, neither the literature about in-class collaborative evaluation nor external collaborative evaluation gives much help to the reader who wants to know how to assign grades.

The literature on in-class collaboration is really about training students to become peer reviewers, not graders. In this literature, the problem of terminology reappears. Some authors talk about peer critiquers; others talk about peer reviewers and student "graders." As we understand the literature, regardless of the variation in terminology, the authors are referring to students who function as readers of other students' papers. Peer reviewers can accomplish three major purposes. First, student readers can provide feedback to their peers so those peers can revise their writing. Second, in learning how to scrutinize a peer's writing, student peer reviewers also learn how to analyze their own writing, becoming better revisers of their own written work. Third, student peer reviewers can participate in evaluating student writing. Training in peer review is required in order for the process to be effective.

For instance, both Selfe and Sims emphasize the necessity to train students to be peer reviewers, and they then attempt to link the work of peer review with grading. In particular, Sims explains a method of training students and says that the peer-review exercise he used was "particularly useful as a grading tool." What Sims means is that students pointed out errors in peers' papers "which might otherwise have been overlooked by faculty or teaching assistants in the process of grading numerous papers on a tight time schedule" (107). Weaver and Cotrell suggest that students might be motivated to participate in the peer-review process by teachers using a system of pluses, checks, and minuses to grade students' evaluations of their peers' writing (37). Neither the basis on which students are awarded a plus, check, or minus nor the relationship between a plus, check, or minus to a grade are clear.

A teacher also can train students to be peer reviewers by using various rubrics, such as checklists and questions (Backscheider; Ellman, "Structuring"; Nash). But the real purpose of these rubrics is to help students identify problems in a paper so the author can revise that paper. For instance, Lamberg states that self-provided feedback and peer-provided feedback using a checklist are important because students must focus on particular problems and fix them in subsequent compositions. Pasternack considers checklists a quality control tool. When students evaluate other students using a checklist, students "are being forced to stop and think of what constitutes a good news story" (18).

Alternatively, Kirby integrates grading into the writing process by comparing her grade of a selection of a student's writing with the student's grade of that same piece of writing. She claims that pointing out discrepancies between the two grades "help[s] students look at their writing with a teacher's eye—that more critical, objective, experienced eye," "[helps] demystify the teacher's grades," and "help[s] students become better and more independent learners who are not totally dependent on teachers for problem solving or evaluation" (44–45). Kirby, however, does not explain how to assign grades. Essentially, Kirby is inducting students into the English-teacher discourse community by teaching them to accept the teacher's authority and look at their writing as a teacher might. Nystrand and Brandt have noted that teachers tend to look at student writing as artifacts, not communicative acts. If what Nystrand and Brandt say is true, Kirby is teaching students to grade texts as artifacts.

While the literature on students as peer reviewers seeks to involve students in the writing process, particularly as critical readers of their own and their peers' writing, the literature on external evaluators seeks to separate the teacher's role as teacher from that of judge. Thus, a teacher can ask other teachers to grade his or her students' writing or a teacher can ask professionals, engineers for example, to judge the quality of students' engineering reports. Those who advocate the use of evaluators external to the participants in a classroom have refocused the problem of assigning grades by focusing on who assigns grades, not how grades are assigned. In a bit of sleight of hand, proponents of external evaluators assume that because the evaluators are experts—either teachers or professionals in a particular discipline—the problem of how grades are assigned is solved.

We agree that collaboration in evaluating writing can aid students in becoming more proficient writers, but that strategy does not solve the problem of how to assign grades. That students can provide useful feedback to their peers and even be trained to become better peer reviewers than they are seems to us a separate and distinct issue from assigning grades to writing. This does not mean that formative evaluation has no relationship to grading, especially when formative evaluation is the basis for revision of writing that will be graded. Indeed, the process approach to writing, if it is to be a complete process, requires links among writing drafts, responding to drafts (formative evaluation), and grading a draft or drafts (summative evaluation). Comments leading to revision are formative comments that point in a particular direction. Summative comments, including grades, are based upon whether a writer got to a particular destination. No one from our reading has shown how a teacher can weigh formative comments when making a summative evaluation resulting in a grade, and vague, generalized talk about "improvement" certainly is not adequate when a teacher wants to understand how the two types of evaluations fit together. While we agree with Ellman that grading should not be confused with learning and formative evaluation ("Peer"), we disagree that the two are radically separate. Both formative and summative evaluation—including grades—are legitimate parts of the writing process. This does not mean that the teacher must be both helper and judge. External graders are extremely important in providing insight into how a teacher can maintain integrity as a helper while ensuring that students receive summative evaluations of their work.

Conclusion

The issues we have raised throughout this chapter revolve around a central concern—how does a teacher assign grades to students' writing using the process model of composing? The literature we have reviewed offers hints, but not a clearly described system for grading. Obviously, we are in need of a descriptive theory about how grades are assigned, if we continue to define a grade without tying that definition to the immediate classroom context. In addition, such a theory is needed if individual teachers hope to explain their grading processes to themselves and to others.

We suggest that the English profession is at the point where fledgling theory about evaluation is beginning to emerge. Researchers in English have recognized that the present methods teachers employ for classroom grading are extremely problematic; in fact, as White has remarked, "The present state of affairs could hardly be worse" (2). The profession's response to that recognition has indeed produced a "babble of competing methods" (Phelps 37), as the literature on grading clearly reveals. Members of the profession have even begun to generate empirical studies that offer support for one technique or another. Griffin goes so far as to say that "research is beginning to look behind methods to the processes themselves" (297), but as our examination of the recent literature has shown, his optimism is somewhat premature. For, we have not really begun to look at the philosophies underlying the grading techniques to discover which ones may or may not be pedagogically sound. Therefore, even though we have made some important strides toward a theory of grading, we are nevertheless still stranded without a philosophy of grading and without any clearly stated procedures for assigning grades.

Notes

1. For a more detailed discussion of how students and instructors interpret grades differently, see Carbone and Daisley's chapter, "Grading As A Rhetorical Construct."

2. For a different argument regarding grading and "real world" evaluations of writing, see Smith and Dunstan's chapter, "Grade the Learning, Not the Writing."

3

Bruce Maylath

Do We Do What We Say?

Contradictions in Composition Teaching and Grading

Ask any of us who teach writing what criteria we use to assess and evaluate student writing, and we will tell you. Many of us teaching writing at the college level and in the high schools alike will say we subscribe to process methods of teaching, thanks to twenty or more years of growing, solid research in composition theory, and thanks also to the National Writing Project and its assorted regional kin. Likewise, encouraged by Paulo Freire and others, we profess to encourage the textual authority of the author/student above the reader/teacher. Furthermore, without a doubt, we universally promote a writing style of efficiency and concision, preaching to every class the merits of chopping out deadwood verbiage and of never using a Latinate word where a good, old Anglo-Saxon word will do. Whether we're talking to peers at conferences, administrators in their offices, or students in our classrooms, we speak with certainty about what we deem important in writing and its instruction. But when we grade students' writing, do we really employ the criteria we profess?

A growing body of research points out the contradictions between what we writing instructors say—and consciously believe—we do, and what in actuality we do unconsciously. A string of studies has revealed writing instructors teach writing processes but grade written products (Appleman and Green), preach the authority of the author/student but honor the authority of the reader/teacher (Connors and Lunsford), teach verbal style but reward nominal style (Hake and Williams), and preach the use of Anglo-Saxon words but reward the use of Greco-Latinate words (Maylath). Witnessing such contradictions, Rosemary Hake has wondered publicly why so little research has been directed at how intended readers process writing, particularly when those readers include evaluators. In 1986, she posed questions about graders that still demand full answers: can judges reproduce their own judgments? Are they consistent in using a particular strategy? Do they, given the same information, agree with one another? Are there systematic emphases in their judgments? Do they ever violate their own strategies (153)?

Since Hake first asked these questions, the answers have begun to take a visible, if dim, shape. What we've discovered about ourselves should at the very least give us pause, if not embarrassment and discomfort. By now, the sheer preponderance of evidence revealing our grading discrepancies places our credibility as evaluators into question.

Some of the earliest evidence of grading contradictions comes from the research in the 1960s by Scannell and Marshall, who discovered a phenomenon that has since become known in the profession as the "halo effect." Told to grade student writing solely on the merits of its content, the prospective teachers in their study nevertheless graded the writing largely on what the researchers called "composition errors," especially punctuation, grammar, and spelling. Nothing indicated that the graders deliberately sought to ignore or repudiate the instructions. Indeed, they appeared to believe that they were doing what was asked of them. Still, they were influenced overwhelmingly by the papers' surface appearances—in the case of those with clean appearances, their "haloes."

We might discount such findings for the profession today since (1) the results predate writing process reforms, and (2) the subjects were not yet full-fledged teachers. However, later research from the 1970s, focusing on full-time teachers, yielded similar results. For example, in W. H. Harris' study of high school teachers of writing, Harris discovered that the criteria teachers indicated as most important for evaluating writing were not the criteria that influenced them most when they actually graded. Worse still, Harris found an "inverse relationship between criteria thought to be used and those actually used" (176). In particular, the teachers based their judgments primarily on the "technical correctness" of sentence structure, rather than such features as the variety of structural elements or the kinds of sentence patterns. Harris summed up the results in traditional, understated academic language: ". . . there appeared to be some discrepancy between theory and practice when student compositions were actually evaluated" (185). "Some discrepancy" may not seem a phrase that should set sirens ablare, but neither does it seem particularly desireable if we can avoid it.

What is there about ourselves as graders that we wish to hide even from ourselves? Unfortunately, our masking of our motives has not disappeared since Harris' study. Rather, increased research has made our masking all the more apparent. Publishing their study from the early 1990s, Appleman and Green write with a hint of horror, ". . . we have been awakened to the insidious nature of pedagogical inconsistency, a problem that pervades all composition classrooms" (198). Like Harris, Appleman and Green discovered inconsistencies between instructors' theories about assessment and their actual practice when assessing and evaluating. In particular, many who consciously espoused evaluating a student's writing process unconsciously conducted their evaluations by concentrating on the student's written product. Appleman and Green confess:

> Like many college instructors, we are essentially—on the surface and deep down—a group of product-process wafflers, flanked on the right by product moderates and on the left by process extremists. Many of us tend to rely on the product—especially its technical elements—as a gauge, especially when faced with evaluative judgments that have serious consequences. . . . (194)

In the same journal issue, Connors and Lunsford published nearly identical results and conclusions from their study, independent of Appleman and Green. Curious to see how instructors in the 1990s were evaluating student writing, Connors and Lunsford state: "What we found, in short, was that most teachers in this sample give evidence of reading student papers in ways antithetical to the reading strategies currently being explored by many critical theorists" (214–15), mainly by attending to products, especially their surface errors, instead of process. Connors and Lunsford's findings might not seem so disturbing if their subjects simply disagreed with critical theorists and openly followed their own criteria with consistency. However, Connors and Lunsford observe: "The judgments expressed in writing by teachers often seemed to come out of some privately held set of ideals about what good writing should look like" (218).

We might ask to what extent teachers keep such ideals private and off limits even from their own consciousness. The findings of these two studies should cause the entire composition profession to sit bolt upright and look into the mirror. Although most of us consider ourselves humanists who research the messy complexities of human culture, often with unique and unrepeatable actions, our colleagues mentioned above have discovered in us something that social scientists long for and natural scientists expect: reproducible results. Given a piece of student writing to grade, we appear consistently capricious.

The contradictions are not limited to process instruction and product evaluation. In our grading, we often contradict what we tell our students about sentence level matters as well. Perhaps the best-known evidence still comes from the study published in 1981 by Hake and Williams, who found that writing teachers in two-thirds of cases rated the "pretentiously indirect style" of nominalizations higher than the plain style of verbalizations. It would be difficult to find a style handbook that advised writing "She made a decision" rather than "She decided." I suspect it would be just as difficult to find a writing instructor who taught students to use a "nominalized style" in their writing. Yet, Hake and Williams found that nominalizations were precisely what a large majority of teachers rewarded when they evaluated student writing. If we were to show such research results to students when they entered writing courses, they would find it difficult not to conclude the following: only the foolhardy do anything other than fill their papers with nominalizations. Given the evidence, I have to conclude that either our handbooks and lectures must be rewritten or our grading practices must be held up to our noses until, like puppies not yet housebroken, we change our behavior.

Further evidence comes from my own study, partly inspired by the results of Hake and Williams' work. The research investigated the effects of Anglo-Saxon vs. Greco-Latinate lexicon on evaluations of student papers (Maylath). Ninety post-secondary writing instructors ranked nine student essays, varied to create three versions: one highly Greco-Latinate, using words like "protrude" and "integrate"; one highly Anglo-Saxon, using words like "stick out" and "mesh"; and one blended. The results were surprising: Of the instructors who showed themselves more sensitive to vocabulary than to other textual features, such as organization, content, and grammar, every one of those who favored the highly Greco-Latinate versions was a novice instructor, with no more than two years' experience teaching writing. Conversely, every one of those who favored the highly Anglo-Saxon versions was a veteran, with a minimum of twenty years' experience teaching writing. Similarly, nearly all those who favored the blends were midway through their careers, averaging a little over fourteen years' experience teaching writing.

Interviews with the instructors revealed the reasons for the differences: The novice instructors, all graduate assistants at the time, felt insecure as new writing teachers and in their positions at the bottom of the academic hierarchy. Projecting their insecurities on to student papers, they were swayed in their judgments by the prestige they associated with Greco-

Latinate words. The veteran instructors, secure in their positions, viewed the use of Greco-Latinate words as obvious attempts to gain prestige. (Their security diminished somewhat, however, when the tables were turned and they were asked to write documents that would be sent to their deans. Some Greco-Latinate words appeared more attractive at that point.) Especially disturbing in the interviews was the contradiction between what the novice instructors thought they were doing when evaluating and what they actually were doing. They professed to teach their students that simple, short, Anglo-Saxon words were preferable to long, complex Greco-Latinate words. They said they often invoked appropriate passages from Strunk and White or George Orwell in their classes. All were first dismayed and then chagrined to find they had preferred the opposite in their rankings of student writings. Veteran instructors were more aware of their biases but didn't realize the extent to which they appeared, through their rankings, to punish students' use of almost all Greco-Latinate words.

When all the studies of writing teachers' grading practices are viewed collectively, we seem surprisingly unaware of our own motives, prejudices, and fears. What's more, we seem oblivious to the effect our subconscious has on our judgments of students' writing. Is this phenomenon unique to writing instructors? Perhaps all persons who evaluate the handiwork of others suffer similiar contradictions.

Perhaps, but not necessarily. Alan Purves says flatly, "People in writing assessment are not as honest as those who judge other forms of competition such as dressage or ice-dancing where the rating is valid for the competition itself" (119). Rosemary Hake has added her own warning: "When graders [of writing] convert their observations into judgments, their ratings can show intolerably large discrepancies" (161). Still, the question lingers, what is there about ourselves as graders that we wish to hide even from ourselves?

Now alert to the discrepancies, perhaps we as a profession can decide how to overcome and reduce them to a tolerable level. Indeed, the contributions by the authors of this book are an attempt to begin a large-scale, critical examination of what we are really doing when we grade writing. Ultimately, however, it is up to each of us, as practitioners, to examine the contradictions between what we say and what we do.

II

The Power and Authority of Graders

Student Voices

My first negative experience with grades occurred in a class where my teacher suddenly gave me a C+ at the end of the semester. In spite of the fact that he was regularly providing us with the info on how we were doing in class, I paid little attention to it because I thought I'd get a good grade anyway as long as I could keep up with the class and assignments. We were graded by our tests and homework, which were collected every week. I turned in all tests (getting 90–100%) and skipped two homeworks at the most. The C+ in the end was a mystery.

I guess the point of this story is that there's something else to a good grading system besides it being clear to students and equally fair to everybody. I thought that as long as I studied conscientiously (and read and understood every single chapter), I'd get what I deserved. Moreover, I really enjoyed the class.

This assumption made me sort of forget about grades and study for the fun of it, without worrying about what I'd get (or rather, I knew the best way to get what I wanted was to behave that way). I think being sure that you'll get a good grade if you study hard, ask questions, and complete assignments is a crucial thing. With a good grading system, students CAN forget about grades as though they are not graded at all. But that wasn't true in the case [of] this class. When I realized that my teacher's grading system was too high, I started counting my points instead of concentrating on the performance itself. In this situation, clear knowledge as to what to expect regarding my grades didn't save me from worrying about them since the grade I desired was almost unfeasible if all I did was enjoy the class, and it required great concentration on the point system, rather than the relaxation needed to learn and study well.

A good grading system should allow students to relax, and be confident that if they take the class seriously and put a lot of effort into it, they will do all right. It should also send a message that little pesky things, like skipping one class or homework, do not matter. When these kinds of things affect your grades greatly, that is what you ultimately start concentrating on. I guess the worst thing about my psych class was *that it made me worry about grades. — Victoria Savalei*

Not having a grade given on my papers made me focus on improving my paper instead of trying to improve my grade. — *Daniel Paknia*

4

Kathleen Blake Yancey
Brian Huot

Construction, Deconstruction, and (Over)Determination

A Foucaultian Analysis of Grades

Grades are ubiquitous, so much a part of the educational landscape that most of us can hardly think about teaching and learning without them. Their effect on us—on teachers as well as on students and on the classroom—is, however, worthy of examination, which is precisely what we do in the chapter that follows. The dialogue, as you'll see, is email-based, but retroactively crafted, as we hope to uncover and critique our assumptions about grades and to locate the effects of grading-as-practice. Instead of focusing on a single characteristic or set of characteristics, we employ a discursive format, incorporating as many different voices, our own and others, to demonstrate the complexity and pervasiveness of grades' relationship with and impact on teaching and learning in American education, in general, and in composition, in particular. Our goal is to display the acontextual nature of grades and to advocate the use of negotiation between the graded and the grader to mediate grades' objectifying force and to preserve the contextual, personal nature of learning. On the basis of this multivocal discussion, we close with two suggestions that we hope will enhance whatever benefits grades may produce.

Let's assume here that grades are text; if so, what is the context? Put differently, why grade? Good question. According to F. Allen Hanson's Testing Testing, *grading is part of something much larger. Our culture, Hanson says, is infected with a hunger to grade* everything, *a hunger that is decidedly unhealthy. But—for the sake of this essay, if not for the sake of argument—let's assume that educational institutions must have grades. If so, we should interrogate them:*

- *What is their purpose? In performative terms,what should they do?*
- *What benefits might/do they produce?*
- *What liabilities?*
- *How can we link agency to grading?*
- *If we must have grades, how can we assure that grades perform as we might wish?*

Uncovering Assumptions

Let's begin by agreeing that grades are problematic in lots of ways and for lots of reasons. As a single symbol, each grade carries considerably more information than it can deliver or convey. Research shows that grades are used for a variety of purposes, but primarily for two: (1) to evaluate work; and (2) to motivate students. Cumulatively, of course, grades are used to rank students; that's the function of the GPA, which allows institutions to determine who can speak as valedictorian, and who can only enroll as a remedial student. Given that some grades stipulate achievement (or lack thereof), and others are used as a pedagogical device, don't we have a problem from the get-go? Even if we assume that—like Gertrude Stein's roses—an A is an A is an A, whether awarded at Harvard or at San Francisco State, whether earned at the University of Alabama or at Rowan Cabarrus Community College, what happens to the purported communicative power of grades when they are used both to motivate and/but to signal achievement? How would we know which was which? Whose grade? What achievement?

The separation of assessment from ranking is one of the basic tenets of criterion-referenced assessment that became popular in the '60s and '70s. Before that, norm-referenced assessment—which depends upon the performance of individuals in relation to each other—was the most widely used method for evaluation. However, it's a mistake to call grading of the typical classroom type "ranking" unless you distribute grades based upon students' performance relative to each other. A teacher who gives mostly As and Bs or mostly Fs is not ranking her students against each other, but rather basing those grades upon some criteria of excellence. Thus, grades can be criterion-referenced. However, eliminating the ranking aspect of grades does not automatically improve their value or effect. Whose criteria is used and what knowledge of this criteria is provided to those who are graded are but two of many issues important to understanding the value of a given measure. For example, standardized tests are usually secure and therefore by definition unknown to the tested.

Even so, grades aren't only a function of some relationship between student work and explicit criteria; they include other, often "invisible" factors, like socioeconomic background and gender. Sadler and Sadler, for instance, confirm in *Failing at Fairness* a continuing, historic pattern of gender bias in grading: girls are awarded higher grades than boys. What such a pattern might mean is thrown into question by another pattern: boys are awarded higher standardized test scores than girls. Given this consistent disparity in achievement on different measures, which—if either—do we trust? And to return to grading specifically, it's clear that criteria of excellence are situated in some very specific ways. One conclusion: by themselves, grades lack the elaboration and context to make any cogent comment about student performance. If, on the other hand, grades are rooted in context and inseparable from a particular classroom/teacher/ student, what value should they hold outside a given context?

> *Ultimately, grades are a part of the ongoing discourse between students and teachers. They define at times the quality and timbre of the relationship itself. This is demonstrated in Melanie Sperling's 1994* RTE *piece on responding to student writing, in which the teacher in her study responded most like a colleague with the student who received the higher grades and likewise in separate studies by Leo Rigsby and Paul Diederich who found that readers who were told that essays were written by honors students gave those essays higher marks than readers who were not.*
>
> *Still, I'm curious about the whole grading thing because it's a topic like plagiarism. I am initially repelled by it because it has so little to do with my ideas about teaching and my theory of language which informs my teaching. I grade every semester. For the most part, I refuse to change those grades when challenged. Where does the grade come from? Grading, I believe, has fostered an objective, atomistic approach to education*

that we in language arts have been resisting for many years. I guess I would hope that we could begin to deconstruct the act of grading.

Agreed. And perhaps better to deconstruct grades—or easier, anyway—when we have only been the object of those grades, not the agent of them. One of my student teachers, Sharon Blumenthal, did this, *before* student teaching, when she had been only the object:

> Well, I just finished reading all of the stuff on grades from ednet [a list-server discussion group], and I must say it really made me think about grades a lot more than I had thought about them before. I think if I was to write about my philosophy of grading before reading the ednet messages, I definitely would've written that they are necessary for students because they define the objectives of a course, and give feedback about achievement; and that they are necessary for teachers, because they make evaluation easier, as well as limit/alter objectives as needed. However, now I really don't feel quite the same anymore. I agree a bit with Dave Kinnaman, that grades are mutual (representative of both teachers and students), but I have a real problem with their purpose. In the classroom, grades serve to formally evaluate students on ability, performance, improvement, but informally they classify students, and therefore have the potential to turn students off to a particular subject matter. Out of the classroom, grades are said to predict future performance (university/jobs), but they're not consistent within THE EDUCATIONAL SYSTEM. Lemoyne Dunn writes that she does want her "children to be creative problem-solvers and risk takers (academically), but [she doesn't] think you can build high-order thinking skills without a low-order base." Reading what she wrote made me think that grades should almost be scrapped. I mean, what's the point of grading anyway? Are teachers (and I realize here that the subject of this sentence will one day be "I") on a power trip? Anyway, in thinking about grading, I really had to stop and think of why I was going to be teaching anyway. (How come all of this always goes back to that?) If I'm teaching to classify or rank students, grading seems okay, but I don't think that's what I want to do.
>
> I don't know. I'm really having trouble figuring this all out. This is a good subject, and that's probably why I'm hating having to write about it.

> *When I first read your note asking me to start off the conversation about grading with some outline of the purposes for grades, I drew a blank. I couldn't think of any purposes offhand. I thought about why I couldn't think of any purposes and went through a few stages.*

Well, we might say, *whose* purposes? Society's? The institution's? Not your purposes, perhaps—nor mine, either—but I have to wonder if that's a common stance. I think plenty of my colleagues see grading as their duty, one that carries with it a kind of moral tenor. Grades as gates, as hoops, wielded in righteous defense of a beleaguered academy.

For me, any positive purposes for grading would have to be related to teaching. Our job is to teach students how to write, so grades should have some pedagogical value. Do they? In whole language, student-centered, process-based writing composition classrooms, response to student writing comprises the most direct teaching we do. What role should grades have as responses to student writing? If we only grade at the end of the semester, do we void the power of grades as a teaching tool, admitting their inherent negative effect on learning? Or is there something we're missing about the power of grades to teach?

Initially, I thought, "There are no legitimate purposes for grades, end of story." Then I thought that perhaps they might be useful for record keeping. When I started thinking of my own teaching, I rejected the record keeping idea. I went back to the records I kept of the last few classes I taught and looked at the grades. Some grades and students seemed to click in my head, but for several I found myself wondering, since the grade and the student weren't always easily comprehensible to me. I then went back to my responsesto students' writing; because I write them on a wordprocessor, I can keep copies of my responses. These responses, it seemed to me, were a better, or at least clearer, record of student work.

Sure, responses are a better indicator—precisely because they are elaborated in a way that grades are not, yes?

> *I don't have copies of the writing they did, but my response evoked that writing in me, and I could connect the student to the writing, to the response. I think then grades are not necessarily good for record keeping, at least not for my teaching. This leads me to another stage in my quest for the purposes of grades. Grades do not figure very much in my teaching. I don't grade students' pieces individually. I don't use grades as a carrot for further revisions. I don't think of grades very much during a semester. I started to think that grades had very little to do with teaching and learning in the courses I teach.*
>
> *I was comfortable with this idea for awhile, but a line from a Pat Belanoff article about grading being the "dirty little thing we do in our offices" caught me, started to haunt me. I do give grades. I give them alone, after the fact, by myself. While grades are not important to me, do not figure very prominently in my teaching or consciousness about teaching, I bet they matter a helluva lot to my students, though*

> *my pedagogy—with no grading, and portfolios for all—tries to minimize the appearance of grading as a factor in the courses I teach.*

Isn't the language here interesting: "minimize the appearance of grading"? Don't we all do this, only our students understand that only the appearance is altered? In important ways, the successful students do understand about grades and the unsuccessful ones do not. In *Lives On the Boundary,* Mike Rose contends that failure in school is social rather than intellectual. The culture of grades and being the graded and the social implications of that position for our students comprise important but neglected skills and information for those students who are on the boundary, marginalized by society and in school.

> *Patrick Hartwell, in a 1987* Rhetoric Review *article, "Creating a Literate Environment in Freshmen English: How and Why," borrows a William Labov term for literate African-Americans who lack the verbal skills to be articulate in Black English Vernacular and calls English teachers "lames" because they are cut off from the vitality of language use their students bring with them into the classroom. I wonder if we faculty aren't a little lame about grading. Parents proudly display bumper stickers proclaiming that their children are "A Students" at a particular institution, while we try to minimize the importance of grading in our classrooms. Whether we like it or not, grades have power and value for most Americans, and the fact that we teachers see so many problems with grades and grading only serves to increase the gulf between ourselves and our students, a gulf thatcould possibly prevent us from being effective as teachers in the classroom. Ok, so here's the proverbial rock and a hard place. We know too much to accept grading whole hog, but failure to attend to the power and significance of grades ignores the position of our students who need to earn good grades in order to benefit institutionally and often financially from their educational experience.*
>
> *In effect, I came to see that much of what I do as a teacher silences my students about the practice of grading. In this sense, the purpose of grading can be seen as supporting the traditional power structures in the classroom. Obviously, for me this reflection on the purpose of grading has been very helpful. It serves to illustrate the importance of making explicit the practice of grading, since so much grading practice occurs within unarticulatedspaces either created by or created for instructors who are uncomfortable with the practice itself. Certainly my experience illustrates the importance of making explicit ideas, practices, experiences, and reflections about grading. Where are the sites within each of our classrooms in which grades can become explicit, contested, and negotiated?*

I think then that there are many purposes for grading both implied and explicit. I offer the following list as [a] working set of functions within and outside the classroom, each of which carries a set of assumptions, a history, a tradition, and [a] place for reflection about the process of grading itself.

- *Grading as record keeping*
- *Grading as student achievement (how well a student does)*
- *Grading as assessment (how a student does)*
- *Grading as feedback*
- *Grading as school currency, the measure of a particular student or specific academic experience that is also cashable*
- *Grading as supportive of power structures in the classroom*
- *Grading as a site for negotiation between student and teacher*

I think this reflection on grading in my own classes demonstrates one of the problems with grading or perhaps any other educational practice in which teachers fail to make the practice explicit to students or responsive to their own theories of teaching.

Grades as Over/Determiners

You are hitting some important points here—one, for instance, that we like to minimize our connection to grading and find recent innovations like portfolios a mechanism for doing so, while what we in practice do is simply to defer and disguise the practice of grading that we nonetheless continue. Which further disenfranchises students. And then they become so disenfranchised, especially the successful students, that they don't even question the disenfranchisement (of course the less successful on the boundary *students are often not even represented at this level). I asked my graduate class last year, for instance, to put grades on (their) papers after I had responded to the texts and after they'd seen my grades on both another set of papers and midterms. One of the students complained about this, comparing it to a child's being whipped; another chose to decline, comparing herself to a conscientious objector. When asked to participate, when asked to treat the grade-giving as a rhetorical opportunity (in a graduate course in rhetorical theory, mind you), the students replied in tropes of violence. Another took a more Foucaultian perspective, commenting that in her entire academic career, no one had asked her to do this, that it felt "weird," and that she was accustomed to professors determining the quality of her performance. Isn't this over/determining?*

In brief: we've done a good job of disguising what we do, and—better yet—we've convinced our (best) students that our grading is in their best interest. They see being asked to take on this responsibility for judging the quality of their own work as a violent thing—and unreasonable. That's what teachers are for. Which makes me ask, "Is this grading practice serving the needs of learning?"

> *The testing apparatus of the Kentucky Educational Reform Act took another tack in trying to minimize the negative effects of grading (and testing) on students by labeling the four designations for students on state-wide tests as Outstanding, Proficient, Apprentice, and Novice. But even young kids get it, as a story one of my graduate students shared with me demonstrates. His two daughters were fighting over something, and one of them said to the other, "What do you know, you're only a novice."*

Alternative assessments that inscribe just another form for grades don't change what we all understand to be true: an activity in which complex performances and practices are coded into a single variable.

> *I'm not sure I agree that the problem is the single variable. I had an occasion a couple of years ago, in considering a student's request for transfer credit for a writing across the curriculum requirement, to see a transcript from a college that doesn't give grades of any kind. Of course the gradeless transcript served the same purpose any other transcript would and silenced any naysayers about the bureaucratic and transfer snafus in a gradeless institution. My disappointment, though, came in the written descriptions of student progress and achievement. Even though the transcript only contained courses from two semesters, it became apparent that there was a formulaic and repetitive feel to the descriptions. I think the problem lies not in the form of the evaluation, whether it be a descriptive account or a single grade. The problem is one of context—of the very problem of trying evaluate a student for the sake of evaluation and beyond any pedagogical context or purpose. Of course, Hanson, Wiggins, and others have critiqued testing for doing this same thing, but all acontextual evaluations suffer from the same problem. Grades and context: we give and receive them within the specific relationships of a certain class, but they have power meaning beyond the doors of any particular classroom. "You know, the A student in the first row or the C in the back of the room."*

And, of course our assumption here is that assessment should serve learning, and that learning is personal. So a formulaic evaluation sounds like a contradiction in terms. Of course, an important question is why does someone need a grade or description of someone's performance anyway? The institutional, regulatory demand for a standardized measure of student achievement/performance conflicts with and overrides the personal, situated nature of authentic learning.

Two other points are relevant here. First, is a presumed connection between self-assessment and grading. If in fact, as some argue, self-assessment plays a role in the development of learning and writing, then this form of assessment is crucial. In fact, we could argue, as Sam Watson does, that when students self-assess well, they need little if any external assessment. A grade, in this instance, would be superfluous. So perhaps we should focus on what encourages learning: that would mean that we work to eliminate grades, that we work to include dialogue and self-knowledge and reflection, that we focus on the learning, not on an arbitrary symbol acontextually associated with it. But how do we know that what we are doing when we preach the virtues of self-assessment is helping the students? Perhaps we are just asking the students to do our "dirty work" for us, requiring them simply to (re) produce the assessment we would have given them. Couldn't this be (yet) another form of over-determining students?

I'm not sure I agree with your concern about students' being asked to internalize our standards. I think it might start there, but students need to move beyond our standards and develop their own. And here's what I think could be the most problematic aspect of grading. It dupes us into devaluing the importance of evaluation in the teaching of writing. If assessment were an explicit part of the writing curriculum, then internalizing a set of criteria for assessing one's own writing would assume the important place it deserves for someone learning to write. Our recognition that grades can have a deleterious effect on learning has prompted us to do the baby and the bath water scene. There are other kinds of response; for example, Pat Carini's, which focuses on a method for teachers to discuss student work and to use this discussion as the sole means of evaluation. Denny Taylor in a 1990 issue of English Education *outlined a complete system for evaluating student literacy by describing rather than just evaluating. In both Taylor's and Carini's programs there are no grades, no room for them, no reason for them, it seems to me, because they focus on the things of learning: assignments, syllabi, and most important, student work. These schemes disconnect evaluation from grades altogether. In this way we could emphasize and refigure evaluation as an important and necessary element of learning to write, disrupting the automatic negative effects associated with grades or other harmful student labels.*

Still, before we abandon grades altogether, consider another alternative: that grades might become a negotiated space between teacher and student in which assessment criteria and evaluation are shared activities between students and teachers.

I don't know: I think here you and I disagree. I think that you are right about there being an assumed relationship between learning and grades: the entire educational system is predicated on that premise. But you seem to think that grading itself could be an opportunity, or a site, for negotiation. I think that grading, given its historical baggage, contaminates that site. For something other than ersatz negotiation to be possible, we may need to dismiss grading altogether. Or, to reconceive it.

Personally—Contextually

As to internalizing others' standards and that being self-assessment, I think this is a topic that needs additional discussion and exploration and practice. I like particularly the idea of students moving *beyond* our standards, of their developing their own criteria, and I think with electronic discourse such development of standards—which include (but are not limited to) multiple voices, rhetorical page design, integration of text and image—is increasingly possible. In some cases, of course, students are supposed to internalize: take the trivial situation of the misplaced comma or the misused pronoun. But in others, I think it's more a situation, in the best scenario, of writers both internalizing and negotiating—internalizing the standards of others and also negotiating with them, sort of in the way that Bakhtin talks about our use of words—they come inhabited, and then we inhabit them too. But there's another change here required: I think lots of students don't negotiate—they are written by the university, perhaps overwritten, in fact, and grading is one of—if not the primary—agents doing that writing.

Right. That's why we would need to reconceive grades. And no surprise here: I think lots of teachers don't want students to negotiate. It's less hassle to award a grade. They are the experts, after all. I think they'd *rather* grade. The very idea that students could negotiate an evaluation of their own work positions all of us quite differently, less advantageously. It is in our interest, in other words, to prefer to grade: it keeps us authoritative experts.

Students are written by grades. It is common for teachers and others to refer to an A or B student as if grades existed beyond a specific context or evaluation. Grades have a life of their own, and when we use them we are bringing that life into our classrooms, our pedagogies and into the lives of our students.

And grades stratify: they separate the wheat from the chaff, slowly at first, but then in an increasingly deterministic way. The third grader who is not a reader will not find Princeton's doors open. The average prisoner in this country is illiterate: not many good grades there, I'll bet. How much of this pattern is attributable to the grades themselves and the story they presume to tell?

As important: as teachers, we, too, are a function of the grade. Teachers, typically, become faculty because they have compiled good grades, lots of good grades. The grades, seemingly, confirm the fact that these people should become teachers, should exercise authority, especially in a classroom. So right from the start, teachers are determined by grades: having "earned" good grades ourselves, we have the right to become a part of the institution: to grade others. This right confers power, and it's an interesting question as to how many teachers will be, or are, willing to give that power away in some move to negotiate evaluation. Then too, we faculty have another reason not to give up the grading game: through the grades we give, we construct a persona that can be used for our advantage in multiple contexts. In the classroom, our grading patterns construct us: our ability to critique, a sign of our intellectual superiority, takes the form of awarding grades. The smarter the professor, the higher the standards, the harder the grader. In our departments, such faculty earn begrudging respect from others. Beyond our departments, our grading patterns are often used to warrant promotion and tenure: they provide a check against student evaluations that might just be the wee bit too high. And now, I'd like to know: who is being graded? Haven't we here the postmodern teacher par excellence: constructed by the academy; devoted to teaching and, as Don Daiker puts it, to praising our students; but ultimately grading hard? How do we make a whole teacher from such fragments of intellectual life?

More generally, while we are constructing the students with grades, and they are constructing us with evaluations, and administrators are constructing us with both, a lot of energy gets spent, people's careers are on the line, students are receiving grades that they may or may not have earned but that cumulatively provide an increasingly deterministic picture of who they are. To what end?

I really like the tension and levels of construction that you bring to mind. The "To what end" question, though, only works if we reduce the entire activity to the giving of grades. It seems to me that we could also read the situation as a series of evaluative levels that collide, constrict and ultimately create the possibility for the articulation of localized standards, controlled by the people who must work with and through them to learn and teach.

What we have is an inadequate system for evaluation that is so entrenched that it has real, perceived value on its own.

Two Suggestions

Although no one can articulate exactly what grades mean in any meaningful way, few of us would be willing to let go of grades because they have so much value in labeling the worth of individual students, teachers, and institutions. Portfolios, one of the most popular alternatives to grading individual student effort, are often positioned as a way to delay or withhold grades, the assumption being that a grade appears with every student performance. Before we can construct any viable alternative to grading, we need to rethink in terms of purpose and audience the entire notion of evaluating student writing. That is, we need to think of grades rhetorically—as a piece of communication, the response from a teacher to a student. This rethinking, though, will require philosophical and epistemological shifts in the way we conceive of writing and student performance in school. We will have to give up our ideas about writing quality being a recognizable and discernible characteristic in student writing and begin to follow the lead of people like Carini and Denny Taylor, begin to see response and evaluation in terms of our ability to describe the progress and potential of an individual writing within a specific context.

So one recommendation here is to provide more context: in our readings and responses, in articulation of local criteria and standards, for our grades in a given class or course, for our own grading patterns. And to understand that context for grading is more than what we as individuals or department members or even institutional agents experience: there is a larger cultural context that we both participate in and shape. This means that we need to work to become aware of this context, of the factors informing it, of ways we can alter it—and to share this knowledge with both our students and our colleagues.

A second recommendation is to invite students to see grading—and evaluation—as negotiated, to encourage them to articulate their own standards and to bring those to bear in their own texts, to defend their own self-assessments so persuasively that we accommodate their judgments. Of course, this will mean that judgment itself must become part of the curriculum. Benjamin Bloom, long ago, claimed that judgment was in fact what education was ultimately poised to produce, good judgment. But we don't teach judgment, we don't help students learn how to judge, and in fact, we remove most opportunities for making judgments before the ink is dry. This can change. We can begin to ask students to make judgments, informed judgments, good judgments—about rhetorical decisions within a single text, about the choices that go into a portfolio, about the criteria that should govern a piece of writing. If we don't ask them to make judgments, we shouldn't be surprised that they don't.

Grading has been with us in America for a very long time, it's true. But it's also true that like any other form of communication, it can be changed by the people doing the communicating. Given what grades seem to be communicating, it's time to make some change.

5

Michael Bernard-Donals

Peter Elbow and the Cynical Subject

In an essay published in *College English* in early 1993, Peter Elbow put forward a series of ideas on ranking, grading, and evaluating student papers. Much of what he said in that essay, entitled "Ranking, Evaluating, and Liking: Sorting Out Three Forms of Judgment," was uncontroversial—that ranking students can work against their learning, and evaluation might take the place of grades in one form or another—and it had been said before any number of times (see, for example, *What is English?*; some of the essays in Belanoff and Dickson; Anson). At the foundation of Elbow's argument is the idea that grades assume certain standards that guide our idea of what is and isn't good writing, but because everybody's standards are different, we need a way to understand student writing and—to get our students to understand their *own* writing—we need evaluation that is flexible and context-specific. Such evaluation gets students to see teachers less as institutional watchdogs and more as gatekeepers or coaches whose role it is to help their charges over institutional hurdles and, we hope, into productive lives as citizens.

Elbow's essay on evaluation is interesting to me for a couple of reasons. First, I was one of Elbow's students in the 1980s during a time when he and Pat Belanoff were piloting the textbook, *A Community of Writers*, in Stony Brook's writing program, and so I began as quite sympathetic to his pedagogies. Over the years I have grown more and more skeptical of some of the assumptions that guide Elbow's work, but have found nevertheless that what he says more often than not *works*. So, some of what I have to say here is a way of working through a pedagogical loyalty and at the same time a resistance, both pedagogical and political. Second, Elbow's essay repeats a move common to a lot of "antifoundational" theoretical and pedagogical work: evaluation is context-specific because we have learned that universal norms and objective criteria for the ajudication of criteria are themselves constructs, and so should also be treated as contingent upon the forces of their production. Grading our students is something like an act of bad faith, since we should know better than to believe in the fiction that there is something like an ideal "A" out there somewhere to which we should hold our students, and since it leads our students to wonder whose side we're really on. What I want to do in this essay is briefly recapitulate Elbow's argument, and in so doing to examine the theoretical underpinnings of his three-pronged approach to writing ("ranking, evaluating, liking"). Then I will examine in some detail the practical implications of this approach (since, as I've said, it's something to which I'm sympathetic). My hypothesis is this: even if more evaluation and less ranking encourages students to write well for themselves in context-specific situations, writing well for oneself establishes an antifoundational foundation—in this case, an atomistic "self." Moreover, though Elbow would like such a student to understand her place among other students and in the institution, this student is more likely to adopt what Zizek has called the "cynical stance": though she may know better, she will do what the teacher wants rather than what may get her to "write better" because evaluation, and even "liking," works to reinforce institutional norms even while militating against them.

Ranking, Evaluating, and Liking

Elbow's premise, in "Ranking, Evaluating and Liking," is that if assessment in one form or another is truly going to drive our teaching, then we had better understand how it works both productively and also against pedagogy (187). Elbow devotes the first part of his essay to outlining the difference between ranking, which he defines as "summing up one's judgment of a performance or person into a single, holistic number or score," and evaluating, which is defines as "the act of expressing one's judgment" by "pointing out the strengths and weaknesses of different features or dimensions" of that performance or person. For Elbow, while it is difficult if not impossible to judge (that is, rank) an entire performance along some arbitrary scale which does that performance justice, it's much easier to understand how each of its aspects can be placed into the context of its own production, and to assess them according to criteria specific to that context. Think of this in concrete terms: I get papers all the time that contain moments of sheer brilliance, or in which the middle parts are coherent and smart, but the remainder is unclear or muddled or terribly written. If we were to stick with ranking, suggests Elbow, we might simply score such papers along the "yea-boo" continuum (189), giving them something like a C+ or 3 out of 5 possible points, but while we have "quantif[ied] the degree of approval or disapproval in [the] reader," we haven't done the more important pedagogical work, which is to tell what we "actually approve or disapprove of" and why (190). By ranking the student with a C+ without doing the more careful evaluative work, we have reasserted the institutional pecking order—who got the C+ and who got the A, but also, who wields the ultimate authority (i.e., the teacher)—whereas by noting the criteria with which we evaluate the work, we are at least suggesting that the context in which students write and work is complex (191).

In the main section of the essay, Elbow clearly states that he favors evaluation because it forces us to articulate our own criteria and method for noting a text's dimensions, and we also take account "of the complex context for writing: who the writer is, what the writer's audience and goals are, who we are as readers and how we read, and how we might differ in our reading from other readers the writer might be addressing" (192). All of the methods he lists—portfolios, contract grading, pass-no pass scoring, analytic grids and sharing—fit somewhere in between the institutional *fait accompli*, namely that there will always be ranking in a school or university system that functions hierarchically, and the extra-institutional understanding that all writing is specific to contexts and must be evaluated accordingly. Take the example of contract grading, to which I will return later. Students know from the beginning of a course what they are required to do in order to get the institutionally sanctioned "B" or "C." In order to get a better grade, though, students must do additional work, work Elbow considers fruitful for the production of better writing. As he sees it, contract grading works well to show students "the intersection where my authority crosses their self-interest" (196). But it's more complicated than this, because Elbow's authority is not coincident with institutional authority, or even the Limbaugh-esque "way things ought to be." Rather, contract grading suggests a mid-point, not between (student) subjectivity and (teacher) objectivity, but between two types of context-specific authority.

Immediately after Elbow notes that the major benefit of evaluation is its sliding scale, he suggests it is also its major weakness. He notes that evaluation tends to replace a simple criterion ("your C+ is quite a distance from that A") with several more complicated criteria which, though they're tied to the specificity of contexts, nevertheless imply measurement ("the organization of this paper shows that you didn't generate enough ideas to begin with"). Grading replaces the objective standard with the institutional fiat; evaluation, while it makes students aware of the contingency of the institution's scale, replaces it with a host of smaller scales which function in much the same way. Evaluation-free zones and the notion of "liking"—to which Elbow devotes the last third of his essay—completely divorces the notion of the scale from the subjective inclination to like or dislike a performance or a piece of writing: "'This is terrible, but I like it'" (201). Liking functions much like evaluation ("the middle paragraphs of this paper work really well, but the first, second, and eighth don't") but attaches a subjective reaction ("I really liked those middle paragraphs") with the implied injunction that whatever you did to elicit the subjective reaction should be replicated in the sections that didn't (203).

Antifoundationalism, Institutional Politics, and Practice

As his essay proceeds, Elbow moves from the presumably mistaken objectivity of grading, through evaluation's mid-point which lies between the desire to retain some standards of objectivity while understanding they're always institutionally constructed and therefore contingent, to the apparently nonfoundational idea of "liking" in which the teacher fosters the idea that what *really* matters is the student's *own* understanding of the text and his *own* relation to it. To put this in other terms, Elbow here suggests we need to get students to understand that the criteria used to evaluate their writing are always contested sites regardless of the institutional sanction, and that by foregrounding the contingency of a teacher's expectations and the points at which the student's expectations intersect the teacher's, we are providing those students with a consistently antifoundational pedagogy.

Elbow's position in the antifoundational paradigm has been firmly established elsewhere (see, for example, Berlin, "Rhetoric and Ideology"; Bizzell; Gleason; Myers), as has the idea of contesting sites of writing (Graff). Moreover, the accusation that Elbow has tended to avoid ideological confrontation while simultaneously providing a pedagogy that foregrounds a multiplicity of intellectual positions for students is nothing new. Pat Bizzell and Jim Berlin have been telling us for years that in the end, all of Elbow's talk about the proliferation of voice(s) and the expansion of a student's understanding of her position is ultimately subsumed to an autonomous self that, in the end, is really doing all the writing (see Berlin's polite take on this problem in "Rhetoric and Ideology" and in *Rhetoric and Reality*; and the—at times—less polite debate between Elbow and Bartholomae from a constructivist perspective, the most recent version of which appeared in *CCC* in 1995). My point here isn't to add my voice to the complaints about Elbow's failure, but to more clearly point out that the debates about foundationalism and antifoundationalism finally don't matter. Bartholomae's complaint about Elbow's misunderstanding of student authority and Elbow's response miss the point: it's not that there aren't foundations anymore, it's that authority, which is the only foundation we're left with, is a very complicated matter, and that it determines—at least in part—what a writer can and can't say. My point here is that Elbow understands that ranking, evaluating, and liking *do involve contestation*, but doesn't see how contestation—played out in the social arena not just of the classroom but of the school and the culture—works potentially to prevent students from "changing their minds" if not their locations in that arena.

This myopia is perfectly consistent with the antifoundational dictum that there is no world "out there" separable from our statements about it, and as a result our task is to find ways—both in terms of Richard Rorty's "normal" and "abnormal" discourse—to "cope" with that world. It is also consistent with the antifoundational idea that it is the creative function of language that gives individuals the "freedom" to engage in abnormal discourse, to recognize their "contingency" and thereby overcome it. Elbow is right: the antifoundational paradigm has in effect given teachers of writing the ability to get students to recognize and "re-utter" the language of other students. The problem is that such recognition doesn't necessarily give us (or our students) the capacity to overcome the threats—and the material constraints—imposed by, as Rorty puts it, the "scarcity of food" or "the secret police" (*Philosophy* 389), because it doesn't adequately pursue the connection, direct or indirect, between language and all of the forces with which it is inevitably bound up. This version of social constructionism only really allows us, and our students, to cope with the world by finding new ways to tell stories about their version of it.

It is this "antifoundational" problem that has larger, political implications for the role of evaluation in the institutional lives of our students, one I'll flesh out in the remainder of this paper. Briefly, the problem can be stated thus: Elbow sees evaluation—rather than "ranking" or "grading"—as a way to foreground for students the complex ways writing works. It is complex at least in part because both the teacher and the student play somewhat different "roles" in the classroom. On the one hand, the teacher is a representative of the institution, which sanctions the class and the rules by which it operates, as well as the writing which takes place within it; on the other hand, by allowing students "evaluation-free zones" or more subtle evaluation in which to "get rolling," "get fluent," and "take risks" (198), the teacher appears to work against those already well established hierarchies. When the teacher uses methods of evaluation that encourage students to break the rules of the classroom or to take chances, he appears to be working against the established norms of the rule-bound academy and becomes, in a word, subversive.

But is he really? Let's look at this from the students' perspective, because their complex use of language is what presumably is at issue here. The students in a class also play a number of different roles, two of which are worth noting. They are well aware that in the institutional setting of the classroom, what the teacher says goes: "Move that comma," "try paragraph eight between paragraphs one and two," "the voice in that third section of paragraph five is wonderful" are all injunctions that, whether put in a final comment after a grade of C+ (or A–, for that matter) or as part of a much more complex system of evalution or even "sayback," will be heeded one way or another when they come from the teacher. Of course, Elbow suggests in his essay that if we detach these "writerly evaluative comments" (193) from a grade or a rank, students will listen to those comments more and pay less attention to the grade, and in effect work with the teacher-as-coach (or perhaps teacher-as-subversive) to produce good writing *in spite of the grade*. But the grade, and the rules of the game, are always there.

To put this in perhaps harsher terms than I would like, even though students may, for the briefest of moments, suspend their fear and loathing of grades or their rank in a class or their parents suspending funding for school, that threat—the material conditions of the academy, with the teacher as authority and the registrar as the recorder of status—remains in place. As much as Elbow would like for more complex evaluation or evaluation-free zones to acknowledge the lack of foundations to which we can appeal to adjudicate "better" or "worse" writing, the attempt to obviate rank or hierarchy and the material conditions from which they originate, hides "the actual, socio-political processes of importance—to hide those moments of indeterminacy, undecidability and ambivalence when real politics is at work" (Shotter 52). By moving to an antifoundational paradigm of evaluation, Elbow comes off as suggesting that if we only ignore for a moment the constraints within which we work we can produce better writing, when it is those very constraints that need to be understood, analyzed and negotiated for students to get a sense of the context-specificity of their writing. The forming of consensus by moving from ranking to evaluation doesn't necessarily have anything to do with the specifics of the writing situation.

There are at least three practical implications of the impasse in Elbow's decidedly antifoundational understanding of evaluation and ranking. The first is that it's difficult to understand how calling attention to the subject matter of the writing, and to the complicated writing situation, makes students better writers. And it's hard to see how calling attention to these features make students more active participants in the discourses beyond the academic community. In short, the first question is whether the kind of evaluation Elbow advocates really works to change students' minds (let alone their lived relations with their worlds). Second, it's difficult to say how Elbow understands the material reality of the institution given what he has to say about the teacher's role in getting students to *ignore* institutional constraints, and how that understanding translates to the practicalities of evaluation itself. Finally, deriving from the first two implications, it's altogether possible that instead of freeing students to write better, Elbow's methods of evaluation may serve to mystify students—may make them what Zizek has called "cynical subjects"—who recognize the mystification and write from that recognition. This is precisely the opposite condition Elbow would like to see his students in, yet it's the one in which I see many students regardless of what kind of evaluation is applied.

As I've suggested, Elbow's utlimate aim in giving students the kind of feedback he puts forward in "Ranking, Evaluating, and Liking" is to suggest that writing is much more complicated than students think, and this complexity arises from the different priorities, different agendas, and different locations of readers (192). The responses students provide one another, and the evaluation teachers provide students, allow students to "change their minds" about themselves and their worlds, and allow students to become more aware of their writing and its place in the transformation. As I said earlier, I'm drawn to this notion of evaluation and the role of writing, and yet I'm also skeptical whether getting students to "write better papers" or "understand more clearly the way language affects people" will translate into more critical students and more critical subjects. One of the reasons for this skepticism is that I've tried this kind of evaluation, and the classroom context in which it functions, and it doesn't work quite the way Elbow suggests. Some years ago, I wrote an essay describing a class in which I combined Elbow's methods of teaching and evaluation with what I called then a "Bakhtinian theory of answerability" ("Answering and Authoring in the Classroom"). As it turned out, the class was much more clearly Elbow's than Bakhtin's. In that class, I'd assigned a number of short pieces, among them a lecture or two by Adrienne Rich and some very brief excerpts by Helene Cixous, Claudine Hermann, Chantal Chawaf, and other French feminists. I'd assigned the students a page-long writing in which they were to describe their reactions to the essays, and told them to bring them to class for work in small groups in which they would simply discuss the issues that were raised in the writing but not the writing itself (a derivation of one of Elbow's evaluation-free activities and a modification of Elbow and Belanoff's "sayback," from the *Sharing and Responding* companion volume to their textbook, *A Community of Writers* [*SR* 22–24]).

What surprised me at the time was the extent to which the students—primarily women between the ages of 18 and 25—described the tone of the essays as strident or bitchy, and wrote that the kind of language (and, several added, that kind of politics) was not necessary twenty years after the women's movement. Women, they said, had made all kinds of gains, were seen as the equals of men, and many in the class wondered whether the kind of writing they were reading was relevant to their lives at all.

Drawing on Elbow, as well as Sommers and Knoblauch and Brannon, I tried to direct student responses and evaluations by trying to get students to ask each other questions about their brief writing. One female student who'd written a particularly dismissive response was asked by a member of her group whether she felt equal to men at the university. After responding yes, she was then asked if she'd ever felt she'd been treated badly or been insulted because she was a woman. What occurred was, I thought, confirmation that the open-ended evaluation Elbow advocates, works: in class, the student told her group about an incident in which a drunk male friend had made a lewd advance; she also proceeded to relate two or three other moments in which she felt threatened or inferior because of her gender. The longer paper she turned in at the end of the unit was a strong assessment of the first incident that contextualized the essays by Chawaf and others and the student's understanding of gender politics in the late 1980s. Truth be told, it wasn't a bad paper. There it is: the evaluative, "writerly" comments made by other members of the class worked to produce much better writing, the kind of writing that a single grade, or a "yea" or "boo," could not have elicited.

Looking back on this incident, and my willingness to see it as an instance of freeing a student to see, through ungraded writing, something she had not seen before, I am disturbed by the following: not only did this student, and others in the class, continue to write papers that were just plain bad (somewhere near a Bronx cheer on the "yea-boo" continuum), but she and many other students didn't seem to make the connection between their political insight in that one piece of writing and anything else they did in the class or outside of it (from what I could tell from their journals). It turned out that the insight was not so much political as it was institutional. The student whose opinion changed because of the evaluative, writerly comments she got from her small group wrote a paper based on what she believed was the "going opinion" in the group. That is, the student saw the tide of opinion change in her small group, and took an incident—which I'm sure was real and which I'm sure produced a jolt of recognition—and built around it the group consensus that the language of feminism wasn't all that shrill after all.

My point is that far from getting students—or, at least, the students I've known and taught—to take risks, produce better writing, or work their experiences against the already-existing institutional assumptions about writing or anything else, open-ended evaluation seems to work pretty much like ranking or grading. If ranking and grading establishes a set of norms or a foundation from which holistic judgments can be made, evaluation—in which writing is seen as bound to the contexts of its production—replaces it with another foundation: classroom consensus. This classroom consensus may not be the teacher's opinion, and it may not even be a consensus to be found outside the classroom community. But because even the most subjective, grade-free evaluations require the suspension of the institutional requirement of the grade, in effect the suspension calls back that which we're forced to ignore—grades—forcing students into something like a *false* consensus. In the case of the students from my class, the foundation of the right answer has been replaced by the consensus that they'd better reconcile this disturbing incident with the *institutional* law which says "papers are written for class on topics produced in the class." It's clear the student changed her mind about something, but it's not clear (a) whether this was a decision about class or about her lived life, or (b) whether, if it was the latter, it made any difference *in* that lived life.

Institutions and Cynicism

This leads me to my second question about the practicalities of evaluation versus grading, the question of institutional politics. One of the things Ira Shor, Henry Giroux, and Dick Ohmann have been telling us for years is that American schools and universities—with their high dropout rates, high levels of student apathy and anxiety, tired teachers, and vast inequities between the haves and have-nots—haven't failed, but rather have *succeeded* in hierarchizing students (embryonic workers and consumers). It's no surprise, then, that colleges and universities also thrive on the grades that rank students to be channelled onto different tracks or into different disciplines. And it's pretty clear this is precisely the situation Elbow decries in his call for the use of more evaluation and less ranking. Shor's call for a dialogic education as part of a broader reform project that will eventually lead to a "change [in] students' experience[s] of learning, encouraging them to learn more and to develop the intellectual and affective powers to think about transforming society" (111) sounds a lot like what Elbow is getting at in his essay (and in his project overall).

But it's the last part of Shor's call for change that seems to distinguish his project from Elbow's. In her essay with Elbow on portfolios (see Belanoff and Dickson), Pat Belanoff notes several problems involving the apparently contradictory aims of evaluative feedback unattached to a grade, and the institutional context in which portfolios are used, in which portfolios are a substitute for letter grades on individual papers. This is one problem students sometimes have when a paper their own teacher likes is failed by a committee of readers. The student might object, "but *you* liked it," to which the teacher might respond "I suspect your piece [didn't] work so well for a reader who is a stranger to you" (25).

A second problem is that teachers often find themselves spending a great deal more time on the papers that will be included in the portfolio—the instrument of evaluation—than on the other papers written during the term (32–33). I confronted both of these problems while I taught in the Writing Program at Stony Brook, and I never had a good way to resolve them, probably because I was unaware that both problems exhibit the political blind spot of Elbow's evaluative methods: evaluation is always part and parcel of an institutional framework, well established before the student ever gets into the writing classroom, a framework of which the student is acutely aware but one which he can't see a way to get past because the teacher is also working within it. Our students are often a lot smarter than we think, and one of the problems with the types of evaluation Elbow would like us to engage in is that it assumes students can (or will) suspend their awareness of the institutional apparatuses that work against their taking chances with writing. There may be no more foundations dictating right or wrong—knowledge is, we are well aware, constructed not given—but the institution that controls who gets into calculus and who doesn't (and, further on down the road, who gets the service-sector job in the fast-food industry and who gets the interview at the accounting firm) *does* dictate right or wrong. Suggesting to students that evaluation helps them produce better writing by providing places to write, isolated from the dicey matter of institutional control, in effect prevents writing from making a difference, even though students know better.

This brings me to the third problem in Elbow's scheme, the problem of cynicism. A number of places in "Ranking, Evaluating, and Liking" suggest it's because of student passivity—"tell me what to write and I'll write it," or "what do I have to do to get an A?"—that Elbow wants to get students to forget about grades for a while and simply listen to the teacher's writerly comments on how to make their writing better, or more lively, or more appropriate to their audience. As Elbow says quite bluntly at one point, "In effect, I'm [uncoupling evaluations from a grade] because I'm so fed up with students *following* or *obeying* my evaluations too blindly" (196). As Elbow recognizes, students and teachers "inhabit a ranking culture in most of their courses" (192). But let's go back to that student in my course on the essay. I was working with evaluative methods that didn't have much to do with grades because I also recognized too much ranking was going on, and it was perhaps stifling creativity, good writing, and good thinking. I was also getting fed up with students asking me "what do I need to do to get" a particular grade (usually an A). The result in that class—or at least that particular instance of the class—was a student not so much suspending, even momentarily, the desire to get a good grade or to write what the teacher (or her peers) thought she ought to write, but writing precisely *for* the teacher and her peers. Far from loosening the institutional grip on the student by replacing grades with evaluation (or even *no* evaluation at all), I was perhaps more insidiously reinforcing institutional hegemony by asking students to forget the very thing that, in having to forget it, they are forced to remember possibly even more chronically. Elbow notes that the worst thing about grades is they "make students obey us without carefully thinking about the merits of what we say" (196), but the merits of what we say derive at least part of their authority from the institution that employs us and that teaches (some might go so far as to say "indoctrinates") our students. A graduate student in one of my Rhetoric and Composition courses noted that Elbow seems to want to have it both ways: grant students the freedom to take chances and write from their own concerns and their own community, while keeping the lid on by reserving the right to impose the law of the institutional community, thereby rendering what goes on in the classroom ultimately artificial. And students, by writing for the consensus even while taking the "liberties" suggested by flexible evaluative methods, know this, and write accordingly.

Slavoj Zizek calls this "cynical reason," after a term made popular by Peter Sloterdijk (Zizek 11–53 passim; esp. 28–31). Traditional left theorists, in literary study as well as in composition, have long held that our understanding of social reality (in this case, the relation between the inculcation going on in schools and universities and the relations of production in the marketplace) is shaped by ideology, the "imaginary" relations to those real relations. The emancipatory move in left pedagogy—something to which Elbow might not subscribe, but toward which his gestures of subversion point—is not to "show things as the really are" but to show how we live is made possible by the "misrecognition" ideology forces upon us. For example, we don't understand, in Shor's scheme, that secondary and postsecondary students are being systematically ranked and tiered (real social relations) because we are led to *believe* that "smartness" or "preparedness" is a marker of ability in the world of work, and that our workaday world functions well if we have the better-prepared people in certain jobs. We're led to believe this—and so are our students—because of the system of work and reward intellectuals are forced to subscribe to by trudging toward the uncertainties of tenure, by a culture that continues to divide the labor relations of employment and unemployment from the dizzying heights of the stock market, and by the notion that if you write better papers," you'll get the A. The critical teacher's job is to lead students to see that ideology functions to allow for this kind of division (and, in the classroom, sorting and ranking), and also makes it seem benign, or—mistakenly—"the way things really are."

Zizek's notion of cynicism alters this equation. First, critical teaching may show ideology at work, but it'll never get students to see social reality *apart from* the "spin" ideology puts on it. It may get students to understand the relation between, say, layoffs at AT&T and the counter-intuitive rise in the company's stock price, but because the connection between their place in the classroom and the laid-off white-collar worker seems remote, the student may just shrug and continue her work. Second, students are quite aware of the division between social reality and our understanding of it, and in spite of what their teachers tell them about the way the institution (whatever institution) works to shape them, they're *in* that very institution. Zizek concludes, it is precisely the students' *understanding* that they're being ranked and the effect it has on them, that they're able to write in the first place. A student may be able to write a paper brilliantly, exposing the problems inherent in a multilayered, late-capitalist culture, but may not be able to deal with—or more to the point, may refuse to be bothered by—the fact that her disappointment at not getting a grade but only comments on her paper (or at getting a B–), is the result of the very same set of ideological circumstances she wrote about. The student knows, in other words, that writing the paper and waiting for the grade isn't commensurable with the very analysis of the paper, but she has good reason to wait for the grade anyway.

Now, let me return to Elbow, and his discussion of contract grading as one of these grade-free methods of evaluation, a method that's never worked well for me. Elbow's proposition is that students will see the contract as a framework—he has to do *this* for the C, this much *more* for the B, etc.—within which the student can take as many chances as he likes, the effect of which will be that he'll listen to the teacher and produce better writing. But Zizek (and here, I) would suggest that something else happens: the contract functions as the "illusion" of no grading or ranking going on, and it's precisely that it *is* a device or an illusion that structures the student's writing. The student knows quite well all this is a ruse, and he'll be graded at the end of the term, and so he does precisely what Elbow doesn't want: he either writes for the teacher, or writes for the low-ball C (or B, or whatever grade the student has decided he wants). My point here is this: contract grading (and other non-ranking methods of evaluation or even "evaluation-free zones") make sense if you see it as a way to foreground the dialogic, transactional nature of an antifoundational classroom whose members require the opportunity to contest the traditional understandings of self, culture, gender, and the institution itself. But even evaluating and liking don't divert our very intelligent students from knowing even safe grading practices, inserted into a culture characterized by competition and hierarchy, are something of a ruse. In other words, our students are better readers of culture than we give them credit for, and when they see us try to do an end-run around grades, they rightfully chuckle out loud, but then quietly decide for themselves how to face an institution we won't.

Conclusion

So, if less grading and more evaluation really does foster cynicism and the insidious mystification of institutional politics, what are the alternatives? My university recently passed around a survey on grading, which asked professors to respond to thirty-seven questions or statements about grading on a scale ranging from "strongly agree" to "strongly disagree." The one statement from the survey I remember most was something like, "Grades give a student a well-needed dose of reality." It took me ten or fifteen minutes to finally circle the number corresponding with "strongly agree." It took me a long time because, as I suggested earlier, I am highly sympathetic to Elbow's desire to make teaching and evaluation compatible, and to make them more humane. And yet, I finally answered the way I did because I'm well aware that most of my students are Zizek's "cynical subjects," who are *so* aware of grades that my attempts to divert attention from them often become counterproductive and serve to reinforce their grade anxiety (and a certain lurking mistrust of me as their teacher). I am not willing to go so far as to advocate the kind of adversarial teaching put forward by Mas'ud Zavarzadeh and several others, which suggests it's precisely *reality* (or some version of it) we ought to use to do something like beat our students over the head with (see Zavarzadeh; Zavarzadeh and Morton; my response to Zavarzadeh, "Reading 'Reading my Readers'"). But I do know there really is no way to avoid the problem of the material constraints (one example of which is *ranking*) imposed by institutions, including the university and the classroom, but also the lab, the office, and the home. Perhaps what I'm advocating is for us to be much more honest about the conundrum we face as teachers and the tight spot our students currently inhabit in a service economy and a reactionary cultural space. Ira Shor is right: "By itself, dialogic education cannot change inequality in society. . . . But it can change the students' experience of learning, encouraging them . . . to think about transforming society" (111). In part, I'm advocating that we shouldn't give our students the idea that the classroom is a safe environment in which to test ideas, but rather it's one of those contested sites—contested materially as well as discursively—and grading and evaluation are, fair or not, one of those elements that must be negotiated.

6

Peter Elbow
Michael Bernard-Donals

Differences of Opinion

An Exchange of Views

An Epistolary Exchange

June 22, 1996

Dear Michael,

I'm flattered at the close attention you pay to my essay; and at the amount of complicated thinking you bring to it. And I appreciate your saying that you find yourself instinctively or temperamentally sympathetic with my views.

Still I resist your criticism. I want to do so as concretely and practically as I can. (For example, I will put aside all your talk about foundationalism. I think you were closer to the mark when you said that a person's position on foundationalism doesn't really matter much. After all, what people say or imply about their epistemological or ontological stand is surely less important than what they do: how they actually teach, treat students, and treat colleagues—and how fruitful their insights are. But I must admit that it's refreshing to have you criticize me for being anti-foundational—after so often being blamed for thinking there's a world out there.)

As you note, my essay discusses an array of evaluative practices, but you focus mostly on one of them, and it's one I'm deeply interested in: the use of contracts to separate or insulate evaluation from grading. This approach means that students' course grades depend solely on how they fulfill the terms of the contract—and those terms have nothing to do with our evaluation of the quality of their writing. I put comments on student papers, but no grades.

Let's look at the students' concrete situation here. I write responses to their papers; these comments are often evaluative in one way or another: I may talk about what I find strong or weak or give suggestions for revising. But students know that these comments are decoupled from my grading; and whether they go along with my judgments or suggestions has no effect on their grades. After a while, students get a clear sense of my tastes and values, and they are very liable to feel a pressure from this—because I am the teacher, an adult, someone who presumably knows more about writing than they do—and some students will have very strong habits of deferring to the teacher. Nevertheless, they know that however they respond to my values or suggestions has no effect on their grades. Students also get responses from other students—and their reactions too may exert pressure but again have no effect on the grade. Of course one of the terms of the contract is that students must revise their drafts—and more than perfunctorily—but the same rules prevail here too, regarding my judgment about the revisions: as I say bluntly to students, "According to the contract, your revision doesn't have to be better, but it must be different."

Here's how you describe this situation: "The contract functions as the illusion that there's no grading or ranking going on, and it's precisely the fact that it *is* a device or an illusion that structures the student's writing. The student knows quite well that all of this is a put-on, and that she'll be graded at the end of the term, and so she does precisely what Elbow doesn't want: she either writes for the teacher, or writes for the low-ball C (or B . . .)."

I'm trying to figure out what you mean here—and not succeeding. I can't believe that you don't understand the system—or that you think I cheat on it. Or did you base your whole comment on the gap between the grades of B and A?—on the fact that when I wrote my essay I was still using a contract only for the grade of B and was telling student that for the grade of A, they were still stuck having to deal with my evaluations of quality? (Now I have a contract for the A as well.) What is your basis for saying that the student knows that all this is an illusion or put on?

What's more, you clearly imply writing for the teacher or for the low-ball C are the only two responses that students will have. What's your basis for saying that? You yourself later acknowledge a third student response to your use of a contract: you describe a student who didn't cave in to the teacher, but rather caved into the group. (But in telling that incident, you never mention her getting any feedback from you.) I certainly find students taking other paths besides the two you mention.

I want to call attention to how your essay follows the logic of conventional adversarial argument to an extreme degree. You give only negative arguments, no positive ones. You describe only what you are against and not at all what you are for. Your total argument says, in effect, that my approach "doesn't work"—thus implying by means of silence that you believe conventional grading does work or at least works better than a contract. Do you *really* believe that conventional grading does better at keeping students from writing for the teacher or trying to calculate the best grade for the least work? I find it hard to believe, and you give no reasons or evidence about the superior effects of conventional grading.

One of your negative arguments, however, does end up with a more definitely positive implication. That is, you argue that "we shouldn't give our students the idea that the classroom is a safe environment in which to test ideas" (27); that my approach fosters an "insidious mystification of institutional politics" (26) and of other inequities in culture and society. In making this particular negative argument you seem to imply an explicit affirmation: that conventional grading—because it is such a naked exercise of institutional politics—is superior at helping students understand it, helping students understand how they live in a "culture characterized by competition and hierarchy, and helping students come to work against it and against other plays of power and inequity. You seem to be arguing that conventional grading helps students think and act more clearly about "real politics."

But I would ask you to think more about this and consider changing your mind. Let's compare the two situations here. When teachers use a contract, they return papers to students with evaluative comments but no grades, and the students know that the teacher's evaluation has no effect on their grades. When teachers use conventional grading, they return papers to students with evaluative comments *along with* a grade based on that evaluation—and the grade affects the final grade.

You are claiming that students will think more about the play of institutional politics when they get conventional grades because they are feeling the *force* of institutional politics in that very grading. You object to a contract because it gives them a safer refuge out of that line of force. Your view seems plausible at first, but really it is an argument that the best way to get fish to think about water is to leave them immersed. I'm arguing that we stand a better chance of getting them to think about water by removing them from it.

Let's look in more detail at these fish out of water—students in a contract system. They write papers and then get teacher comments. In the past they have become accustomed to going along with the teacher's comments because of the institutional pressure of grades. But now the grading pressure has been removed. In the past they've often wanted to resist the teacher's comment but the price has been awfully high. Now, too they often want to resist the teacher's comment—and now at last they can thumb their nose at it. And yet they know there is every chance that the teacher's opinion is sound.

This is the way in which the contract system faces them with a wonderful perplexity. It invites them (of course it cannot force them) to think—to think about what their own tastes or values are and how they compare to the teacher's tastes and values—and to think about how they themselves tend to react to pressures from teachers and the institution. Naturally some students simply cave in just try to please the teacher anyway. But to find yourself caving in when you know it doesn't help your grade is surely another incentive to think about your relation to the institutional pressures of grades and teacher comments. When, on the other hand, students are in the conventional situation where the evaluative comment and the grade are both rolled into a single powerful package, I find students less likely to think with any perspective about the play of politics and more likely simply to cave in or, in the case of some students, to fight reflexively. Over the years, students develop ways of dealing with institutional grading and authority relations; when I leave the conventional authority/grading situation unchanged, they seem less thoughtful, more stuck in their habits of coping. You complain that a safe classroom undermines thinking. I think I see students *not* thinking well unless they have a degree of safety.

In short, I am arguing that more choices makes for more thinking: the more forks we can build into their road so that they have to decide among them, the more they are likely to think about those choices. You are arguing that *fewer* choices makes for more thinking. A contract doesn't *force* critical thoughtfulness. (Critical thoughtfulness cannot be forced—by definition.) But it does force additional choice-making—and that is an added incentive for thinking.

Finally, I have to bring up one troublesome issue. You tend to state and imply the criterion of whether the contract makes student writing *better*. Frankly I doubt whether the contract is superior by this measure; I have a sinking feeling that teachers who are good at grading (I am not) get their students' writing *better* than I get mine to write. My real reasons for using a contract are to improve my relationship with students and my relationship with myself. I think the contract makes my students' writing more lively and genuine, but it also gives them more space to write the way they want rather than the way I want.

But I've come to feel more and more troubled, anxious, and intellectually dishonest when I use conventional grading. I don't believe that grading decisions of quality have genuine reliability, and I don't like what grading does to the classroom. Perhaps I've become a conscientious objector to grading. Many years ago, when I struggled my way to the position of being an actual conscientious objector to war, I had to admit that the position could not be defended on the grounds of how well it "worked." It didn't make wars or armies less functional. But it seemed to me the only honest way I could proceed.

Best,
Peter Elbow

June 28, 1996

Dear Peter,

Thank you for your very thoughtful response to my essay. I, too, am flattered by the close attention you've given it, and have the sense that we are, after all, trying to get to the same place.

That place, I believe, is one where students recognize the complexity of writing and the value of it. And in the classroom, I believe we are both at pains to have students come to recognize both what they can and what they cannot control—in writing and in the situations in which writing intervenes—in the most ethical ways possible. Where we disagree, I think, is on the best way to do this. There is no escaping, in those concrete writing situations—in the classroom, in the seminar, at work, in our responses to others—the problem of those real situations, those others who exert a certain pressure on what we are able to say and do. I think for both of us the task is to deal with, rather than to escape, those pressures, those material and discursive circumstances that you and I face in our writing and in our jobs, and that the first-year students in our writing classrooms face when confronted by you and by me.

So how can we deal best with these constraints? Part of your suggestion is that contract grading allows students both to recognize the practical know-how the teacher can bring to bear upon their writing through the teacher's advice, and their own resistance to that know-how (in the form of their own experiences as writers or simply their experience as eighteen or nineteen-year-old people) through their freedom to experiment within the constraints of the contract. Of course, I do not believe that you cheat on the contract system; and of course I understand how it works. I've used it myself.

The problem, however, is that contract grading is—like any other form of grading (or evaluation, for that matter)—inherently tied to arbitrary standards. Even your requirement that the writing doesn't have to be better in revision, but must be different is tied to what you think ought to occur in the writing classroom. I remember well being enthusiastic about the unit on revision in *A Community of Writers*: it worked because it allowed students to take chances and rework a piece of writing that the students may well have thought was already pretty good. But it became increasingly hard for the student—and for me—to justify going through the rigmarole of changing something that we both recognized was a thoughtful response to a complicated issue simply because we—no, I—wanted the student to put the paper through revision. At some point in contract grading, or any method of evaluation (grade or no grade), the student will either recognize that there really is quite a bit of pressure coming from the teacher after all, or that there has been all along. It's this recognition that I want to deal with, and that I fear contract grading, or any evaluation-free zone, doesn't deal with as honestly as it ought.

This is my essay's positive implication, not that grading is better than not grading: rather than try to open up a safe place where students feel as though they can temporarily escape the pressures of the institution or the teacher or even each other, I think it's much more honest that we acknowledge that college—and a lot more than just college—isn't a safe place at all. What I would like to suggest that we do in the classroom is provide students with the tools that allow them to analyze the ways in which they are encumbered by institutions, people, material circumstances or, to make this as concrete as possible, by their college's goals for retention and for the writing skills their students leave with, by their classmates, by their teacher, and by their two part-time jobs—and that grading, evaluating, and perhaps even liking, are effects of those institutions and circumstances. By these lights, students are always writing for someone or something, even when they are presumably writing for themselves, because what students do and how students think is a product of those circumstances. The positive implication of the essay, then, is that teachers understand the complex host of pressures that are brought to bear when students write (and when anyone writes) and provide ways of dealing with them honestly rather than try to mitigate against them.

One final thought: if it's true that the real reasons you use contract grading—and by implication, the other methods you mention in your essay?—are to improve your relationship with students and your relationship to yourself, I'd want to suggest that these aren't the sorts of things students are truly concerned about. I know this, to my dismay, from reading countless student evaluations of grade-heavy and grade-light first year writing classes. Students are trying to figure out what the teacher wants, and how what the teacher wants will help them. Whether I use grades or a contract, I want to be sure that my students know that I know that this is what they want, and that I can show them whether this is a useful way to proceed (and if so, how to proceed). I don't like what grading does in my classrooms either. But it's there, students are concerned about it, and since it's part and parcel of their, and my, work situation, the most valuable thing I feel I can do is deal with it honestly and intellectually.

Best,
Michael

July 23, 1996

Dear Mike,

Fran and Chris have invited me to have the last turn and I can't resist it. I will try to articulate our agreements and disagreements briefly from my point of view.

I agree with you that contract grading, like any grading, is tied to arbitrary standards, and that there is always some pressure on students from the teacher and the institution. But where you feel that the contract doesn't deal honestly enough with these standards and pressures, I feel it is more honest. That is, the contract makes it nakedly clear that all these requirements and standards are being imposed by a particular person who takes responsibility for them. One of the things I don't like about regular grading is the inevitable ambiguity about whether requirements and grades represent the personal preferences of the particular teacher, or institutional standards, or societal or universe-wide standards. The student doesn't quite know whose measuring stick is being held up to her writing.

I agree with you that college (like the rest of society) is not completely safe. But you seem uninterested in distinguishing between more and less safety—or in distinguishing between situations of more and less pressure. If there's always *some* danger and pressure, does it follow that there is no point in looking for ways to have less?

I agree with you that we should try to help students figure out what they can and can't control and to develop tools to deal with the unsafety of classrooms and the world. But you seem to imply that you can help students develop these tools better by keeping pressure and danger at their normally high levels. I think I can help them develop these tools better by creating spaces of less pressure. I want them to feel the difference between more and less pressure—not just get numb to pressure. Most of all, I think students can deal better with tricky pressures and constraints if they have a clearer and more vivid sense of *what they themselves think and want*; and that they can figure this out better in situations of lower pressure and danger; and that they often get bamboozled about what they think and want when they always operate under conditions of maximum pressure and danger.

I agree with you that the contract is somewhat *tricky*. It is liable to put students off balance by giving them at once more freedom and yet more blatant, pushy constraints. I don't want to be mean to students, but I don't mind confusing them a bit in a friendly way to make them think about the nature of constraints and quality. They are often unsure how much to be suspicious. They have to try to figure out whether this is just a scam from Publishers Clearing House.

But you imply that the contract confuses students much more radically than that: fools them into thinking that school is a safe place and that teachers are trustworthy and nice, and that they can be wholly free. I don't think students are so easily fooled; I don't see a contract blinding them to the realities of school and society.

Best,
Peter

III

How Students See Grades as Signifiers

Student Voices

Colleges seem more worried about GPAs than whether students have learned anything in a class. Ideally, education of students should take precedence over a quick way of pushing students through school. Today colleges seem to be more of mental fast food joint[s] than a place of higher education. — Russell Gilchrist

One story that comes to mind is my final exam in literature in high school. In Russian high schools, we used to have a comprehensive exam in literature. The exam consisted of two parts. The first was to write a four-hour in-class composition, the hardest part of which, for me, was that we were not given the subject to write about until we sat in class with a pen and a blank notebook. Boy, I was scared! The Exam Committee, usually three or four teachers, watched us from the table in front of the class, making sure nobody cheated. Only enormous bouquets of flowers on the committee's table separated the poor victims from the jury. When I felt a watchful eye on me, all the words would immediately drain out, and suddenly my brain would become blank. To regain confidence, I had to drag my chair to that corner of my table where I could hide behind the white cloud of roses. . . . I was the last to turn in my composition, but somewhere inside, I had a feeling what I wrote was good. I liked the words, and I knew they would not let me down.

The second part of the exam was the next day. We had to pull out a ticket with two questions. My questions were about Mayakovsky's poem—he was a Russian poet of the beginning of the century—and a biographical question on Chernyshevsky, one of the many authors we had studied in the course. I had about twenty minutes to get ready. When they called my name, I panicked. Why was I so unsure of myself? I knew the answers. I was well-prepared, but three teachers at one table—they were intimidating. I started. I recited Mayakovsky's poetry, and my answers went smoothly until I had to remember some dates from Chernyshevsky's biography. They seem to have disappeared from my memory. I stumbled, blushed, and felt unable to continue. The silence hung in the air.

My examiners asked me a couple of questions, but I was numb and lost, although they were trying to help me find my way. Then, one of the teachers reached for a pile of notebooks on the side of the table. My eyes followed the teacher's hands. She sorted the pile, and pulled out a notebook. She opened it and handed it to me. At first, I noticed a thick red 5/5 (5 is a grade of A) at the bottom of the page, and after that, I recognized the hand-writing. It was my composition. The tips of my fingers became warm, and the same warmth was spreading in the middle of my chest. I smiled. Confidence stepped out of nowhere. I remembered all the facts, dates, and answers my teachers had expected me to know. I smiled. The exam went on. — *Yana Polyakova*

7

Nick Carbone
Margaret Daisley

Grading as a Rhetorical Construct

We first started thinking about grading as rhetoric amidst the usual rhetoric about grading that percolates at the end of every semester. This rhetoric permeates the air of our hallways and offices, hangs in the glances and questions of students in our classrooms, and becomes a long and sustained conversational thread in our electronic discussion groups. Along with the complaints about the drudgery and distractions of computing grades, the conversations wend to thoughtful—although sometimes quixotic—observations about the nature of grading, teachers' grading systems, and about the institutional demands that attend to grading.

In our take on these conversations about grading, we began to see a rhetorical paradox emerging. The paradox is that we spend a semester teaching students to think about audience carefully, to write and revise arguments and explications specific and appropriate to their audience's time and context—and yet, at semester's end, we, their instructors, write an argument or explication for how well students did in our courses in a "text" that consists of one or two letters of the alphabet, a "text" that we know becomes decontextualized, detached from the arguments and criteria that inform it. Thus, we write a grade in ways antithetical to how we teach our students what writing is and should be.

In order to explore this paradox further, we hit upon a simple rhetorical model that proved to be very useful for us, and began imagining a grade as a text, no different in many respects from an essay we might assign: a grade is written, it is read, and it makes an argument about a student and a student's writing. We knew from our own practices as teachers, and from talking with colleagues, that this rhetorical act—writing down an actual letter or two—could be easy or gut-wrenching, or provoke a range of feelings in-between, depending upon the student in question and how we envision our courses as well as a host of other factors. Whatever the case, each teacher's grading methods are for the most part privately determined. Even in departments such as ours where formal criteria have been agreed upon, where fixed attendance policies and rules govern how those will effect a grade, the actual grading of a paper or a portfolio, or the assigning a final grade for a course, ultimately is done in isolation by a lone teacher who sits in judgment.

Our goal was to take these texts—these grades—written by isolated, individual teachers and to consider them within the rhetorical context of their writing. In doing so, we hoped to illuminate the paradox that we felt described our own situations (teaching process writing methods, while grading written products). In addition, we began to formulate other hypotheses we wanted to explore which grew out of our readings, discussions, and thinking about a grade as a rhetorical construct. We present our investigation in two parts: (1) a report on a survey we devised and administered, which examines teachers' and students' understandings of the audiences and arguments of grades and of grading as a rhetorical construct; and (2) a consideration of how current theoretical frameworks in composition studies might provide a rhetorical framework for grading.

Our conclusions, based both on our survey findings and our readings in rhetoric and the literature of grading, are actually quite simple. Current models of rhetoric which serve as theoretical frameworks for composition instruction should also be translatable to theoretical frameworks for grading practices. These current models are based on making the metaphorical leap from seeing a text as static and decontextualized, to being able to see texts as dialogues, written and read by multiple rhetors and audiences. In addition, these models see "meaning" as the result of negotiating a shared language within a given context.

Translated to the practice of grading, this means that grades-as-texts must represent dialogues between teachers and students who develop a common vocabulary for reading grades as signifying texts. If criteria can be made more explicit, those criteria can be developed only within particular contexts through the process of dialogue and negotiation. This notion is not new, of course; many teachers work with students to develop the criteria used for grading, and work to build a common vocabulary of evaluation. Indeed, many of the teachers we surveyed indicated they did as much. However, the majority of teachers and students, we found, seemed to be speaking different languages or rhetorics when they spoke about grading, especially in the grade ranges of "C" and above. In addition, our survey results indicate that a significant number of students seem to feel they have no speaking role in the "dialogue" that grades should represent.

The Survey

We distributed a survey to all ninety instructors and eighteen hundred students in the spring 1993 College Writing classes held at the University of Massachusetts at Amherst where we both taught.[1] Forty-nine percent of students (802) and 38 percent of instructors (30) responded. Our survey relied on a rhetorical model of teachers writing grades in the belief that the primary audiences for those grades—students—would understand a grade's meaning as a written text. We assumed that, in writing a grade, a teacher would envision other audiences besides students—parents, departments, teachers outside the discipline, deans, graduate schools, employers, and perhaps legislators (our university is a state school)—but that teachers would expect these other audiences would be much less likely to understand their grading criteria and the arguments embedded in these texts called "grades."

We used the standard rhetorical model (rhetor, audience, text) to help us fashion our inquiry, and devised a short, four-question survey which focused on indicators of grading as a rhetorical construct. The first two questions explored students' and teachers' sense of audience and values of grades. In the second two questions, we invited students and teachers to use their own language to describe their perceptions of what grades told students about their writing and their perceptions of the criteria for writing those grades.

In the responses to the survey questions, we looked for obvious concurrences and significant differences of opinion between students and instructors, and we were able to isolate four specific findings. First, both teachers and students did envision multiple audiences as readers of grades, but they differed in the amount of importance they felt grades had for those audiences. Secondly, most teachers and students did not believe a C was a good grade. At best, nearly half felt C was a "neutral" grade, but for about one-fourth, it was actually an out and out "bad" grade. Third, many students used some of the common language of grading and evaluation—words like "work," "effort," "improvement," "progress"—in a decidedly ambiguous manner, whereas teachers had much more specific ideas of what those terms meant. Fourth, and most significantly, teachers said they applied criteria based primarily on student effort and classroom performance in assigning lower range grades (C, D, F), while their criteria for assigning As and Bs were specifically and heavily text-based. In contrast, the majority of students seemed to assume that *all* grades are based primarily on their own efforts and classroom diligence, or lack thereof, or on natural talents or disadvantages. Students and instructors, then, had remarkably different perceptions of the criteria which led to As and Bs. In the following, we describe each survey question and the responses to it in more detail.

Survey Question One

As Tricia Evans notes in *Teaching English* (1982), students and instructors view grades as symbols that speak to many audiences: students themselves, peers, parents/guardians, our colleagues, other professors in other courses, college administrators, graduate schools, employers, and legislators. These observations were reflected and tested in a nationwide survey on college grades reported on by Milton, Pollio, and Elison in *Making Sense of College Grades* (1986). Our first question is adapted from that survey, modified slightly to fit our time and place. In this question, we asked students and instructors to place a value (on a scale of one to five) on the "importance" of the grade to various audiences (see fig. 7.1).

Overall, the responses to this question indicated that neither students nor instructors perceive the grade to be a text which has importance only among themselves. Instead, both acknowledged that it had some importance to multiple audiences. Teachers saw grades as being slightly more important to the school and their department than did students. However, students—more so than instructors—felt grades were important to other students and future employers. This suggests that each group sees the audiences closest to them as more important. Our hypothesis at this point is that for students (more so than teachers), other students' grades are important because they know grade standards are used for comparison, for ranking purposes, and they know employers will look at these rankings. Teachers know their department and school will look at their grading patterns to see if they are demanding and rigorous enough, and so teachers naturally place more importance on these audiences than do students.

Survey Question Two

We suspect that students and instructors have different perspectives regarding the relative value of specific grades. We tested this hypothesis by asking a survey question that invoked students' and teachers' perceptions of the value of the grade of C. Our department's position on delineating the values between grades of C or above is that Cs are "respectable" grades, and As and Bs are "Honor Grades," reserved for outstanding work.[2] Additionally,

FIGURE 7.1

Question 1: How important is the grade for the course to the following people?

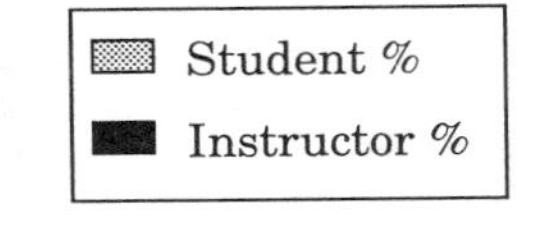

1 = of little importance
2 = of slight importance
3 = of moderate importance
4 = of great importance
5 = of crucial importance

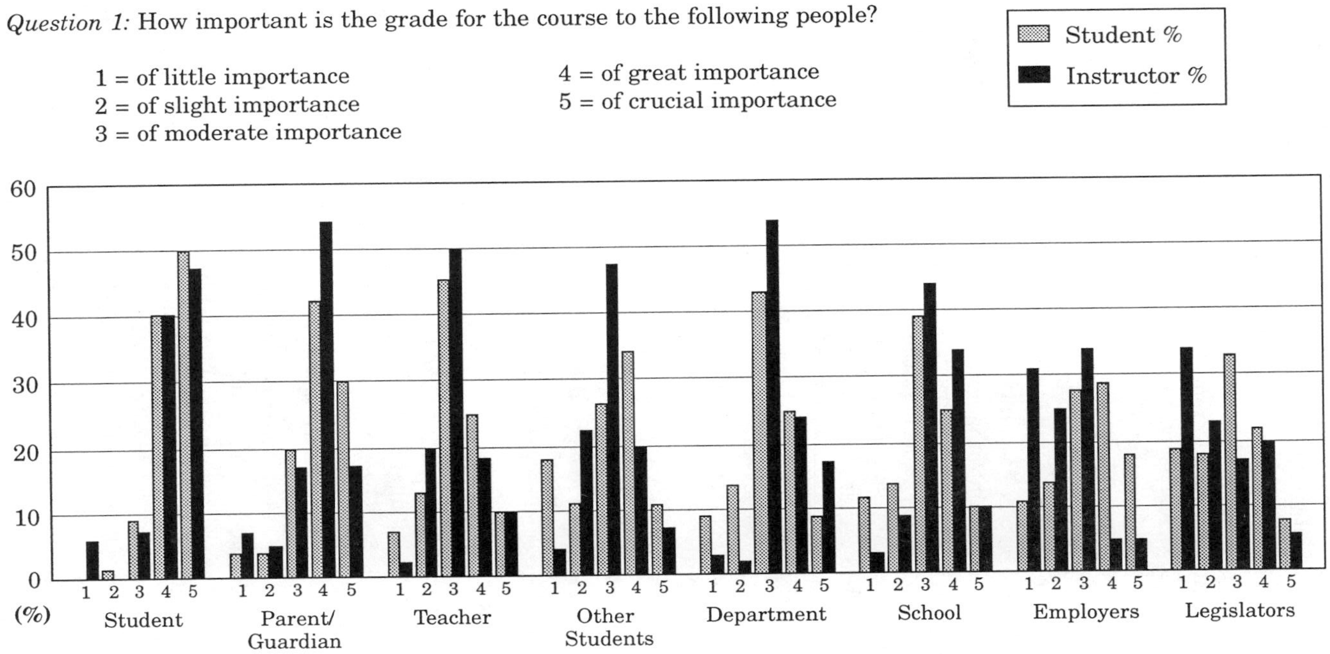

60
50
40
30
20
10
0
(%)

1 2 3 4 5 Student
1 2 3 4 5 Parent/ Guardian
1 2 3 4 5 Teacher
1 2 3 4 5 Other Students
1 2 3 4 5 Department
1 2 3 4 5 School
1 2 3 4 5 Employers
1 2 3 4 5 Legislators

Percentages are based on total number of surveys completed.

it is not an uncommon story for instructors to console students who have received Cs by telling them it is a "respectable" or even a "good" grade. Yet, that teachers sometimes feel it necessary to "console" students for receiving such a grade would indicate that Cs are neither "good" nor "respectable." We took Question #2 *verbatim* from a national survey done by Milton, Pollio, and Elison (1972), and asked students and instructors to assign importance to, or more accurately, a personal feeling about, particular grades—A, B, C, D, and F (see fig. 7.2). The scale of 1–7 is used to offset the tendency to simply equate A–F as a 1–5 ranking system.

Predictably, all respondents' scores fell into a bell-shaped curve, with As and Bs perceived as favorable grades, Ds and Fs perceived as unfavorable, and Cs falling into the mid range. However, more interesting to us was that, while 50% of all instructors and 43% of students assigned a neutral number ("4") to a grade of C, the other half of instructors and students were almost equally split between feeling that a grade of C was a "good" grade or a "bad" grade. While over one-fourth of students (28%) and one-fifth of instructors (20%) placed a C in the "good" range, 29% of students and 30% of teachers felt it was in the "bad" range. Most students and teachers, it appears, do not really believe a grade of C is "good." Our hunch is that the majority of respondents also would not describe "neutral" as being synonymous with "respectable," though official policy in our department at the time indicated that it was.

Survey Questions Three and Four

The second set of questions, #3 and #4, asked students and instructors to use their own language to describe what various grades "say" about a students' writing (#3), and how those grades are written or determined (#4). However, because our own methodology in categorizing the responses to #3 seemed to highlight inherent rhetorical ambiguities of the grading process, we will first discuss findings from Question #4.

Question Four

In Question #4, we asked instructors to describe how they arrived at the grade they assigned students, and students to describe how they thought their instructor arrived at their grade. Our intention here was to slant the focus towards the instructor as the writer of the grade, whereas in Question #3 we deliberately phrased our question to focus on the meaning or argument a grade makes about a student's writing. Although we both believe, as Hillocks (1986) and Elbow (1993) specifically recommend, that evaluation and grading is a process in which both instructors and students should participate, our experiences and conversations with other teachers led us to hypothesize that many students did not feel as if they were participants in that process.

FIGURE 7.2

Question 2: Use this 7-point rating scale to describe your personal feeling about each of the grades, A–F.

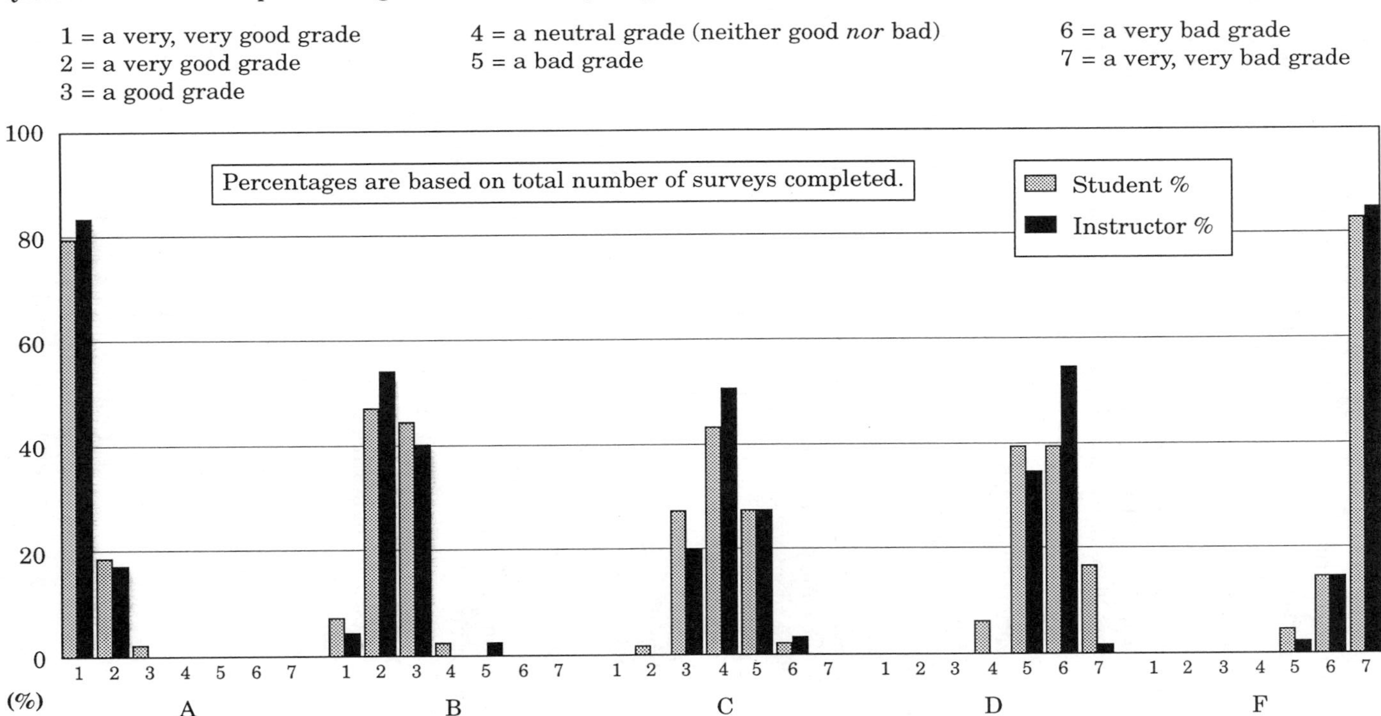

Responses to Question #4 were grouped into the following four categories of criteria: course-based criteria; student performance-based criteria; instructor preference-based criteria; and text-based criteria. These criteria evolved from the language of the responses. Course-based comments commonly referred to syllabus details about attendance and meeting due dates. Student-performance comments were those that used words and phrases that reflected student actions in a more general way—"did the work," "worked hard," "put in a lot of effort." Instructor-preference comments were those that indicated that grades were arrived at subjectively—"student writes the way the t.a. likes." And, text-based criteria referred to features of writing—any mention of punctuation, coherence, organization, spelling, quality of ideas, and so on were grouped under this heading.

A small number of student respondents (1.8%) left this section blank. Another 2.6% indicated that grading was a somewhat mysterious process. Examples of comments of this sort are: "I have no idea" or "Not sure" or even "Eenie meanie minie mo' syndrome." We grouped comments, or portions of comments, as editorials when they contained language like this: "It's hard to give a letter grade on an individual's creativity or lack of! I think it should be a pass/fail class." About equal numbers of respondents, 3.6% for students, 3% for teachers, offered editorial comments of this kind (see fig. 7.3).

Overall, and not so surprisingly, instructors were much more articulate and specific than students were about the criteria they used for arriving at grades. Of the students who did respond with specific comments to this question, there was a ratio of 2.87 comments per completed survey, while instructors as an aggregate made 7.64 comments per survey. Only a small number of students comments (8.2%) linked the grading process to teacher preference, prejudice, or inexplicit subjectivity; an even smaller number of instructors (3.9%) indicated this was the case. There was a very close percentage of "course-based" comments between students (29.5%) and teachers (29.3%), indicating that a similar number perceived grades to be determined as a result of factors spelled out on the syllabus or as part of the course outline.

However, our most significant finding in the responses to Question #4 was that, while it seemed there was some concurrence of opinion that "course-based criteria" is a determinant of grades, significant disagreement between instructors and students about what these criteria mean in practice was evident. In the category of "student performance-based criteria," almost one-third of student comments (32.8%) linked grades to these factors, while less than one-fourth of instructor comments (23.6%) fell into the same category. And, an even more significant difference can be seen in the category of "text-based features" as criteria for grades, where there is an

FIGURE 7.3

Question 4: (Teachers) How do you arrive at the grade you give a student?
(Students) How do you think the instructor arrives at your grade?

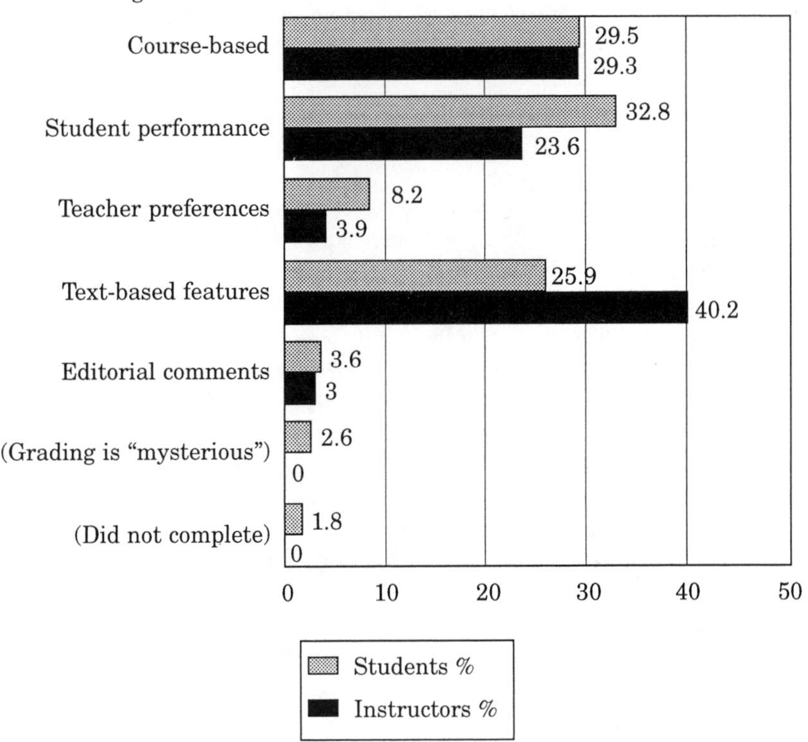

Student percentages are based on 802 returned surveys, less 71 in which this section was not completed, and less 51 in which students seemed to indicate that grading was a somewhat "mysterious" process. Therefore, the base number of surveys on which percentages were figured for students = 680.

Students: Total number of criteria = 1,949 in 680 surveys. Ratio of comments per survey = 2.87

Instructors: Total number of criteria = 229 in 30 surveys. Ratio of comments per survey = 7.64

almost 15% difference between student and instructor perceptions. Of instructor comments, slightly over 40% linked grading to text-based features, while only about 26% of students made this connection.

This last finding seemed to confirm one of our initial hypothesis: that students and their instructors are speaking different languages, or using different rhetorics, in their constructions of how grades are determined. Instructors, much more so than students, seemed to focus on evidence found in the product of writing. Students, much more so than instructors, seemed to focus on evidence found in the processes of writing—or perhaps more accurately, in the processes of being a student. After looking at Question #3, we will return to this finding.

Question Three

As mentioned previously, Question #3 presented problems of ambiguity in trying to categorize students' responses, and we will discuss these ambiguities in detail in the next section. In this question, we asked students and instructors to describe what each grade—A, B, C, D, and F—"told a student about his or her writing." Our intention in asking this question, within the rhetorical framework we had established, was to focus on the letter grade as a text, and the student as a reader of that text. We identified four major categories in the responses to Question #3—Student, Instructor, Text, and Apriori-based—which overlapped the categories identified in responses to Question #4 (see fig. 7.4).

Frequently, responses to this question fell into more than one category, as many were phrased in terms of either/or statements, as in: "they didn't put any time into it [a student-based comment], *or,* they are immigrants from another country" [an apriori-based comment]. Just as frequently, compound statements would be joined by a conjunction, comma, or semi-colon: "they are good writers [apriori] *and* put in a lot of effort [student]"; "the writing was of average quality [text-based comment] ; could use more effort to bring it to another level [student]"; or, "they're not bad writers [apriori] *but* could use a little help on their revision, organization, etc. [text]."

We discerned an overall pattern from the responses to Question #3, similar to the one found in Question #4, in which the majority of students seemed to perceive grades as texts that primarily reflected features of their own performance and efforts, rather than features about their writing. In the A and B range, however, a much higher percentage of comments in student surveys than instructor surveys connected grades to what we called "apriori" factors—i.e. some students are just "born" writers, or the letter grades of A, B, C, D, F simply translate to mean Excellent, Good, Satisfactory, Poor, and Failing, respectively. The majority of instructors, on the other hand, connected the meaning of A and B to specific text-based features, and connected Cs, Ds, and Fs to student effort and performance.

FIGURE 7.4

Question 3: What does a grade of A, B, C, D, or F tell a student about his/her writing?

Student-based comments: Indicate grades result primarily from student effort; a clear connection between time, energy, attention, care put forth by the student, and the grade (e.g., a grade of A "tells the student his effort was put into his work").

Instructor-based comments: Indicate that grades reflect meeting instructor preferences or idiosyncrasies, or that for some reason the student cannot or does not understand something about writing without help from the instructor (e.g., a grade of A tells a student "absolutely nothing except that her TA happened to like it").

Text-based comments: Here the focus is on the writing (e.g., "a grade of A tells a student that his writing is excellent. The ideas flow well, the piece is clear, and there are few or no grammatical errors").

Apriori-based comments: "Apriori" in its most common form represents a simple system used by students for the A–F grading system (Excellent, Good, Satisfactory, Poor, Failing). "Apriori" was also used as a code for comments that seemed to indicate that some students were "born" writers (e.g., a grade of A tells a student "that you're very good at writing"). Occasionally, students referred to other pre-existing conditions that effected one's writing, for instance problems incurred when English was not one's first language.

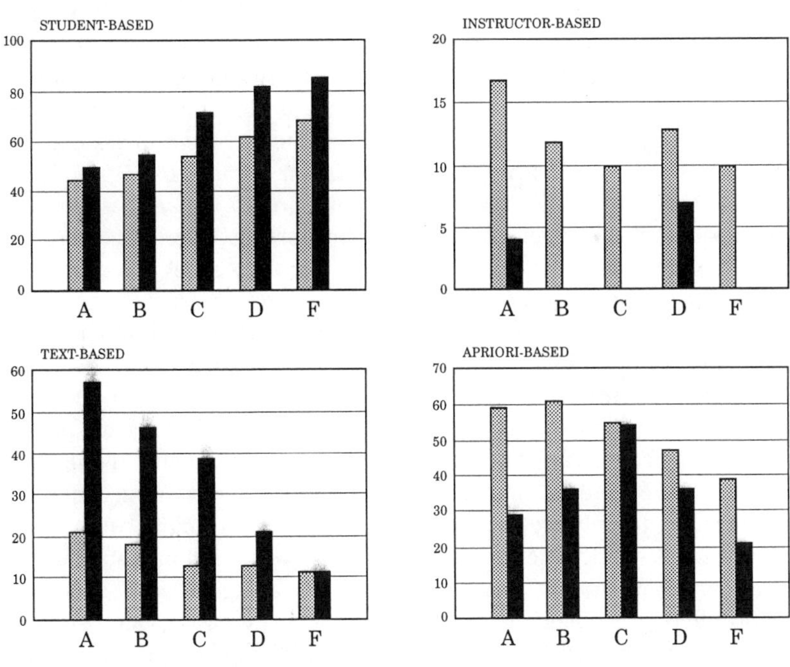

Numbers shown are percentages of frequency of occurrence of types of comments made at each grade level, based on a total number of comments made in student and instructor surveys.
Note: Only about half (418) the student surveys were coded for this section

These patterns seemed to confirm and further clarify our findings in the responses to Question #4. At the "Honors Grades" level, instructors seemed to switch grading criteria. Up through the C– level, instructors connected grades to student effort and performance, but in the A and B range they focused more on text-based criteria. Students as an aggregate group, alternatively, were less likely to detect or articulate this transition, and continued to assume that As and Bs, as with other grades, reflected either the amount of energy and compliance they put into the work, or some sense that an A or B means the student is inherently a good writer.

Ambiguities That Arise When Process Becomes Product

Given the difference in how teachers and students understand what As and Bs say about writing, and given that students mention text-based features of writing significantly less often than their teachers do, there is a schism between process pedagogy and a grading system that in many respects looks at writing in a more current-traditional, product-based way. As teachers, we know our students will be judged primarily on text-based features, especially the more grievous kinds of errors, as identified by Connors and Lunsford (1993) and Hairston (1981). Yet, students seem to assume they are being graded primarily on their efforts, or on pre-existing conditions beyond their control. We suspect that while process pedagogies guide the course, in the end, when it comes to grading, product-based considerations figure into the dividing lines between Cs, Bs, and As. Yet, many students are not clear about where these lines come into play, how they're being defined, and why. Consequently, students and teachers fall into divergent vocabularies when talking about the higher grades, what they mean, and how they are earned.

As we gradually began to narrow down the types of words and phrases that seemed to create ambiguity in categorizing students' responses to Question #3, the most prominent were the words "work" and "effort." In some cases, these words seemed to clearly signify a link between grades and student effort; for example, a grade of A "would tell me that I worked real hard to deserve it." In other cases, the meaning of "work" and/or student "effort" was vague. For example, a grade of C says about a student's writing: "Not a good paper. Needs more work." In this type of response, which was frequent, it is not clear whether work means simply student effort, or whether work means paying attention to particular features of writing such as organization, punctuation, and clear thinking. Another set of words that seemed to be used ambiguously included "improvement" and "progress." When used more decisively, they were frequently also linked with a student's efforts. For example: "a grade of A tells the student that a lot of progress was made over the semester. A conscious effort to improve was present." When used ambiguously, the student and the writing appeared separated. For example: a grade of A says, about a student's writing, that "it showed much improvement and is now a very talented writer [sic]."

We might dismiss the problems with Question #3 as the result of a poorly designed survey question. Upon reflection, however, we also noticed that although the question invited both teachers and students to reflect on what they thought a grade "said about a student's writing," many respondents offered comments about what grades said about the students themselves. Few were able to view the grades entirely as statements about the writing done in the course. Grading, then, *is* about the work—the writing—done in the course, but because grading speaks directly to and of the person being graded, it is also about the person doing the work. Subsequently, we surmise that the locus of the process/product schism is in the recursive, work-intensive nature of process writing pedagogies.

Writing class strategies at UMass include workshops, conferences, and multiple layers of feedback, with emphasis on doing the work—completing assignments on time, coming to class with completed drafts, and revising. During the course, teachers spend, in many cases, more time emphasizing the "effort" because they believe in the value of doing the work—writers learn to write by writing. Teachers follow these precepts, it should be said, not for the sake of "effort" itself, but as a way to guide students to good writing, writing that is clear, mechanically correct, as well as interesting and persuasive reading. So the stress on process is not simply some "touchy-feely" approach; it is a rigorous attempt to encourage students to think and work like writers. Much of the evaluation teachers give students along the way attempts to address the thinking and reasoning, the exploring and experimenting needed to make writing interesting and effective. However, at some level, many teachers experience a conflict between the pedagogy and the grading practices, evident, at the very least, in the conflict between how teachers and students read and perceive grades. Many teachers experience this in the occasional student who complains about a grade and does so *not* on the merits of their writing, but with arguments about performance, claiming that since they worked hard, they deserve an A for "effort." Teachers praise and encourage effort, but they cannot, or do not often, give As and Bs for effort alone. Our survey and particularly, coding the responses to Question #3, has confirmed this central ambiguity.

Revising Our Framework for Grading as a Rhetorical Construct

What was missing in our survey was a more current model of rhetoric, one that offers an image of teachers and students as collaborators, active participants in dialogue, negotiating consensus about the grades students receive for their work and their writing. What types of questions would we ask, if we were to redesign our survey with a more current model clearly in mind? What would such a model look like, in regard to grading as a rhetorical construct? How would such a model work in practice?

To frame such a rhetorical model for grading, we would draw upon the work of scholars who conceive of texts as dialogue, and dialogue as texts. We would incorporate the practice and theory of dialogics which begins with Plato and continues in the work of many theorists and composition teachers today.[3] However, in constructing this model, we would keep in mind what Donald Stewart (1984) calls "the fundamental paradox" of Plato—the impossibility of using "ineffable" language in order to arrive at the truth. We feel this ineffability is reflected in the ambiguity of language in the responses to Question #3, and in the overall gap between teachers' and students' perceptions of grading criteria, especially in the A and B range. John T. Gage (1984) offers a way out of this paradox by claiming that uses of language take two directions: (1) technique; and (2) the use of rhetoric to both discover and validate knowledge (153). In this sense, "knowledge is seen as an activity . . . rather than a commodity which is contained in one mind and transferred to another" (156). Gage argues that the only way to learn rhetoric in both senses of the word is through "tacit" experience. That is, one must be confronted with specific tasks (such as evaluating writing) and practical goals (earning a grade for the course) and then be allowed or required to actively use the techniques in question (in this case, rhetoric) to accomplish the tasks and attain the goals. In our rhetorical construct, this would translate into a situation where students, as well as teachers, are engaged in using evaluative language which would ultimately lead them towards consensus about grade assignation.

In thinking about a grade as the consensual outcome of a dialogue between students and instructors, we would rely on Aristotle's construction of knowledge and truth, which continues in Kenneth Burke's construction of rhetoric as identification, and Kenneth Bruffee's social constructionist theories of teaching and learning. However, the notion of "consensus" is as problematic as the problem of the ineffability of language. In thinking about consensus, and grades and grading as "dialogue" between teachers and students, we would also need to consider what Kenneth Burke identifies as the inevitable hierarchies of rhetorical situations, the problem of power and authority. This is an important point when we imagine students entering the dialogue of evaluation where, as our survey demonstrated, they address more, and different, "voices of authority" than their instructors. Burke also notes that, although the hierarchic principle itself is inevitable, it is a natural part of the process of growth and development. Problems arise, however, when the "inevitableness" of these processes acts to "rhetorically reinforce the protection of privilege," which then "interfere[s] with the very process of development that was its reason for being" (141) .

According to Foucault, as Bruce Herzberg (1991) observes, rhetoric is always about reconstituting power relationships, rather than about the purported subject matter. Within Foucault's framework "students collaborate not with one another so much as with the educational system, the disciplines, and the social forces they reproduce" (79) . However, Don Bialostosky (1991) sees a way through this potential rhetorical stalemate by adopting a Bakhtinian approach which recognizes the polyglot nature of both authoritative and internal discourse, and which allows for the fact that instructors and students alike, as we found, address multiple audiences in the grading process. Bialostosky advocates giving students an "open space in which to "retell or even parody" the words or texts of authoritative others in order to bring them within the realm of the "internally persuasive" voice (17) . Within this model of rhetoric, students would not simply assume their instructor's evaluative language, but would reconstitute or critique that language in their own words.

Using these theoretical models for the rhetorical situation, we can begin to imagine a way in which instructors and students, through dialogue, can acquire a mutual understanding of the evaluation and grading process, and come to some kind of consensus about what grades mean. However, underlying this model there still seems to be an assumption that once invited, or instructed, students will take an active role in such a dialogue. In the composition classroom, using a workshop-style pedagogy, we are encouraged to transform our writing classes into "communities of writers."[4] Many students, however, seem to resist the notion that they are writers, much less part of a community of writers. For example, one of our students, in our end-of-the-semester portfolio review, seemed to suddenly rebel against the very idea of self-evaluation and assessment. In response to the question "What has changed since the beginning of the semester?" (posed as part of the end-of-semester portfolio preparation), the student wrote that nothing had changed because she still—as she had mentioned at the beginning of the semester—didn't like to write:

> I really hate these questions because I feel that I have to analyze myself and that is not fair. . . . I wrote because I had to make the grade. . . . Yes, I have seen changes. I have become more independent and responsible, but in writing I guess I wouldn't see a change unless I was really into it

> like you or a writer or even a journalist. I'm just a freshman trying to get a good grade . . . by doing the work, passing it in on time, participating, and having good attendance. (May 1993)

This student's resistance seems to reflect the perceptions of many students in our survey who indicated they felt writing skills are acquired apriori to the situation, that teachers determine grades, and that students succeed when they do what they are told to do. This student could not conceive herself as "writer"; she could only imagine herself as "student." Yet, because part of her grade rested on her own participation in the evaluative process, she was forced to articulate her own criteria; these criteria then became part of the discussion about her grade for the course.

Conclusion

Early in their book, Courts and McInerney (1993) state a premise we find useful: "If the assessment movement cannot or will not lead to major changes and improvements in the teaching/learning enterprise, it has no good reason for being" (3). This statement, modified for grading in the writing classroom, might read like this: If a grading system cannot or will not lead to major changes and improvements in the teaching/learning of writing, it has no reason for being. We believe this means grading systems should be an extension of what teachers are trying to do. For example, Haswell and Wyche-Smith (1994) describe the efforts at their institution to develop a writing placement exam and scoring system for incoming first year students that reflects what goes on in first year writing courses. We share this view and believe that any form of assessment, including grading, should grow out of the need to privilege learning.

Simply stated, if grades are rhetorical constructs, and rhetoric is a complex dialectic involving negotiations of meaning, then it follows that students should be active in the dialogues that lead to their grades. Additionally, because the instructional situation is automatically embued with unequal relations of power and authority, students should be encouraged to share their own language, also, in developing a rhetoric of evaluation. Perhaps we are being idealistic, but our goal at semester's end is for students to be able to say they got a grade of "X" in the course and be able to describe the writing they did. They should be able to articulate what they learned about it and from it, and where they need to go, or can go next, in order to make it better. Our goal is to conclude the course in agreement with our students that their grades represent not so much a terminal judgment (although outsiders may read it as such), but a sign that recalls specific and useful memories about their writing, and which guides them on the road to further learning.

How would our more current rhetorical model for grading work in practice? When we began asking ourselves that question, both of us began trying to incorporate such a model into our courses, involving students as active participants in determining what the criteria really mean and what the grade, as a representative symbol of those criteria, denotes about them as writers. One possibility is to ask students to write arguments for their grades at the end of the semester. The instructor can then meet his students in final conferences where they mediate—looking for places of agreement as a starting point—what the grade for the student should be. In so doing, they can work together to clarify the criteria and rationale for the grade. The groundwork for this procedure is established throughout the semester by a series of evaluative writings required of the students, and in the kinds of questions they ask in peer review exercises used to promote revision and further writing.

We both feel our grading practices are evolving, in order to reflect a more current model of rhetoric; the design of our survey reflected the very process/product tension we were investigating. What types of questions would we ask if we were to redesign the survey with this current rhetorical model more clearly in mind? We continue to consider this question, and hope others will find it an equally challenging pursuit.

Notes

1. "College Writing" is the name of the entry-level writing course required for all undergraduates at the University of Massachusetts at Amherst, unless students "test out" of the requirement in a placement exam. In addition, UMass matriculated undergraduates are required to take a junior year writing course more closely aligned with the genres and conventions of their disciplines. Participants in these junior year writing courses, however, were not included in our survey.

2. Every year, the UMass Writing Program provides a generic, or model syllabus to be used especially by teaching assistants who are new to the program. When we first began teaching through the program, the word "respectable" was regularly connected to a grade of C. The current (1994–95) model syllabus states: "If you satisfy the minimum requirements for the course, you will receive the average of "C." If you performance falls below the minimum, you will earn a lower grade. On the other hand, if you work conscientiously and consistently on your writing and related work, you will earn a higher grade. Honor grades—A, A/B, and B—are reserved for outstanding work, work that is within everyone's reach."

As another example of this phenomenon, the myth of the acceptable C was deconstructed in a rather ironic form, during the time of our study at U Mass. In 1994 the president of the university system released a report on the state of the university. Like some teacher comments, it was long and detailed, filled with both praise and criticism. However, what made the headlines was the grade he gave the university: a C+. The grade incensed members of the community when it was announced—they thought it unduly harsh and hardly respectable. In this case, the grade became a rhetorical symbol, read by a wide range of audiences who then used it as currency when a faculty contract, negotiated with the university's board of trustees, was rejected by the legislature, in part because of the C+ grade. The president tried to explain that the C+ was a good grade, intended to encourage the university by symbolizing areas of success, while pointing to areas where more progress could be made. Still, as the answers to our first two questions showed, those who receive the grade, rather than those who write the grade, are generally more sensitive and attuned to the reality of the currency those grades will have in a larger context.

3. See, especially, Irene Ward's *Literacy, Ideology, and Dialogue: Towards a Dialogic Pedagogy*, (State University of New York Press, 1994) which presents concise descriptions of how dialogic constructions are used in the works of scholars such as Peter Elbow, Don Murray, Marilyn Cooper, Kenneth Bruffee, Paulo Freire, Ira Shor, and Gregory Ulmer.

4. The phrase "community of writers" comes from Peter Elbow and Pat Belanoff's *A Community of Writers* (New York: McGraw-Hill, 1989). The term is used to denote the ideals of the writing workshop, where the focus is on the "social and socializing" aspects of language use, and where students are encouraged to think of themselves as writers because they are *treated* as writers. As Elbow and Belanoff note, "No one can teach you how to write; others can only create a situation in which you learn for yourself from what you're doing" (4).

8

Steven VanderStaay

Resisting Reform

Grading and Social Reproduction in a Secondary Classroom

Current research in the teaching of writing within primary and secondary schools holds much in common with contemporary research in college composition, including a heightened attention to issues of power, difference, and democracy. These commonalities are expressed in many forms, including the call—first heralded by John Trimbur within composition, and Henry Giroux within education—to embrace the terms and methodologies of cultural studies. Tracing the genesis of this development within his own teaching, Raymond Williams notes that its guiding impulse was not merely one of "remedying deficit" but of making teaching and learning "part of the process of social change itself" (quoted in Giroux, "The Discourse of Critical Pedagogy" 201). While widely evident in research on composition at both the secondary and college level,[1] this impulse becomes distinguished within K–12 research by the attention educational researchers give to the complicity of schools and teachers in resisting social change and perpetuating the forces of "social reproduction" which explain, as the subtitle to Paul Willis' *Learning to Labour* declares: *How Working Class Kids Get Working Class Jobs.*

The roots of current attention to this "complicity" go deep into the history of educational research and wrap around cultural studies as well as the structural sociology it seeks to replace.[2] While manifest in many forms, few are as noteworthy as the consistency with which educational researchers have excoriated grading, tracking, and standardized testing as inherently biased tools which perpetuate the stratification of society along existing lines of race and class.[3] As Henry Giroux makes clear in "Doing Cultural Studies: Youth and the Challenge of Pedagogy," this research demands that teachers "critically address the politics of their own location" and consider how their very "vocation as educators supports, challenges, or subverts institutional practices that are at odds with democratic processes and the hopes and opportunities we provide for the nation's youth" (279). Consequently, progressive and radical educational reforms almost always include features designed to subvert the functions of testing, tracking, and grading, or to abolish them altogether. In broad reform efforts, testing and tracking get the most attention. But for individual teachers, their own use of grades becomes the most important, if simply because it is the one form of institutional assessment they control. Yet there is precious little data on such teacher attempts to reform or subvert the grading process, and literally no existing attempt to describe what such efforts suggest about the phenomena of grading itself.

I seek in this chapter to fill this gap by describing "The A Plan," a grading reform effort of my own, and by accounting for its effect upon my students, the notion of "schooling" we created together, and my teaching—both in high school classrooms and the university setting where I now work. Ultimately, I hope my experience will shed light on both the function of grades in social reproduction, and the nature and limitations of attempting to subvert that function through reform efforts like my own.

Contexts

I spent the first year of my teaching career in a large, inner-city high school and the second in a tiny, rural district on the Iowa prairie. The differences were more than geographic. The urban school, which housed the humanities division of Seattle's magnet school program, was like a caricature of social reproduction models: middle to upper-class white and Asian-American students dominated the A.P. and honors classes, a diversity of working-class students filled the "regular" courses, and teachers who worked with "remedial" and "special needs" students looked out on classrooms which were often entirely black.

The Iowa school, in contrast, was almost entirely white, very mixed economically (20 percent of students received free lunches—a broadly accepted proxy for "poor"), and virtually egalitarian in appearance. Too small to track its students into ability groups and too rural to serve neighborhoods divided by class, the school appeared to mirror few of the great economic divides that distinguished local, land-owning farmers from those whose families rented land or did seasonal labor. Social markers, like popularity among peers, largely followed athletic and personality traits—characteristics only marginally impacted by socio-economic distinctions.

It may be to the disadvantage of teachers from tiny districts like the one I taught in to know so much about the demographics of their students. Research in expectancy bias has repeatedly demonstrated that overhearing even vague descriptions of students will bias grading. These biases become self-fulfilling for students at all levels since teachers give higher grades to high expectancy students and lower marks to low expectancy students. Yet familiarity with my students also made subtle patterns of social reproduction obvious. The strata of students in my 12th-grade English course who went to college was quite clearly drawn from those families with college-educated parents or large farms, for example. And, as I became more aware of it, I saw the beginnings of this pattern in the grades sophomores earned. The correlation wasn't perfect: a few of my working-class students were A students. But no student of mine from a college-educated or farm-owning family earned less than a B, and many of the others did.

Returning to graduate school in the fourth year of my tenure in this district, I began to reflect on this realization in light of contemporary educational research. This drew my attention to the patterns of expectancy bias described above, the "deficit orientation" teachers adopt with respect to working class students, and the school—home mismatch of speech registers, discourse practices, and conceptions of literacy so thoroughly documented by Shirley Brice Heath and Courteney Cazden.

At this point in my career, I taught writing from an expressivist perspective, characteristic of writing process models typical of the early 1980s. I saw the research in bias I've described above as an affirmation of my emphasis upon student experience and personal writing and, in response, my pedagogy became yet more pointedly expressivist. I became more accepting of the informal, working-class registers that emerged in my students' writing, and I sought out topics and writing assignments that would tie more explicitly to their homelife and experience. Within the 10th-grade language arts course (an integrated, year-long course in the "language arts" of reading, writing, and speaking), for example, much of our writing became focused upon the farm crisis of that period. I remember with particular fondness the rigor and enthusiasm with which the students critiqued, and responded to, a reporter who wrote a lengthy piece on the farm crisis in Iowa for the *Atlantic Monthly*.

These reforms made me more attentive to my own biases and they made my students more fluid and enthusiastic as writers. Interestingly, they also encouraged the same sense of collaboration, of "pooling of resources," and the "social engagement in intellectual pursuits" that Kenneth Bruffee was about to advocate in "Collaborative Learning and the 'Conversation of Mankind.'" But they did not eradicate the grading patterns I had previously observed and associated with the stratification of the community into an upper class of college-educated professionals and land-owning farmers, and a lower class of blue collar and seasonal farm-workers. In fact, by helping to transform my classroom into a community of writers and learners, these reforms made the socioeconomic distinctions yet more painfully evident. For while the processes by which my students wrote, debated, and researched had changed, the products they turned in for grades had not.

For example, many of my working-class students became deeply engaged in our class discussions of the farm crisis and wrote blistering critiques of the *Atlantic* article they never turned in. Others refused to participate in our peer-editing sessions and then railed at me for lowering their grades on account of surface errors. In this way, the process of grading, and distributing the grades in class, created distinctions between successes and failures that had literally not existed during the writing, reading, and learning together that comprised our consideration of the farm crisis.

First Drafts

These experiences placed me in a position which, while not uncommon, is rarely remarked upon. On the one hand, I fit James Berlin's characterization of the expressivists of this period as I was "unsparingly critical of the dominant social, political, and cultural practices of the time" ("Rhetoric and Ideology in the Writing Class" 485). I very much wanted to make the "writing classroom work explicitly toward liberating students from the shackles of a corrupt society" (485). But I taught composition to 10th graders, not college freshmen. And I was a graduate student in education, not rhetoric or composition. I certainly believed that power "is a function of finding one's unique voice" ("Rhetoric and Ideology" 486). But I also had come to believe that the politics of my position as a teacher who handed out grades made me complicit in the institutional oppression of my working-class students.

In short, I believed that grading is formative in both a social reproductive and pedagogic manner. Indeed, apart from its role in reinscribing the socioeconomic patterns I'd seen emerging in my classroom, my grading of the farm-crisis papers reframed all that we had done. What had been experienced as collaborative became recorded as competitive. Stratification both preceded and superseded the democracy of the learning community we had created. And I became convinced that I needed a grading system that would empower my students to find their voice while subverting—perhaps even reversing—the damage done by grading.

I settled, first, on a modified "mastery learning" system that emphasized contracts wherein students determined what grade they wanted and worked to fulfill the requirements I'd specified for that grade. For my 10th-grade language arts course, most of these requirements referred to portfolios of written work and daily progress checks. I specified a set number of pages to be written for each grade, and I also used subjective criteria—such as my own notion of a "strong personal voice" and "above average." As is typical of mastery learning systems, the plan assumed that all students can attain a high level of success if they receive adequate assistance and have adequate time. I strove to provide both by allowing students to resubmit a paper, portfolio, or other product, as many times as they needed to make the revisions necessary to reach the criteria specified for the grade they sought.

Ultimately, this system boosted more of my "C" students into As and Bs and turned more control over the evaluative process to my students. More importantly, the "mastery learning" feature reconfigured that process. Our class time continued to be spent in collaborative, process centered activities, like those that had characterized our farm crisis unit. But whereas the bulk of my evaluative work had previously been to append terse comments explaining why I had judged a finished product A, B, or whatever, I now faced the much harder task of providing the kind of in-process, formative advice that would help a student get a paper to meet the criteria she'd contracted for. I read more drafts, held more conferences. Students took home more homework and came by after school to see me. I came to school earlier, stayed later and, while exhausted by the work load of teaching this class and five others, felt like a success.

Then gradually, as if by degrees, I became less satisfied with the contracts. My work may have changed, but the grading curve had merely been revised, not rewritten. Students grew frustrated at the number of revisions required to reach a grade goal. Others began to lower their sites and contract for Cs. And, despite the increased attention to collaboration, the classroom milieu remained individualistic—if simply because the class continued to earn a range of grades. The success of one student did not mean the failure of another, as it may in a classic bell curve, but neither did it mean other students were better off for the success.

Then, in a single gasp of insight and desperation that struck me while driving home from school one day, I conceived The A Plan.

The A Plan

As I saw it, The A Plan would maintain the strengths of my mastery/contract system while subverting the stratifying function of grade competition by awarding each of my students an A. In essence, I wanted everyone to contract for an A and to work together in a context marked by the collective assumption of cooperative assistance and high standards.

This collective feature struck me as the key. Whereas my traditional grading system had stratified my class on the basis of performance, my contracts had ultimately stratified the class on the basis of school ambition—a feature heavily influenced by socio-cultural orientations toward literacy and schooling, and previous experiences in school. The A Plan couldn't alter the knowledge and skills my students came to class with. But it could help democratize both performance and ambition by institutionalizing and rewarding the collaboration that had characterized our best activities. The only catch was to get my students to go for it.

I made the pitch to one of my sophomore language arts classes the next day, asking them to commit to a four—week test-pilot of the plan for the *Julius Caesar* unit my district required of all 10th graders. I explained that I would indicate the exact criteria required to fulfill each portion of The A Plan and that I would schedule no more homework than would be assigned were we not on The A Plan. In turn, I would ask them to approach each class with an eye to what needed to be accomplished; to commit themselves to drafting papers, retaking exams, and resubmitting portfolios until they met The A Plan criteria; and to work together so that the class, as a collective whole, fulfilled the plan. All but one student, Bob, a consistent contrarian, agreed to the plan. I said that was good enough and we were off.

The unit emphasized collaborative retellings of *Julius Caesar,* readers' theater performances of specific scenes, and a final exam to include character identification questions and an in-class essay. To help students prepare for the exam, I gave a pretest of the essay questions, each of which had been drawn from our class discussions. Each group took one essay question, mulled it over, and then gave a brief, class presentation on how it might be answered. I "published" my grading criteria by copying it to the blackboard as they did the group work, and we contrasted each group's advice about the essays with the scale I would use to evaluate them. In this way I sought to help prepare the students, to be explicit about the criteria I considered "mastery," and to use the quiz to reinforce the culture of mutual assistance I sought to create.

I gave students the choice of answering any of the essay questions that had been discussed. Yet nearly half of each class had to polish their essays or retake the quotation identification section. In order to avoid giving the identification questions again, I had students who had not reached mastery on that section write modern English versions of the speeches they had failed to identify. Students whose essays didn't meet the criteria I had specified had to resubmit them.

Many of the students had not, in fact, resubmitted their essays by the end of the unit, but most had. I conferenced with each student, offering congratulations for staying on The A Plan, or a description of the work he or she still had to redo. Rather than lowering grades, I stuck to the positive bias inherent in the plan and simply marked anything not up to the "mastery" criteria as incomplete. Report cards for these students looked something like this:

Week 1: A.Week 2: A.Week 3: A. Exam: Incomplete.

The students, to my surprise, were elated. Those with straight As "high fived" each other or flashed their cards to a friend, as if to confirm their success. Others, seeing that the exam was their only blemish, begged me to let them work on their revisions right then and there. These students bent over their rewrites, struggling to see if they could get the "incomplete" scratched out by the end of the period.

I explained that the next unit was an "I Search" paper, and a team-taught project wherein they worked on their paper as part of both their English and social studies courses. "We can continue The A Plan," I explained, "Or we can go back to business as usual."

I wanted so much for them to continue the plan: for those who had learned to be habitual failures to succeed—if just for this once—for an entire quarter. I wanted the students to see themselves as "A" students, to be able to look back on school with the memory of how they had succeeded. And I wanted student success to reflect a cooperative culture of mutual assistance and achievement, rather than the socio-economically stratified world of work they would soon enter. But I didn't want to push them into it. Consequently, I made the pitch purposefully gruff and business-like, in order to mask this agenda.

"Whether we continue the plan or not is up to you," I explained. "I simply need to know what you want so I can do my part to help you get there. If you want to continue, I'll structure the plan just as I did for this unit. I'll define weekly criteria for the paper. Meet each's week's criteria and you'll be on the plan and on your way to mastery work."

"Let's go for it!" someone shouted. There was a second, then a third. Ultimately, everyone but Bob, my lone hold-out, agreed to continue and pledged themselves to the plan.

We began by searching for questions the students would be interested in pursuing through research. "Mastery" criteria required everyone to combine book research with personal interviewing, or some other form of real-world data collection, and to write with a strong, personal voice. We brainstormed ways to do this by drawing up lists of questions that grew out of each students' experiences.

After finding questions, we made our first inroads into the library. Mastery for this week meant a question, a research plan, and three pages of writing. We worked at the library each day and I did my best to get to every student, to give feedback, advice, inspiration.

It wasn't enough. Students grew frustrated and complained that the daily "mastery" criteria were unreasonable; I grew angry and told them they would meet the criteria if they worked more and complained less. Then, somehow, I caught myself. I saw that trying to make the class succeed undercut the role of their individual commitments and the power of the classroom culture of cooperation and mutual assistance they, if only briefly, had achieved. I loosened up, relaxed my "mastery" standards for daily work, and strove to demonstrate a positive bias of high expectations that assumed their eventual success. The students, surprisingly, became more dedicated and engaged. I kept my room open afternoon and evening. Students called me at home; others brought dinner and came to see me, or worked together with a partner after basketball or wrestling practice.

In this way we worked through three weeks of drafting, researching, and peer-editing. Ultimately, nearly half of the students turned in papers that met the "mastery" criteria and received an "A" for sophomore English on their midterm report card. Most others received a "B." They were the highest grades my sophomores had ever achieved; some had never earned an "A" before. But when we came back after midterms and voted on whether to continue the plan, the class turned it down by a wide margin.

"But you liked it!" I objected. "You were successful; we worked together and earned great grades!"

"Maybe so," a student ventured, "But it was too hard. Too much work."

"But the plan did not change the work-load," I added. "You would have had the same tests, the same assignments."

"Yeah," the student said. "But this way we had to do it."

Reflections

Despite its ultimate rejection, The A Plan met most of my hopes and expectations. Most importantly, it created a learning setting characterized by the attributes Lilia Bartolome has described as necessary for schools to foster progressive, social change ("Beyond the Methods Fetish: Toward a Humanizing Pedagogy"). That is, it fostered a collaborative context, marked by high expectations, in which low status students perceived as "poor learners" could achieve success and "demonstrate their possession of knowledge and expertise" (44).

These are the attributes I try most to encourage in my present grading practices in my university classes, where I continue to use contracts specifying the number of books and articles to be read and the number of papers to be written. I also continue to permit assignments and papers to be revised indefinitely. Students must find the time for these revisions on their own, of course, but since I respond to each draft, the process increases the amount of assistance students receive. However, I no longer attempt to talk an entire class into "going for an A."

Students applaud the system in their course evaluations for a number of reasons. Those with family or work responsibilities say it allows them greater control over the amount of work they wish to take on. Others say that it rewards effort and encourages goal setting, or that my openness to revision allows them to give more attention to the material and less to their worries about grades. Students who have had little success in college often find it empowering—a conclusion that Ronald Gentile and Laura Cox Wainwright's recent reevaluation of criterion-referenced and mastery learning systems supports ("The Case for Criterion-Referenced Grading"). That many of these students come from working-class backgrounds confirms their marginalization in the university and points to the role of grading reform measures in resisting the role schooling plays in the social reproduction of class divisions and inequities.

To the extent that The A Plan did momentarily set my classroom apart from these processes, it did so by shifting assessment to the front end of my curriculum. This thrust more attention upon my assessment procedures and led, in turn, to my efforts to reframe "A work" as a minimal standard students met in a context of mutual support and collective progress.

There were numerous consequences to this, many of which continue to interest me. For the most part, I had been won over by the view that writing and reading are best learned in contexts that replicate the conditions under which we all first acquired spoken language as children. These conditions are broadly understood as being context-rich, meaningful, and characterized by a positive bias that reframes "errors" as a natural part of growing and learning. Consequently, arguments, like that of Frances Zak, that responses to student writing should be "exclusively positive" ("Exclusively Positive Responses to Student Writing") made a world of sense to me, and for most of my career I followed them.

The A Plan—by far my most successful experience of assessment—was a glaring exception. Faced with the challenge of helping my students achieve the criteria I had specified as "mastery," I responded to student writing in an aggressively pointed manner that focused on "weaknesses," and my thoughts on how they might be overcome. Yet no one in my class objected. Indeed, The A Plan drove my students to be so goal-oriented that they rather demanded prescriptive advice. They didn't stew over how they felt about my response; they used it to get down to the rewrite.

If this example makes me sound like a firm and exacting coach, that is exactly my point. I have long been persuaded that Peter Elbow was right in pointing out that writing teachers do well to distinguish their coaching and judging functions. But I had always been tripped up by the process of actually doing so, except in this case. Similarly, The A Plan rather institutionalized the recommendations Elbow makes in "Ranking, Evaluating, and Liking" to give more attention to evaluating and less to ranking and grading. After all, under The A Plan, evaluation meant providing feedback to help a student achieve "mastery." This occupied virtually all of my time. Ranking, in contrast, merely meant determining—not how good a piece of writing was—but whether it was good enough. Liking was of little consequence, though, like Elbow, I found it helped both me and my students when I could say, "I like this very much but am afraid it does not yet meet 'mastery' criteria."

Of course, this was also The A Plan's greatest weakness. It didn't encourage students to find the act of reading *Julius Caesar* intrinsically rewarding. Nor did it foster the kinds of intrinsic rewards and self-reflexivity we associate with learning to see oneself as a writer. Indeed, in forcing me to define "mastery" so explicitly, and in structuring the course in such a goal-directed fashion, The A Plan exaggerated my coaching function to an almost ridiculous extreme. This made a charade of the notion that my students were to keep in mind an intended audience other than myself. And while the bulk of my work remained evaluative, my evaluations were so criterion-specific that an impartial observer might have commented that the coach was doing everything he could to get his students to please the judge. Ultimately, revising was reduced to a high-bar, of sorts, to leap over.

Yet leap my students did: for half a semester. And then they gave up—or at least those who had previously earned the lowest grades did. Ironically, these were the very students whose grades had profited the most by the plan.

I've had a wide variety of thoughts about this in the years since The A Plan. At times, I've taken these students at their word and decided they simply didn't want to work that hard. At other moments, I've been persuaded by Jay MacLeod's argument that students from our lower socio-economic tiers know, for them, there *Ain't No Makin' It*, so why try? From this perspective, the rejection of The A Plan may have implied a rejection of my own attempt to seduce my marginalized students into believing that they could achieve the kind of school success that would translate into economic success.

Conversely, the students may simply not have valued their grades as much as I expected them to. Emerging research on "resilient" students who succeed in spite of great obstacles and institutional marginalization, such as Sonia Nieto's "Lessons From Students on Creating a Chance to Dream," reveals that teachers often give more attention to grades than such students do. And an interesting study by Maureen Hallinan and Ruy Teixeira suggests that teachers who downplay the importance of standardized testing and grades can reduce status differences between black and white students and facilitate more cross-race friendships within their classrooms.

Embracing Cultural Studies

Each of these explanations suggests the complicity of students in the formation and maintenance of grading practices. In this sense, they point both to the role of grading in social reproduction, *and* to the inadequacy of describing grading as a *social construction,* framed by power elites and imposed on teachers and students. Talking, and writing, about this is difficult. Reflecting on The A Plan in light of these concerns, I find myself challenged to attend to the subjectivity of the students I graded, the place of that grading in our power relations, and the larger, socio-economic context of Iowa in the early 1980s, in which the grading occurred. Fortunately, this is the very balancing act that cultural studies permits. As James Berlin puts it in "Composition Studies and Cultural Studies: Collapsing the Boundaries," "cultural studies concerns itself with the ways social formations and practices shape consciousness," *and* with the manner in which "this shaping is mediated by language and situated in concrete historical conditions" (101).

For example, The A Plan was "successful" for my students only to the extent that they accepted the essentially middle class norms and values it rested on—norms and values which, as the earlier sections of this paper demonstrate, denigrate the "cultural capital" of working-class students and otherwise institutionalize biases against them. In this sense, my enthusiasm for their participation in The A Plan can be read as prototypically hegemonic, because it encouraged them to choose to participate in a system which oppressed them.

Similarly, it can be argued that by participating in the plan, my working-class students forfeited their right to assert their own norms and values by opposing it in acts of resistance. Henry Giroux argues that this resistance enables marginalized students to form and assert their own subjectivity, their own sense of who they are. This probably explains the motivations of Bob, the lone "hold out" who refused to participate. Like the working-class students who wrote great rebuttals to the *Atlantic* essay they never bothered to turn in, Bob strove to present himself as a skilled reader and writer who rejected schooling. He liked to read novels while we wrote and to write short stories while we read. And he loved for his work to be praised. But participating in The A Plan meant wanting to be an "A" student—exactly what he worked so hard to prove he didn't want.

Would The A Plan have worked in a class of middle and upper-middle class students? Perhaps. It did work for the middle and upper-middle class students in the class I've described, and I expect it would be more successful in a class with more such students. But while orientations toward schooling and grades correlate with some socio-economic distinctions, they don't predict them. And the collective nature of The A Plan, however pedagogically laudable, created a homogeneity that even a class full of "A" students might be expected to rebel against.

These arguments don't disprove that grades serve to reproduce our class divisions and inequities. Nor do they suggest that marginalized students can't be empowered by reform efforts that facilitate their "success" in school. However, they do suggest caution in enacting reforms on behalf of marginalized students. And they point to the value of reframing our discourse about grading so that we can examine its forms and functions while simultaneously attending to the issues of subjectivity, power, and resistance it inevitably raises.

Notes

1. This is particularly the case in Freirian and post-Freirian theory. Consider, for example, the many similarities among Kutz and Roskelly's *An Unquiet Pedagogy: Transforming Practice in the English Classroom*, Cooper and Holzman's *Writing As Social Action*, and Hurlbert and Blitz's *Composition and Resistance.*

2. "Modern" analyses of the link between schooling and class stratification grew out of the sociological notion of class "conflict theory," derived from Max Weber. Randall Collins' "Functional and Conflict Theories of Educational Stratification," is the quintessential example of these analyses. Contrasting the technical-functional explanation that the key function of education is to train specialists required by our modern, industrial society with the conflict theory explanation—that the key function of education is to create a "contest mobility" system to contain the power struggle among status groups—Collins demonstrates that the conflict theory explanation is more persuasive.

3. Educational theories of social reproduction have changed considerably. Early analyses, such as Samuel Bowles and Herbert Gintis' *Schooling in Capitalist America: Educational Reform and the Contradictions of Economic Life*, were rigidly Marxist. More recent explanations, including Giroux's *Theory and Resistance in Education*, build on Pierre Bourdieu's notion of "cultural capital," or the disposition, background, knowledge, and skills of cultural groups and socioeconomic classes. This literature notes that schools value the "cultural capital" of middle-upper class students and devalue the "cultural capital" of marginalized and working-class students. Schools then exacerbate these differences by seeking to inculcate middle-upper class "cultural capital" in all students.

IV

Institutional Entanglements

Student Voices

In my first writing class, grades had a dual effect on me, and that is why I'm not sure at all how I feel about the traditional grading system. The first effect of a single letter grade on my paper was that it made me work (proportionally to how high the grade was—the lower it was, the more work I did to improve the writing). The second effect was that I experienced all the "by-products" of negative feedback possible when my grades were low: anxiety, depression—the whole bouquet. . . . The system my teacher used was this: we had three opportunities to turn in the work to her—three drafts. The first drafts she never graded—she would just give us a lot of feedback and suggestions for improvements. The second draft was graded, and if you weren't satisfied with the grade, you had a chance to turn your paper in once again (a deadline was given) for a grade improvement.

As a diligent student, I had used all the feedback I got from my teacher on my first draft and considered it in revising. (All right, I'll admit, at first I was following it blindly, but as time passed I learned to judge for myself.) I also went to the Learning Center a couple of times. Students do all they can to get away with doing as little work as possible and getting good grades, so I figured I shouldn't waste my time on rewriting my paper a third time—might as well get an A for my second draft and get it over with. So I worked hard.

My paper came back to me with a B+ and a bunch of comments which I, of course, (and in accordance with all the research done) saw in the light of the grade and thought of my teacher as an extremely evil being. I remember crying over that poor paper (the other problem was that the topic was very personal and something that I wanted to write WELL about), and I also remember thinking that "I'm gonna go and make this paper perfect so she doesn't dare touch it with her green pen ever again!" I went to the Learning Center again and was told that the paper is very "nice" (oh those student tutors just love giving such feedback) and no one understood neither any of the comments, nor why the paper was given a B+ (hysterical, come to think of it now).

So I summoned all my courage up and signed up at the Learning Center to meet with the "evil being"—my teacher. Evil Being turned out to be a very nice lady whose first words were "I knew this grade was gonna piss you off!" and second—"I was just teasing you!" I, of course, felt better after the session. I realized that our teacher was deliberately not giving As (or giving them very reluctantly) on the second drafts—so that we have some motivation to revise for the third time. (I almost hear you saying that that is the behavior of an undeveloped writer, that the motives for revising should be different, but—believe it or not—and I'm sure you experience the same thing when you write—deadlines and evaluation work just as great as the awareness of possible readers.)

By the end of the semester, I really felt that I'd gained the feeling of the "writing process"—or at least the very primitive, beginning form of it: I now knew that anything I write will have to go through several stages (our "three drafts") before it's any good, and I should never count on getting a high grade on the first drafts, since our drafts were graded as they were final products. Think twice before you share something that hasn't been worked on long enough, in other words!

Overall, I' m not sure how I feel about traditional grading, and this teacher's grading system in particular. Although I have nothing bad to say about it, it's being widely criticized, as I've noticed, in the comp literature; and I see why. The "side effects" I have experienced taught me a lot and cost me a lot, *but* the amount I learned by the end of the semester was as great. — *Victoria Savalei*

9

Pauline Uchmanowicz

The Politics of Cross-Institutional Grading

An Adjunct's Dilemma

In recent years college compositionists have sought to demystify the acts of reading and grading student writing. Charles Bazerman admits that the veracity of how we read student papers remains "secret and obscure, hidden in unexamined private experience" in conflict with the comments we write on them, "visible and open to inspection" (139). Robert Schwegler recommends that writing teachers unmask this dichotomy by acknowledging in evaluative comments how our perceptions of a text's meanings are conditioned by our social, cultural, or political concerns (204). Lad Tobin suggests that instructors practice self-recognition and self-disclosure when assessing student writing, as he himself has done in constructing a list of things he thinks about when grading "that teachers are not suppose to think about when we give grades" (58–65 passim; 69). As these comments suggest, many have called for teachers to examine their own reading and grading practices and to situate their responses in terms of both their personal experience and their cultural condition. But calls to demystify grading practices largely ignore the work of teachers who are not situated in a single school; for this vast population of instructors the culture of grading is cross-institutional. By overlooking their experiences, current conversations about grading fail to adequately address the concerns of those deeply affected by grader culture: instructors forced to vary their practices across institutions, and students situated in their cross-institutional classrooms.

Perhaps no postsecondary instructional staff is better prepared to demystify grading practices than are college writing instructors who teach at more than one school on a part-time basis, or who move from place to place in a string of temporary appointments. For along with transporting the individualized politics of various institutions to multiple locations in order to manage the exchanges they share with dozens of personalities, these teachers do a good deal of grading student writing. Recent reports bear out this claim. In October 1994 the National Center for Educational Statistics (NCES) estimated that over a quarter million (approximately one-third of the total) faculty and instructional staff serving United States colleges and universities were employed part time (v), including 42 percent of the estimated 64,000 instructors in English (Tables 6 and 7; 14–16). The NCES also indicated that nearly 125,000 full-time faculty were instructors, lecturers, or "others" (Table 2; 10); nontenure track, temporary contract workers likely swelled these ranks. A year later *The Wall Street Journal* claimed that part-timers made up 38 percent of the postsecondary teaching faculty in the U.S. (Kean 49), a number that can double at two-year community colleges (Gappa and Leslie 1), where roughly one-third of all undergraduates are educated (Sommer 8). At four-year colleges the number of full-time teachers has dropped from 80 to 71 percent over the past twenty years (Brodie 12); a 1988 American Association of University Professors study found that even the nation's most prestigious research universities classified nearly 17 percent of the total faculty as part-time, not including teaching assistants (Sommer 7). Since most part-time instructors teach introductory and lower division courses—composition being a conspicuous example—these figures indicate that "[m]any American students now complete at least the first two years of college taught [and graded] largely by instructors and graduate students who are not on the tenure track" (Gappa and Leslie 5).

As a long-standing member of the teaching population contained in these statistics, I wish to argue that unmasking the politics of grading student writing from a position of multi-institutional situatedness can revitalize grader culture as well as lead to new ways of producing knowledge in the composition classroom. Using descriptions of research and classroom dialogues about grading as well as evaluative comments on student writing as a basis for my discussion, in the sections that follow, I describe grading processes that emerged for me while teaching writing at five institutions during a recent five-year period. Since my discussion remains partial and local I also wish to encourage college faculty—particularly those economically forced to divide their labor and practices among divergent locations—to keep track of institutional and related power structures that surround the culture of grading in order to disclose options and alternatives for transformative classroom praxis (West 213).

Making Grading Visible

Compositionists seeking to transform grader culture must make its often concealed institutional uses visible. For example, as Peter Elbow stresses, "assessment tends so much to drive and control teaching" (187). The grades students earn likewise can influence the economic well-being of academic institutions, a causality I wish to explore through the lens of cross-institutional teaching experience.[1]

During the spring of 1991, the writing program director at a state university where I was a teaching assistant issued a memo to all first-year writing instructors. It reported that the dean wanted to know why class averages during the fall of 1990 were higher for some writing courses (the sections and averages were listed) than for comparable introductory courses in other disciplines. Soon after, a rumor began to circulate among writing instructors: we should be prepared to justify to the director of writing, final class averages of above B minus (i.e., 80 percent). Irritated, I doubted anyone at the private college, where I also taught writing, would question such an average; students admitted there were deemed capable of earning high marks, I reasoned.

I also sensed more than a simple lack or show of confidence lurking behind these contrary institutional positions. For instance, I suspect that at state schools where funds are limited administrators typically want to "weed students out," while at private ones they wish to "keep students in," particularly those who can pay the tuition. A writing instructor relying on semester-to-semester work contracts, whose institutional survival potential, as determined by evaluation, correlates positively with that of first-year students in general, may find my speculations on variable dismissal and retention tactics familiar. For while a student may be dismissed from an institution for low grades, a part-timer may choose not to assign low grades for fear of receiving poor course evaluations, which can affect whether she gets rehired or fired. Noticing as well how other ranking structures related to departmental budgets—pay based on my rank of visiting assistant professor or teaching assistant, number of students per course, access to an office or support staff—shifted my instructional identity across the two institutions, a growing urge to unmask my portable grading practices took hold within me.

So I posed the question: Do I give higher grades to students who attend more prestigious institutions? To address the question I created "The $5,000–$25,000 Exchange," a research design which calls for two groups of writing students who attend economically disparate colleges to generate "clean" copies of papers previously graded by their instructors, to exchange these samples across the institutions, and to read, comment on, and grade them. I conducted my first exchange during the spring of 1991, when a group of first-year writers attending a flagship state university traded papers with those attending a private college. In spring of 1994, I had intermediate writing students (all English majors) at a regional campus of a state university exchange papers with first-year writing students at a private business college. Sampling these four groups of my own students I wanted to see what they could teach me about the politics of cross-institutional assessment. In summarizing how their participation in the exchanges made many of my own grading practices visible to me, I call them "readers" and "writers," and use the designation 5K to refer to students who attended an institution where the tuition was roughly $5,000 per year; 25K refers to those who attended an institution where tuition and fees equaled roughly $25,000 per year.

At the time of the first exchange, conditions surrounding my institutional identities, as well as those of the participants in the study, differed vastly across the two schools. A teaching assistant at the 5K setting, I followed departmental guidelines for course design provided by full-time faculty who monitored and observed my classes. The 5K participants enrolled in my course were in school to improve their economic status; they took their academic commitment to our course very seriously, and did whatever I recommended they do to improve their writing and standing in the class. At the 25K school, where roughly 40 percent of the students paid full tuition, I was a visiting assistant professor granted complete autonomy in designing and teaching my course. A few of the students who participated in the exchange felt simply showing up for class should translate to a final grade of B; another, who did not attend many classes, submitted assignments at her convenience, expecting a semester grade of A. Regarding my credibility as a teacher with suspicion, still another looked up a grammar rule I had recited in class, admitting to me, "I thought you made it up." I found myself not only tolerating but accommodating the desires of these students.

Despite institutional distinctions dividing them, both groups in the exchange adopted many of my evaluative techniques. For instance, most 5K and 25K students wrote "protocol" marginal comments, alluded to grammar, spelling, and punctuation errors, and wrote a general comment and a grade at the end of the papers. Likewise, both 5K and 25K readers frequently used the pronouns "I" and "you" in their comments; while I want to read this information as proof that students had learned to situate their responses in terms of their cultural circumstances, more likely they were mimicking formulaic patterns I universally used in constructing my grader identity.

The samples did, however, reveal to me variable grading practices I brought to specific institutional settings. For example, voicing what they liked about ideas or word play in 5K writers' papers, 25K readers tended to be high graders. On the other hand, the 5K readers typically pointed out mechanical errors, or searched the 25K papers for claims closely supported by warrants; they were not generous graders. The "tough" vs. "easy" grader variance embedded in their cross-institutional assessments appeared patterned on the fact that at the 5K institution I tended to judge student papers foremost on standardized criteria (e.g., mechanics and organization) imposed on me by full-time faculty, while at the 25K institution I granted more for strong ideas and creativity and did not emphasize foundational concerns as pervasively in assigning grades. Not surprisingly, both 5K and 25K readers typically arrived at grades reflecting this dichotomy, so that 5K readers tended to heavily weight discursive strategies ("not clear"; "where do you state your claim?"; "good but maybe belongs at end of 1st ¶"), while 25K readers tended to grade based on individual responses to innovative ideas ("I love this idea of the 'normal family' [. . .] Congratulations on a paper well done"), and "creative" expression ("I . . . like the use of little phrases like 'a hunted fowl on open water'"). Moreover, compared to the grades I had assigned the papers before the exchange, of the 25K sample (assigned to 5K readers), 73 percent of the grades went down; of the 5K sample (assigned to 25K readers), 58 percent of the grades went up. For my part, I did not believe one group of participants wrote better than the other, yet the grades I previously had assigned the 25K papers generally were higher than their 5K counterparts.

I decided, then, to confront my variable grader habits by practicing demystification. Transporting interactive teacher-student processes to all the institutions where I taught in the ensuing years, I sought first and foremost to unmask invisible ranking structures related to grader culture. Differing institutional expectations, my socioeconomic status as a part-timer, the explicit ideologies I owned: all these factors, I let students know at the start of a semester, would partially influence the grades they earned in my courses.

Before they began writing I revealed to students how papers with topics engaging or unfamiliar to me sometimes earned higher praise or grades than those with themes I had encountered dozens of times in the past.

Attempting to expose my proclivities toward style and content, I put check marks on early drafts I read straight through on the first reading. I conducted open discussions about grading by asking students selected by index card lottery to read comments I'd written on their papers out loud to the class, or invited students to write back (anonymously if necessary) to my comments and grades on their papers. When students read final drafts aloud and the class discussed what the final grades "should be" and why, if we reached consensus I would announce, "Great! I don't have to take that one home!" (If we didn't agree, I'd admit my own institutional power, explaining the final decision would come down to me.) Periodically, I conducted cross-institutional follow up tests, reading an already graded 5K paper to a 25K class (or vice versa) and asking students to grade, while keeping its institutional identity "blind." Here, I hoped to discover whether or not my grading habits remained relatively consistent across institutions. Each of these gestures asked students to question my evaluative praxis, to view comments and grades not as personal secrets, but as legitimate subjects of classroom discussion.

Though my institutionally prescribed grader habits did not completely disappear, enacting processes aimed at unmasking them helped to erode the variable identities I brought to cross-institutional classrooms. For example, I found myself granting more in the writings of 5K students and caving in less to the institutional demands of 25K ones. And while my 25K class averages stayed at a consistent level, those of my 5K classes steadily climbed. Consequently, at the time of the second exchange, 1994, I wanted to test whether my identity relative to reading and grading student papers cross-institutionally had shifted. Universally steeped in reader-based rather than text-based discourse, the participants' cross-institutional responses revealed that this was partially the case.

Readers in both sample populations overwhelmingly wrote lengthy end comments, several of which explicitly illustrate the act of creating mental images of the writers they evaluated. Typical value-laden and identity driven comments on the part of both 5K and 25K readers expressed a shared sense of cross-institutional identification by responding to ethos with ethos, for example: "I also feel that artists succumb to the government just because they need a paycheck to provide food and pay the rent. They are, I feel, robbed of their chance to show their true artistic talents. I really enjoyed reading this. A" [happy face]; and to pathos with pathos: "Very sorry to hear about your father's situation—Your anger towards God, and your bitterness is evident throughout your essay. It may have been therapeutic for you to write about it. [. . .] It is good that your father has a wonderful son like you & I'm sorry about the MS." And students in general also seemed more interested in each other's identities than in each other's writing skills; "what's this person like?" was a question frequently asked of me when a reader returned a writing sample.

Initially, some comments in this exchange did suggest that what the teacher "wants" remains situational and variable acress institutions. For example, a 25K reader's query to a 5K writer, "Where's the E-Prime [a movement in General Semantics to remove all forms of the verb 'to be' from written English] or explicit quotes to keep my attention?" reads like a direct challenge to my praxis. It is another way of asking, "Aren't the 5K students required to follow the same style and content standards as 25K students?" Indeed, the 25K reader's grade on the paper, "at best a C," sharply contrasted with the A—it earned from me, seeming to indicate less than uniform cross-institutional evaluation on my part. Yet, unbeknownst to the 25K reader, the criteria he stresses in his comment reflect my former demands put pervasively to 5K writers; I'd also been a tougher 5K grader. Thus, while the 5K paper in question might have been an exception, I saw myself moving towards more universal evaluative standards.

Plagued by the passion and quality of comments evenly distributed on the part of both groups, I questioned how the probable lives of these students beyond their present institutional ones also might be less than uniform. For while students at my 25K gig prepared for writing tasks they might undertake in law school, those at the 5K one learned memorandum formats for middle management positions in textile factories. How might my acknowledgment of such lived-out expressions of uneven social power work to modify my grading practices across institutions, I wondered. Can a classroom aiming to make the cross-institutional basis of assessment transparent reveal grading practices as sites of institutional contestation, "inevitably lead[ing] to the [bases] of these contestations, which are social class, gender, race, and labor relations" (Zavarzadeh 35)?[2] In the next section I confront as sites of contestation the cultural situatedness of myself and my students in a single institutional setting. I do so in order to examine my grader identity in relation to the production of knowledge in the writing classroom.

Demystifying Difference

As of this writing, my occupational identity—once categorically fragmented across institutions of differing prestige—has shifted to that of full-time, temporary replacement lecturer in composition. I believe this position as a temporary outsider inside a permanent faculty enables me to construct a grader identity in ways that neither a scrutinized semester-to-semester contractor nor visible tenure-tracker could afford.[3] In addition, teaching on a state-run campus (with, according to an October 1995 survey published in *The Chronicle of Higher Education*, tuition among the lowest in the nation) where a university education in the minds of most students translates to moving up the ranks of the employed, makes me sensitive to the fact that many students in my writing classes attend college part-time, work full-time in manufacturing or service industries, and support or contribute to the support of a family. Thus, a primary goal for investigating how sites of institutional contestation (race, gender, class) affect the politics of grading at this inner-city campus concerns "the intersection where my [teacher] authority crosses their [student] self-interest" (Elbow 196).

In order to assess our collective self-interest, on the first day of classes during the fall of 1995, I asked students in my intermediate writing class (which fulfilled a general university requirement for most majors, not including English) to share their goals for our course, "Barbie and Ken: Growing Up with the Mass Media"; I likewise shared my own. Though two years earlier my number one goal in all my writing classes cross-institutionally read: "To understand the relationship between institutional power and knowledge," my amended list—which speaks to the specific institutional situatedness of these students—began: "To give only As and Bs." I explained my position to students by making statements such as "I don't like bad grades. I won't grade less than a C on any paper. Okay, if I do think it's less than that we'll conference to discuss a rewrite." I followed up these remarks as the semester progressed by striking independent deals with students for a semester grade of B or A, sealing the agreements with simple handshakes while reminding them that the syllabus served as a contract for work to be completed and the terms of its completion. As I once had acquiesced to the desires of 25K students, I now tried to accommodate those of these 5K students, who largely shared as a primary goal for our course: "To pass with an A or B." Additionally, I wanted to address the concerns of students whose obsessions with, or fears about, grades block them from A or B writing.

As the semester wore on, I gave my students a more frank explanation for striving to assign high grades: the act correlated with my own self-interest in institutional survival (and transformation to permanent faculty status). I admitted to inflating their grades at times where I might have asked for a third revision, or scheduled a second conference, in order to clear time for my own writing and publishing. I justified my decision in such cases (more to myself, since students hardly protested) by periodically whipping out my pay check and reciting the amount to the class. "For that amount of money, I can't afford to spend a lot of time evaluating your rough drafts," I told them.

But at the same time, I tried to honestly convey to students that marketplace assessors might not be as forgiving as I. Illustrating the idea by exposing my own vulnerability within the academic marketplace, I circulated among them the handwritten comments an evaluator had penned in rejecting one of my scholarly articles: "This paper is . . . badly written . . . irritatingly self referential . . . incomprehensible . . . innocent of an accurate sense of audience . . . wastes my time & energy & I resent that." Explaining how the "invisible" subjectivity of the evaluator (the comment was unsigned) constructed in these remarks illustrates why Joseph Harris, in assuming the editorship of College Composition and Communication, asked reviewers to sign their critiques, I, in kind, defended my wish to expose my cultural biases in reading and commenting on their writing. For while Harris worries that anonymity "may sometimes allow people to speak in a less responsible or collegial manner than they would if they were held to account for their remarks" (305), I worry that holding back biases may produce comments which do not accurately reveal to students the source of grades which accompany them.

Though throughout the term I tried to expose to students, through my comments on their papers, how many of my cultural biases (such as a predisposition towards atheism) divided me from certain kinds of knowledge, at times making me a difficult reader and grader, the following evaluative extract from a student draft illustrates how demystifying grading does not necessarily lead to transformative practice.[4]

> I am, as I admitted in class, a very difficult reader on this subject since I'm extremely cynical about xmas; (I wouldn't think of spelling the word any other way, deliberately "x-ing" Christ). Now, I'm prepared to read about and attempt to understand an alternate view on the subject, but after reading your paper, I feel as cynical as ever! Somehow, I'm more interested in what the ads/wish books [alluded to in the paper] say than what your story says. Perhaps you need to analyze and explain what your story tells us about "Christmas" [student's word] spirit vs. the over-commercialization of the holiday constructed in the media.

The critique of consumer ideologies I embed in my reading of the draft asks the student to fill in epistemic schisms I perceive in the paper; later in the comment, I intimate that without these additions the paper probably will earn a grade of C. Appearing to justify the "average" feel I attribute to the draft by judging it on features it supposedly lacks (explanation and analysis), in reality I am asking the writer to rewrite to my strongly held beliefs.

On another intermediate writing student's paper I wrote: "I feel this is an average, or slightly above average piece of writing, and yet I'm not sure why, exactly." But as I later reveal in the comment, an ideological investment in my own manner of conducting scholarship and producing knowledge (a mark of my institutional identity within academe) partly mediates my "feel" for the paper and its topic (does violent children's television programming cause violent behavior in children?):

> Perhaps [I find this paper average] because you generalize from childhood memory [as opposed to watching and analyzing a TV show directly]? Perhaps you wish to "edit down" some of the long, descriptions of your childhood actions, and sit and actually watch (pencil in hand) some Saturday morning cartoons—or WWF [a wrestling program mentioned in the paper]! Perhaps you will discover deeper, critical insights about these shows, particularly about how they construct violence. I'm very interested in the topic. In fact, I wrote my PhD dissertation on violence in American popular culture, which also might explain why I'm a tough reader on this subject.

As the two evaluative extracts pointing to my ideas about average writing illustrate, I don't always succeed in assigning only As and Bs, in part because I cannot at all times separate my cultural biases and institutional self-interests from my instructional goals.

As I contemplated the two comments above in the course of writing this article, the very questions of what constitutes a C paper and who formulates the criteria, reinforced my wish to assign students in this intermediate writing class final grades of As and Bs.[5] Though one of these students eventually earned a grade of A, and the other a B, had I graded them earlier in my career as an instructor at the 5K regional state university described in the section above, this probably would not have been the case. For many full-time faculty in that English department prided themselves on the belief that no one in a university-wide required writing course should earn a semester grade of A. During a fall semester especially, their proverbial wisdom filtered down to part-timers who competed for a reduced number of spring contracts. Thus, one fall term I assigned a single A out of three sections of first-year writing; my spring contract was renewed. Conversely, knowing in fall of 1995 I could not be fired in the spring, I did not feel institutionally bound to avoiding high grades; sixteen of my intermediate writing students earned As, and eleven earned Bs.

Meanwhile, as a temporary instructor who probably would be at another institution a year later, I felt more open than I had in the past to examining my cultural concerns about grading during class discussions, as well as more receptive to pedagogy that reinforced these feelings. For example, I was inspired to read of bell hooks: "Like other feminists she is deeply critical of the separation of public and private, and she writes that it is crucial to be open about 'personal stuff' in order to oppose ongoing practices of domination" (Faigley 18). Might Bazerman's characterization of instructors reading and commenting on papers in "secret," and within "unexamined private experience" equally apply to students reacting to graded papers, and might their reactions relate to practices of domination they perceive on the part of instructors? To address this concern as a white teacher at a multiethnic university, I decided to openly discuss "personal stuff" about race with the African-American, Asian, middle-Eastern, and white students in my intermediate writing class. For as bell hooks admonishes, pedagogy must "make productive space for critical dissent dialogue even as we express intense emotions" (109).

So, during one particularly heated debate on affirmative action, I admitted to the class that, because of material conditions shaping race and class divisions in our society, I had in certain situations "trusted white people more than black people." The white students were shocked by my strategy of confrontation, and at first, many tried to deny the existence of such a position in their own lives; for the most part, the students of color found nothing remarkable about the statement, and augmented it by discussing their own experiences. The contestatory discussion led us to examine how our seemingly natural and self-selecting views often are not chosen, and to recognize the hope of transforming our negative ones.

Speaking frankly about my thoughts on race in relation to affirmative action allowed me to later raise the topic in dialogues about grading, for example, by pointing to social and political allegiances (including to Standard American English) often held by those who historically have done the ranking in university classrooms. These discussions were especially meaningful for the African-American students, who, by virtue of witnessing popular slang phrases from their communities get absorbed by larger culture, recognized that while they "have the ability to change language . . ." (Mack and Zebroski 158) their college teachers did not always acknowledge it when evaluating their writing.

Since social realities that influence cultural biases in the classroom often are played out in the context of grading, in evaluating their papers I tried to grant all my intermediate writing students their particular ways of making knowledge. When a Chinese student's paper was selected by another student and read aloud in the class, revealing mechanical errors because Standard American English (SAE) was not her native language, I stated to the group, "Who could go to China right now and enroll in a writing class for native speakers? I know I couldn't." A short discussion followed in which the other students in the class praised the writer, both for the paper's engaging topic (media censorship in China compared to the United States) as well as its felicity. I next admitted to the group, "I'm not taking any of the mechanical errors into consideration when I grade the paper. But if you're a native speaker [of SAE], I will take it into consideration." At the same time, I assured the writer that we would discuss any SAE issues contained in her writing privately in a conference. Before the class ended we all reached a consensus together; the paper earned a grade of B.

Neither native nor non-native speakers in the class publicly or privately disclosed to me dissent regarding the decision I made in grading the Chinese student's paper. I want to believe this is partly because our open dialogues about relationships between cultural differences and institutional expectations led students to encourage rather than denounce the possibilities in a piece of writing. In fact, when in open discussions students stumbled over their articulations of ranking (assigning a grade to) each others' writing—particularly when the social identities or levels of literacy between assessors and assessed diverged—they voiced the difficulties they were experiencing in attempting to evaluate a piece of writing based on preconceived, ambiguous, or prescriptive institutional formulas.

"Thanks for understanding my situation," the Chinese student, who publicly had earned the B, later told me when we met in conference to discuss her paper. "I tried so hard to fix my grammar in my 102 [first-year writing] class. But the teacher just gave me a C on everything, and told me to go to the writing center."

"What did you get in the course?" I asked.

"C," she said. We immediately struck a deal for a B in intermediate writing.

Teaching cross-institutionally in the past on a part-time basis, I probably would not have adopted—never mind disclosed—grading practices that differed according to students' levels of literacy relative to SAE. In fact, I largely had ascribed to departmental guidelines concerning English for Speakers of Other Languages (ESOL) and basic writers, and in some cases had railroaded these students out of my traditional writing classrooms and into pre-college level courses, often in service of my own self-interest. For example, during a semester when I taught five writing courses simultaneously at three schools and also worked in a writing center, I hardly had the energy to devote extra time to needy students.

Back then, I also learned how specific departmental attitudes regarding ESOL and basic writers not only differed between institutions, but also influenced variable institutional policies—once again—related to economics. For instance, at one of the 25K schools where I had taught, students who took ESOL writing did so in place of the required first-year writing course and earned credits towards graduation; while the official institutional line logically argued for parity with foreign language study, it also encouraged a steady supply of wealthy internationals. At a 5K school across the state, no credit toward graduation was awarded to students (many from newly arrived immigrant families) who passed ESOL; instead, surviving the course simply moved them into basic writing, which they then had to successfully complete before graduating into the traditional first-year course. The three-step sequence cost them money. But rather than sympathize with ESOL students, or acknowledge how their existence helped provide teaching assistant stipends or finance their own scholarly activities, faculty at the 5K institution thought many of these students should not be in college at all. "They'd be laughed out of the classroom in another country," as a tenured professor put it to me. But as Nancy Mack and James Zebroski put it, "The university seems content to have the income from these students, yet at the same time the university finds these students to be an embarrassment to its elite image of itself" (155).

As differing institutional policies toward ESOL study show, the act of grading student writing can have visible, real-world consequences that are inextricably bound to the graders. For instance, despite the theoretical temporality of part-time and temporary (a synecdoche for the "temp agencies" destined to employ many 5K students) writing instructors, the grades we assign students form part of their permanent records, influencing their access to timely graduation schedules, scholarships and fellowships, graduate and law school acceptances, as well as to career placements. Indeed, as *The Chronicle of Higher Education* reported, using the tremendous economic and political power of grade records to retaliate against administrators at Yale University who struck down their demands of unionization, 200 teaching assistants refused to provide grades for students in their fall 1995 courses (Crystal A15).

More traditional courses of action available to underpaid faculty responding to oppressive work conditions may partially operate to send underprepared workers into the marketplace. For, even if we want to take Elbow's advice for "evaluating" student writing (using grids, assessment sheets, and portfolios) over "ranking" or "judging" it, our grading practices may continue to illustrate his claim that "evaluation takes more time, effort, and money" (192). For example, an overworked and underpaid teacher traveling lengthy distances between more than one school might choose to give a simple evaluative comment and a high grade on an early draft of a paper rather than preparing a more in-depth comment, discussing it in a conference, and asking for a re-write later.

In the fall of 1995, finding my institutional identity firmly situated in a school with an urban mission, and, for the time being, no longer plagued by divergent cross-institutional politics, I was able to rethink my grading practices and radically alter my standards in assigning final marks. Certainly, the years of transporting and transforming my own standards and politics to the various institutions where I taught contributed to the creation of my newly exercised grading criteria, which perhaps nonetheless conflicted with those of my department or with the university in general. Adjunct teachers and graders who likewise travel across institutions also contribute to the creation of uneven, inconsistent and even conflicting standards at those schools. Postsecondary faculty and administrators need to assess the possible impact these variations have on students—in and beyond the institution.

In the final analysis, then, I believe the large numbers of us who teach writing across institutionally divergent class, race, gender, and ideological lines have much to contribute to conversations about grader culture. Therefore, I believe we must—in the public arena of the classroom or in the private space of evaluative comments, in departmental or research dialogues—continue to demystify grader culture, to make its invisible institutional uses visible. In so doing we can provide compositionists and writing students with alternative tools for creating and evaluating knowledge, or for participating in institutional change.

Notes

1. Some of the discussion in the paragraphs that follow in this section is directly quoted or paraphrased from my article, "The $5,000–$25,000 Exchange," *College English* 57 (1995): 426–47. I wish to thank the students who participated in this study for their permission to quote from their comments.

2. While I take up the politics of institutional difference in grading along race lines in a provisional way in this discussion, and, unlike in my everyday classroom praxis, merely allude to considerations of gender, a more thorough investigation of grader culture would involve a sustained exploration of both these categories. The NCES Survey provides a statistical starting point for such a discussion, for example, breaking down the percent of full and part-time postsecondary staffs by race and gender. Also, for a feminist rendering of differences among higher education's instructional and research staffs, see Nadya Aisenberg and Mona Harrington.

3. I do not confront the use of part-time faculty at the university characterized in this section of my discussion; however, according to an external evaluators' report of March 1996, 70 percent of its courses in English (almost all in writing) are allotted to adjunct faculty and graduate students.

4. I wish to thank the students who allowed me to quote from my evaluative comments on their papers in the paragraphs that follow.

5. In regards to the "unavailability of agreement" on grading criteria Peter Elbow relates the following familiar news: "[R]esearch in evaluation has shown many times that if we give a paper to a set of readers, those readers tend to give it the full range of grades" (188).

10

Maureen Neal

The Politics and Perils of Portfolio Grading

I first experienced some of the conflict inherent in grading practices when I was a student teacher a little over twenty years ago. At that time, paper-by-paper grading systems were the norm; portfolio evaluation was unheard of in public schools. When I gave out my first set of grades, a student named Kevin Williams was so upset by his "C" that he spat on his report card in disgust—not once, but three times. I've sometimes thought the use of portfolio evaluation would have soothed the wounds in that situation. However, I've come to realize that, rather than solving most problems related to grading, portfolio evaluation can create conflicts—both institutional and theoretical—much more disturbing and problematic than those represented by a student spitting on a report card.

This past semester, for example, in a feeling very much like Eleanor Agnew's in "Departmental Grade Quotas," I found myself alarmed at the number of As and Bs in my researched writing course, which employed a portfolio system of grading. As I figured grades, I scrounged to find someone who legitimately deserved an F or a D (not many) or a C (a few). I felt uneasy, ashamed of the obvious lack of adherence to anything remotely resembling a traditional grade distribution. I wondered what my traditionalist colleague down the hall would say if he were to see my grade book. I wondered, too, if my department chair ever looked at my grade distributions with dismay or concern. I felt as if I were negligent in doing my job, so much so that I briefly toyed with the idea of curving my grades or using a less generous grading scale. I believe portfolio evaluation is a good thing;

so do countless others in the profession. Then why do I often feel uncertain about grades in my portfolio-based writing courses?

To be sure, in any kind of writing classroom, there is bound to be some conflict, even anguish, over the assignment of grades to student texts because issues of consistency, autonomy, role relationships, and institutional politics accompany our evaluative behaviors. Not long ago, I might have argued that my life as an instructor of composition would have been less anxiety-ridden and more effective had I used portfolio grading in all of my teaching experiences, including the practice teaching stint mentioned above. I now believe that portfolio grading, though increasingly widespread, poses unique problems for the field of composition studies. If these problematic issues are ignored, I fear we may be creating a breeding ground for a serious backlash against portfolio work.

It should be noted that portfolios are used in a variety of ways: portfolios are sometimes used for placement in lieu of traditional entrance or exit exams, portfolio assessment is sometimes mandated as a program-wide method of evaluation; and portfolio grading may be employed in individual classrooms as a pedagogical tool. In this essay, I'm concerned with the latter two purposes, which seem to present the most problematic issues. Some of the conflicts related to these uses for portfolios include questions about grade inflation, reliability, the appropriateness of scoring techniques and who should oversee them, and competing means and ends for classroom portfolios. These contested issues mar the promise of portfolio evaluation and contribute to a climate in which a backlash against portfolio evaluation is a real possibility.

My purposes in this essay are several: first, to investigate the claims of those who are critical of portfolio work and to call attention to the potential for backlash; second, to send a cautionary message to those who embrace portfolio work without considering the political and practical issues involved; and third, to show that new research is absolutely necessary if portfolio work is to move beyond its current status as an exciting—but largely untested—mode of composition pedagogy and evaluation. If it is to live up to its promise as an assessment tool which is a "natural outgrowth of a process-centered classroom" (Rycik 27), those who favor portfolio assessment must become aware of the conditions and the issues which may support a backlash against it.

Makings of a Backlash

By the term "backlash," I'm not referring to expressions of reservation or caution associated with portfolios, which appear as caveats in almost all articles and presentations on portfolio work. A backlash implies a reaction, a pendulum-like movement away from theoretical and practical principles of one thing to something else; a backlash is symptomatic of a fluid kind of tension between two forces. I recall a quotation from an old film describing this motion in relation to institutional change: "Radical ideas threaten institutions, then become institutions which are threatened by radical ideas." In the case of portfolio grading, I fear the backlash, if strong enough, could signal an unwelcome return to traditional forms of grading.

Given apparent broad-based support and enthusiasm for portfolio systems (see, for example, the October 1995 report of the CCCC Committee on Assessment), I was surprised to encounter any form of resistance to portfolios. However, in small-group discussion at a recent national conference, I attended a session on portfolio assessment a woman who identified herself as a department chair expressed skepticism about the use of portfolios in individual writing classrooms because, as she explained, "The problem is, the grades are so much higher with portfolios, all As and Bs." She attributed higher grades to the way portfolio-driven courses are taught. I was surprised to hear the concern for grade inflation linked so directly to portfolio-based pedagogy. In the same discussion, a graduate teaching assistant admitted that the effort, energy, and rigid requirements for grading in his department's portfolio program had become so oppressive it would be a "relief" to not have to work in a program which mandated portfolio assessment. This comment, again surprising, nevertheless made me aware that for some instructors, the use of portfolios has become not a solution for instructional and assessment problems, but an unwelcome burden instead.

A third negative response to portfolio grading comes from my own department, which recently implemented a portfolio system for its basic writing courses. During a discussion in which we evaluated the new system, two instructors made their opposition clear: one was opposed because he noted that his methods of teaching contrasted sharply with the requirements for portfolio grading. Additionally, he was apologetic for criticizing the student portfolios in his colleague's classes. Overall, he claimed, the use of portfolios was divisive and destructive, although he also mentioned he had come to value the end-of-semester collection of student pieces. But the most critical remarks about portfolio work came from another instructor, who claimed that those who employ portfolios in composition classrooms are "Marxists and feminists" who choose to "coddle" students. Portfolio systems of grading, he claimed, are responsible for an increase in superficial error in student work, a decrease in coherence, and an overall lack of readability. Though he once used portfolio grading, this instructor now absolutely refuses to consider portfolio evaluation in any form.

These caustic remarks represent an idiosyncratic view of portfolio work and are located, I think, a long distance from mainstream thought about portfolios. A more moderate, but still biting, view of portfolios can be found in recent publications. In "On the Running Board of the Portfolio Bandwagon" (1993), Edward Kearns uses the term "bandwagon" regarding portfolios to imply that the concept is being embraced on the basis of its popularity rather than on its substantive merits. Although Kearns claims to "express some doubts and skepticism, rather than opposition" (50) regarding the use of portfolios, his connotations and tone are sometimes more scornful than skeptical. For example, he claims that "portfolio" is a new "buzz word" in composition studies and describes Pat Belanoff and Peter Elbow as "bandmasters" leading the "parade." Kearns claims to be on the "running board" of the portfolio movement because, as he says, "it is relatively easy to jump off" (50), which I assume means it would be relatively simple to return to traditional paper-by-paper evaluation if the problems with portfolio work become too difficult to overcome, suggesting the possibility of a backlash and a threat to return to previous means of assessment.

Kearns raises another issue about the use of portfolios which also reflects the possibility of a backlash. He challenges the theoretical assumptions underlying portfolio assessment by claiming that "Apparently, and I stress the apparent nature of things, the portfolio bandwagon got started on spurious grounds, namely, a series of unexamined assertions against existing practices" (57). Kearns' point is that the field of composition has embraced portfolio work (and discarded traditional assessment) on the basis of narrative reports of classroom or program practice. Brian Huot makes a similar observation when he says, "Most of the work done with portfolios up to this time has been . . . anecdotal or testimonial, what I call show and tell" ("Beyond the Classroom" 326). Huot shares Kearns' concern that perhaps we have come too far too fast with portfolios, and he suggests that the field of composition studies "stop, take stock, and begin to ask some hard questions" (Huot 326) about what we really know about portfolios and the various ways they are employed in writing courses and programs. While I do not suggest that Huot is contributing to a backlash against portfolio systems, I do think that we need to examine portfolio practice on a more empirical basis if we are to counter the kinds of resistance represented by Kearns' commentary.

Another issue which could contribute to a backlash against the use of portfolios, particularly portfolios used in individual classrooms, is the complaint raised by the department chair mentioned earlier, who felt that the use of portfolios caused grade inflation. What, exactly, is meant by the term "grade inflation"? I see grade inflation as an unwarranted preponderance of high(er) grades. Does portfolio grading contribute to that kind of grade inflation? To date, no empirical studies have been published that explore this crucial question, but the need for such research is imperative. Without experimental research which might investigate correlation and/or causality, we must rely on the only kind of information available, which is, as Brian Huot would say, anecdotal and "testimonial." Several theorists discuss grade inflation, although no one, as yet, has been able to offer a definitive answer to this question. Jeffrey Sommers, for example, notes that the possibility of grade inflation in a portfolio-driven course is an important concern, but he points out "the [portfolio] system itself is designed to promote better writing by the students, and it stands to reason that many students are going to be submitting portfolios that consist of writing better than they might be able to produce in a classroom employing a traditional grading system" ("Bringing Practice in Line" 157).

One of the students in an English education course I teach tackled the question of grade inflation which some assume to be associated with portfolio work and came to the conclusion that "[S]tudent grades might rise when compared with either the same teacher's classes prior to using portfolios or compared with another, traditional teacher's classes. Rather than arguing that grades are not higher in classes using a portfolio system, I say they should be" (Merriam 6). The evidence used to support this claim is testimonial, once again, but because it comes directly from a student's experience (rather than from an instructor's), it's worth mentioning. The student writes:

> I'm a pretty conscientious student and write reasonably well. In one class this semester, each essay I write receives a grade, along with thoughtful teacher comments, suggestions and questions. Rather than reworking the piece based on insight from the teacher, I put it completely out of my mind. It's done. On to the next assignment. However, for this class [taught by the author of this chapter] where I'll choose some writing to go into a portfolio, I've rewritten two pieces four times each, changing them substantially each time, based mostly on response from a teacher-reader who questions, suggests, and points out weaknesses not evident to me. I disagree with some of the suggestions and won't change those parts of the piece. But I consider each comment, re-read my work most carefully, and spend a lot more time with it than I do with the assignments in the other class (Merriam 2) .

In other words, the pedagogies that support a portfolio grading system (the emphasis on revision and response; student choice about what is to be evaluated in the portfolio; the opportunity for reflective commentary) contribute to an increased possibility for writing improvement, and therefore, higher grades are warranted for students who improve their writing. Is this a "problem?"

This is indeed a problem if the issue of grade inflation is conflated with the can of worms that is labeled "standards." If a department chair or *Writing Program Administrator* subscribes to the philosophy of standards promoted by Albert Shanker, the late president of the American Federation of Teachers, for example, then portfolio grading in the individual classroom is indeed a site of potential conflict. One of Shanker's positions on standards—and here he is referring to minimum-competency testing—is that educators need to raise educational standards by increments, so that students will be continually challenged and thus continually motivated to excel. He uses an analogy to explain this view: "If you were helping athletes improve their jumping and you got 95 percent of those in your charge to jump six feet, what would you do next? You would raise the bar another inch or so, and when most of them were regularly jumping at that height, you'd raise the bar again, and you would keep on going. But not in the world of education" ("Raising the Bar").

The effective use of portfolio grading in individual classrooms might result in higher grades for students, but many compositionists and instructors might resist "raising the bar" in portfolio-based instructional settings. Jeff Sommers, for example, writes:

> Do grades rise when portfolios are employed? Shouldn't they? If they don't, won't students feel duped and begin to rebel? Although I would like to have my students revise their work for the self-satisfaction of doing so, realistically speaking, much of their motivation is derived from the sense that they are improving their standing in the course. Portfolios ask students (and raters) to do more work; if we raise our standards at the same time that we initiate portfolios, I think we run the risk of alienating our students. . . . I switched to portfolios because I wanted to keep my standards from eroding and felt that giving students more of an opportunity to reach excellence allowed me to do that equitably. In other words, I could be demanding because I had given them ample opportunities to succeed. When they do succeed, my grades reflect that. (Sommers, personal correspondence)

Perhaps the question administrators concerned with grade inflation should be asking is not how many students receive As and Bs, but rather, does working in a portfolio system contribute to the improvement of student writing?

The concern for the possibility of grade inflation associated with classroom portfolios might also be an issue for composition instructors because of another set of expectations: institutional pressures for consistency and rigor in grading standards. Eleanor Agnew describes this problem in "Departmental Grade Quotas: The Silent Saboteur." She claims that "[G]rade deflation is insidiously encouraged in many colleges and universities, especially in freshman writing courses. As a result, grading down has become a point of pride for some writing instructors" ("Departmental Grade Quotas" 2–3). Agnew identifies process-centered pedagogy as a special target for accusations of grade inflation and points to the inequities and the ironies involved in such a distinction:

> I want to focus on the political dilemma in which process writing teachers are caught. Instead of earning reputations as good, caring, committed teachers whose students do well because they, the teachers, have worked hard to create positive and empowering rhetorical contexts, writing instructors with higher grades are often thought to be grade-inflators, not only by administrators, but by more traditional faculty who read the faculty grade distributions. (4)

She goes on to say that administrative attention to grade distribution is sometimes fueled by legislative mandates for "standards" which are then passed on to writing programs offices (6) and that the push for consistency and "standards," while admirable, is also driving instructors into a paradoxical situation:

> [S]omehow in this well-intentioned journey towards academic excellence, lower grades in freshman courses have become associated with better teaching while higher grades have become associated with slack teaching. Although it is easy to understand how institutions have evolved towards that outlook, the underlying logic has been questioned by scholars on grading practices. (6)

If institutional concerns for grade inflation are to be countered by those who use portfolio assessment, at least two things are desperately needed: (1) education/awareness for administrators, government agencies, and legislators about the value and potential for student learning in portfolio-driven classrooms, and (2) empirical research that investigates the assumption of a causal relationship between portfolios and high(er) grades.

Contested Issues: Scoring, Reliability, and Institutional Pressures

It's fair to say that portfolio evaluation does present some thorny problems when compared to more conventional means of writing assessment and language testing. Because a portfolio, as a cumulative writing product, can include a variety of genres for a variety of audiences and purposes, and may also include work that illustrates different stages of the drafting process, it is admittedly difficult to evaluate as a whole. Many theorists

(Elbow; Hamp-Lyons; Huot; White) have identified and discussed this problem, which is one of reliability (consistency and predictability) and validity (fairness and accuracy). But some solutions to this dilemma may contribute, in an ironic and unintentional way, to the backlash against portfolios because the "cure" for these ills can sometimes be more destructive than the "disease" itself.

Because portfolios are unlike standardized tests of language ability and are more like direct writing samples, the assumption is that what "works" for scoring direct writing samples should also work for evaluating portfolios. This is, however, not necessarily so, as portfolios represent a unique kind of direct writing product. Thus, trying to respond to pressures for program consistency via the application of holistic scoring techniques may help create conditions for a backlash. Issues related to the politics of scoring that need to be addressed are several: the use of evaluative criteria generated and/or imposed by someone other than readers, instructors, or graders of portfolios themselves; issues of power and status which arise when participation in a portfolio system is mandatory rather than voluntary; and the appropriation and misapplication of holistic scoring procedures initially designed for large-scale direct writing assessment of single samples.

The first two of these issues are related: the practice of using specific criteria for scoring portfolios evolved as a response to the need for evaluating portfolio work fairly and consistently, especially when blind readers are used. Ironically, the means by which such criteria are developed could contribute to a negative response to portfolio systems. This is particularly true when the development of grading criteria is not an egalitarian effort, as many theorists believe it should be: for example, Pat Belanoff has written that "when portfolios are read by more than the classroom teacher—whether during or at the end of the term—development of criteria obviously needs to be the responsibility of everyone involved" ("Portfolios" 7). Marcia Dickson, too, maintains that criteria developed in community is essential to the success of a writing assessment program because the debate and discussion that produces scoring criteria is valuable: "Instead of a singular system of evaluation set up by the lone professor or some other faculty member in the ivory tower, the standards in portfolio evaluation are the result of collaborative actions, criteria that evolve from much discussed and sometimes hotly debated issues in the discipline of composition" (Dickson 275–76). Edward White also assumes that all participants in the grading process will take part in the development of scoring criteria ("Assigning, Responding, Evaluating" 67). Liz Hamp-Lyons and William Condon concur: "We must search for an approach that permits criteria that are constantly open to negotiation, open to the changes that a recursive process of teaching and reading portfolios must involve" ("Questioning Assumptions" 188).

Theorists, then, have widely supported the principle of collaborative development of scoring criteria for portfolios. In contrast to this aim, however, institutional expectations and practical constraints often work against what these theorists have proposed, resulting in the imposition of scoring guides, rubrics, or criteria which are generated not by the people directly working/teaching with portfolios, but by people outside that circle such as government agencies, institutional committees developing "standards," or writing program administrators.

An example of what I mean by the "imposition" of guidelines and/or criteria for scoring can be found in the handouts writing programs make available to students and evaluators. One such handout explains: "When your portfolio is submitted, it will be read by another teacher. . . . Before the portfolio is read, however, all of the teachers meet to read sample portfolios. The teachers agree on the standards that will be used to determine whether or not a portfolio passes. This is what the reader of your portfolio will be looking for. . . ." Two pages of specific criteria for evaluation follow. The list includes questions relating to "development," "organization," "quality," "effectiveness of revision," and so on. Reductive as it may seem, I wondered how readers of the portfolios could have already agreed on the scoring rubric before the term begins; either the criteria were developed and presented to instructors for approval (saying they all "agree on the standards" is not the same thing as saying they have all collaborated in creating them), or instructors have met prior to the start of the term in training sessions with sample portfolios and have hammered out the existing criteria, possibly without compensation for the additional time and effort this kind of participation would require.

An imposed set of criteria can also be as innocuous and well-intentioned as the following statements taken from a departmental handbook given to instructors prior to the start of a basic writing course: "All students are required to complete a portfolio as a final project. . . . All portfolios will be read by the student's instructor and another [basic writing] instructor. We will use the department's rubric for evaluation that is included below." A detailed one-page "portfolio scoring guide" follows, containing descriptors for specific letter grades, including the following markers for a failing portfolio: "Individual papers may be characterized by . . . little or no sentence variety; occasional major or pervasive minor errors in grammar and usage; simplistic or inaccurate word choice." As an instructor who was given this handbook, I know these criteria were not generated communally because I had no opportunity to contribute to their creation; however, I was expected to use them to score my colleagues' portfolios. The point in using these examples is not to question the values represented by the scoring rubrics, but to illustrate their mode of development: in the latter example particularly, the criteria clearly have not been generated collaboratively by instructors. An instructor required to use the above criteria might want to argue the values implicit in the descriptors, but would have no opportunity to do so if the criteria are not open to discussion prior to use.

Institutional politics and pressures for grading consistency play a part in these situations. Some administrators, for example, might argue that the imposition of scoring guidelines for portfolios is a practical necessity rather than a breach of collegial ethics. Consider large institutions in which graduate teaching assistants may be the only faculty members who teach entry-level composition courses: inexperience, lack of funds, and a predictably high turnover rate from year to year undermine a program's desire for coherence. (See Smit for an elaboration of this point.) In order to assure some consistency and to allow departmental standards to remain relatively constant, some might contend that criteria are more efficiently designed by WPAs rather than by instructors themselves.

In a lengthy discussion of some of these issues, Marcia Dickson says that "Departments often create elaborate rubrics, exit exams, or proficiency exams to overcome criticism of the uneven quality of instruction" and that "Outwardly, rubrics and exit exams appear to bring order to a department" (275). In addition to the desire for consistency, developing scoring criteria and instructional guidelines for portfolio assessment ahead of the fact (before the semester begins) is a strategy which saves time and is cost-effective; indeed, it would be a luxury for some large research institutions to conform to what the theorists have told us about the need to develop scoring criteria and guidelines collaboratively.

Despite those rationales, however, the imposition of scoring criteria could contribute to a negative reaction to portfolio grading for at least two reasons. First, it violates the concept of academic freedom: if, as Dickson suggests, "Reading portfolios together, determining standards, and arguing for or against various criteria for grading student writing embody the spirit of academic freedom" (276), then anything which takes away the right to discussion and debate of criteria contradicts that spirit. Second, to be invested in the production of portfolios, an instructor needs to be included in the development of standards for their evaluation. If teachers themselves are not involved in the creation of rubrics they "must" use, they have little incentive for following them—which completes an odd circle, then, of the maintenance of idiosyncratic standards and grading practices the use of portfolios is designed to combat.

Further, if the reason criteria are imposed is because the faculty involved are inexperienced, the issue of asymmetrical political power is raised: teaching assistants, part-time and adjunct faculty, and lower-tier faculty who are frequently responsible for entry-level composition courses have little institutional power to begin with. It seems an exploitation of their already-low status and lack of authority to impose scoring criteria for evaluation. It's difficult to imagine a graduate teaching assistant who would feel confident enough to argue for egalitarian control over the production and evaluation of portfolios. On the other hand, why should lack of input by teaching assistants be a problem? Don't graduate students enter a program with the understanding that they will be required to follow some guidelines as part of their pedagogical training?

One response might be that discussion and debate about criteria would be an invaluable part of students' training as writing instructors, and therefore they should be included, rather than excluded, from the development process. In addition, most instructors would chafe under the restrictive covenants, however well-intentioned, provided by some writing programs. An analogy: the imposition of criteria reminds me of a situation in a novel I recall in which the protagonist finds herself cooking, one day, in another person's kitchen. She knows how to use the utensils, the pots and pans, and she knows the ingredients for the dish she's supposed to make, but she also feels a sense of uncertainty and irritation in the expectation that she should produce a beautiful casserole, say, when working in someone else's kitchen, with all its familiar—yet unfamiliar—territory. The novelist called this feeling of insecurity, anxiety, and exasperation the "OPK" (Other People's Kitchen) syndrome. In a similar way, when instructors (at any level of expertise) are asked—or required—to use other people's criteria to evaluate writing portfolios, a sense of discomfort, if not outright resentment, can be the predominant response. In this case, instructors may be resentful of the system that produces these conditions rather than with the imposition of criteria; it would be easier, some might argue, to return to a conventional paper-by-paper system in which they have some control rather than use a portfolio system in which they seem to have very little. One last point about power and status: if it's not hard to understand why the imposition of criteria would trouble a faculty member with low status, consider how infinitely more galling it would be for faculty who have long-term experience and expertise to be required to use externally-generated criteria.

I'm also concerned about the curious situation in which institutional/departmental sensitivity to complaints (Kearns 51–52; Smit) about the lack of reliability in portfolio assessment may contribute to a backlash reaction to portfolios. Program administrators and department heads face pressure—from forces both inside and outside the academy—to be accountable for the success of their writing programs. On different levels, and to varying degrees, public educational organizations, alumni groups, parents, legislative committees on education, and foundations supplying grant monies can bring external pressure to bear on the administration of writing programs. This is especially true when institutions are funded by state legislatures and governed by politically oriented boards of control. In addition to these external forces, interdepartmental political pressures within some institutions may hold the teaching of writing to a higher standard of accountability than other instructional programs. When composition courses are administered and taught as service courses for other departments , yet another kind of pressure may be brought to bear on the need for rigor and consistency in evaluating student writing.

In response to the multiplicity of demands for accountability in writing instruction and assessment, those who administer writing programs may seek to relieve some of these pressures by applying principles of holistic scoring to portfolio evaluation. Many people are aware of Edward M. White's prescriptions for how to conduct controlled sessions to promote reliability and scoring consistency ("Assigning, Responding, Evaluating" ch. 4). For scoring single direct samples, these procedures may indeed be the best approach we can employ at present, but when individual classroom portfolio use is at stake, it may be counterproductive to hold portfolios to the same rigorous standards of reliability—particularly inter-rater reliability—that might be applied to program-wide direct assessments. This might seem a contradiction in terms, but it is precisely this kind of situational use that is problematic.

Such a theoretically unlikely situation is created in a seam of overlap and confusion in which the development of portfolios for classroom evaluation is combined with a writing program's need for accountability or consistency. In circumstances such as these, students create portfolios in individual classroom contexts, but at the end of the semester, the entire writing faculty reads and grades the now departmental portfolios in some form of holistic evaluation.

The conflation of means and ends is problematic partly because the purposes for using portfolios conflict: at the classroom level, portfolios represent a process; at the program level, portfolios represent a product used to test departmental consistency and to satisfy external needs for accountability. While it's certainly true that portfolios represent both a process and a writing product, the mixed-use approach is troublesome. When a department requires classroom portfolio evaluation by all writing faculty involved, a domino effect is created whereby the solution to one problem creates a whole new set of problems to be solved. For example, if all program faculty must evaluate each others' classroom portfolios, then some system of blind reading is indicated; issues of inter-rater reliability and consistency come into play, which suggest the application of techniques for large-scale scoring of direct writing samples, since portfolios are indeed direct writing products. Criteria for scoring must be developed. As a result, a new set of demands is placed on individual portfolios, asking them to carry a burden they—literally—have not been prepared to bear. Liz Hamp-

Lyons and William Condon note that scoring criteria for "traditional essay assessment" are often based on the "expectations of the academy as a whole" and are external to the writing classroom (187), whereas in a situation in which an individual portfolio is the basis for a grade in a course, the "criteria [for grading] are grounded in the curriculum of the course in which the portfolio is produced" (187). There may be a conflict, then, between course expectations and program standards.

Another problem (mentioned above) is the assumption that what "works" to promote reliability in the assessment of single writing samples will be transferable to portfolios. White says, for example, that "Experience with essay tests has shown that reliable readings can take place only in controlled sessions, with all evaluators reading at the same time and place, under the direction of a chief reader. This experience may not hold true for portfolios . . . but it probably will, as the scoring of portfolios seems in every way even more difficult than essay tests" (White 69). If portfolios are even more "difficult" than single samples, it does not necessarily follow that more controls are needed; perhaps a different kind of scoring procedure altogether is necessary. As many theorists (Elbow, citing research by Despain and Hilgers; Condon and Hamp-Lyons; Huot; Schuster) have pointed out, the assumption of transferability from single samples to portfolios is not supported by research.

Creating reliability and consistency in scoring through controlled reading is also at issue. The use of training sessions has been questioned on the grounds that reliability among readers is achieved only by suppressing individual readers' instincts and natural responses to a text. Peter Elbow, for example, claims that "What 'training' means is getting . . . scorers to stop reading the way they normally read—getting them to stop using the conflicting criteria and standards they normally use outside the scoring sessions. . . . The reliability in holistic scoring is not a measure of how texts are valued by real readers in natural settings, but only of how they are valued in artificial settings with imposed agreements" (Elbow 188–89). When "reliability" is achieved this way, it is at the expense of a great deal of time, effort, and authenticity. Is it worth it?

White maintains it is worth it (70), but controlled sessions of the kind suggested by White, in which he recommends that participants "Resist using informal procedures, such as parceling out the portfolios to faculty to take home and treat as they wish" (70) could contribute to a backlash reaction because the effort this kind of reliability requires may only succeed in achieving an artificial and convoluted kind of consistency; in addition, this synthetic construct may be only as dependable as the "chief reader" for that particular scoring session on that particular day. If we are to try to meet any number of demands for accountability, certainly we want portfolio assessment to be reliable, consistent, and fair, but if the administrative task of creating reliability becomes more important and more overwhelming than the task of helping students learn to write, resistance—in the form of a desire to return to a more predictable, more quantifiable (but less direct) type of assessment—would not be surprising.

Beating the Backlash

In the interest of mitigating a backlash possibility and establishing an agenda for enhancing, rather than endangering, the use of portfolio assessment, four suggestions might be helpful: first, administrators need to recognize that portfolios can serve a variety of purposes and they need to distinguish among those purposes in conversations about their use. For example, the kinds of portfolios produced in a classroom context for classroom purposes are not the same as portfolios used to test program credibility or validity and should not be used in the same way. We should avoid the "mixed-use approach whereby portfolios produced in a classroom context for classroom purposes are also used by program administrators to test credibility or program validity. It's a mistake, I think, to confuse portfolios produced by classroom means with a given program's need for consistent ends. I don't propose we should limit the use of portfolios to the writing classroom, but that we need to develop distinctions in the way portfolios are produced to satisfy different ends. As a corollary to this, perhaps the use of outside evaluation should be a more careful, thoughtful decision; many successful portfolio programs (e.g., Weiser) do not employ outside readers or graders because the aims of the writing program focus on pedagogy rather than program accountability.

Second, if portfolio systems do employ outside evaluation, scoring criteria need to be designed and reviewed by all participants in a collaborative, egalitarian effort. Portfolio production and scoring should not be a top-down management decision; all participants need to be involved in decision making if the aims of invested writing and consistency of evaluation are to be achieved. Asymmetrical power and role relationships between those who direct and those who teach are counterproductive to the development of a functional and healthy portfolio program.

Third, when the product under evaluation is a portfolio, we may need to reconsider the very nature of reliability and how it can be achieved. David Smit, for example, argues for more "flexible, circumstantial notions of reliability" (312); Liz Hamp-Lyons, too, supports this notion when she cites research supporting Michael Williamson's claim that "we should privilege teacher expertise and use their contextual knowledge and experience to increase 'conceptual reliability' rather than 'statistical reliability'" (448). No one would argue that the entire notion of reliability should be tossed out the window, but that traditional concepts of reliability simply do not correspond well with the reading processes people use when they read (and evaluate) portfolios as writing products.

Finally, the most urgent need is for the field of composition studies to conduct more systematic research into the paradoxical issues presented here and elsewhere. We need to add experimental research methodologies to the bulk of testimonial and descriptive research already produced and published. We need studies to allow for generalization and replication, not because these methodologies are assumed to be inherently more credible than qualitative methods, but because, in studying portfolio assessment, it would be highly appropriate to argue we cannot accurately assess portfolio work on the basis of a single type of research. We need the capacity to generalize to counter those skeptics who call into question "merely anecdotal" research on the basis of its limited application, its specificity. We must begin to build a comprehensive research portfolio to investigate questions and assumptions about any number of portfolio-related issues. Possible topics for inquiry might include several of the issues raised here: (1) the relationship between portfolios and grade inflation; (2) the creation and maintenance of "standards" and scoring criteria; (3) how scoring rubrics are used by real readers in uncontrolled settings; (4) the question of transference between single-sample scoring and portfolio scoring; (5) the correlation between "conceptual reliability" and traditional views of reliability; (6) the influence of external and institutional pressures on portfolio production and grading. The field is especially ready for experimental research on portfolio work because we are at present so dependent on anecdotal, testimonial material, and new research along these lines would be useful in adding to our understanding of the theory and practice of using portfolios. Common misconceptions and assumptions about portfolio assessment need to be investigated so the threat of a backlash against this most promising practice could be defused as an outcome of information and awareness.

V

Imagining Alternatives

Student Voices

Grades have a way of snapping me back into reality when I've become too confident and nonchalant in my studies. When you've let down your guard and then you're slapped with a paper that has so many red error marks on it that it barely resembles its original form, you tend to take a few steps back and re-evaluate your thinking. — *Andrea Pekovich*

Did I do enough? Was my writing good? The only way I could know was if I had a grade. So, not to be evaluated during the semester is like a double-edged sword. It feels great up until the end of the semester when your performance is graded. — *Craig Banger*

I have always prided myself on the fact that I'm going to college because I like to learn. Of course, then, I should have been elated at the idea of having my first two portfolio classes last semester. Here was my opportunity to spend an entire semester improving my writing before submitting it for a grade. What possibilities! The truth was, though, I was terrified. Without grades, how was I to know when a piece of writing was finished, when it was good enough? I now realize that was the point. I had to be the one to decide when my writing was finished and at its best. And I'm my worst critic. Had I been given my usual A on any one of those papers I did last semester, they would not be what they are today. Instead, I kept at it all semester. I worked hard to improve them, and when I was stuck, the instructors were always there with suggestions and questions to get me rolling again. — *Stacy Taylor*

I do remember well my worst moment in writing. It was when I really worked hard for a paper. I think I spent 44 hours, to be exact, on that paper. I had my paper proofread by five students with 4.0 GPAs. When I got my paper back, I got a C+. I was furious about what happened. I tried to read the comments so I could have an understanding of what I had done wrong. The first comment was that I didn't have much detail in that paragraph. The second comment was that I had a comma splice. The third comment was that I had too much detail in that paragraph. Well, the second comment I can understand, but how about the first and the third! — *Hans Stevenson Go*

From my experience, most teachers I've had graded mostly on whether they liked [a paper] or not and didn't put trying into consideration. This made me not try as hard because I thought I couldn't write something to please them. — *Karen Koprivnik*

Seems to me that getting rid of grades would work great in theories—but who knows what will happen in the real classroom? — *Victoria Savalei*

11

Christopher C. Weaver

Grading in a Process-Based Writing Classroom

Our beliefs about writing, teaching writing, and perhaps about teaching in general, have undergone something of a revolution over the past thirty years or so. This revolution has been characterized by a paradigm shift from a product-based pedagogy to a pedagogy that is process-based. Yet process-based pedagogies, because of their attempt to decenter authority, are particularly vulnerable to being undermined by traditional grading schemes. If we have failed, after three decades of innovation, to truly transform the writing classroom, it is because we have yet to imagine systems of grading that will support our teaching strategies. Our failure on this front is particularly ironic because students are so often receptive to a process-based approach. Many accept our invitation to explore their attitudes and assumptions about writing and to attempt to define for themselves what makes their own writing work in certain situations but not in others. Certainly, most students I have taught prefer feedback groups to lectures, find freewriting and exploratory writing enjoyable and liberating, and appreciate the opportunity to reflect on their work. However, while we are asking—perhaps demanding—that our students engage in activities which help them to explore the complexities of the writing process, they know most of us base our grades not on these activities but on the texts which they produce—the papers that, whether graded individually or as part of a writing portfolio, represent their achievement in our classes.

Such a practice on our part amounts to a breach of faith which undermines not only our process-based approaches but also our students' trust in our good intentions. Even when our grading practices take into account such extratextual factors as effort, participation, and improvement, students are generally most concerned with the one variable they have been conditioned to regard as the most critical: what the finished product is "supposed" to look like. If we truly believe in our process pedagogies, then we need to construct grading systems which foreground the complexities of the writing process and which minimize, defer, or possibly even ignore questions about the quality of the writing our students ultimately produce. I wish to describe one such system of "process grading" and examine what this system suggests about our roles as teachers and evaluators and about the authority on which these roles are based.

Process grading is a system which grew out of my own experience with the contradictions between teaching and grading. After several disappointing years teaching high school English, using some of the truly dreadful textbooks that are quite common there, I was excited to discover Peter Elbow and Pat Belanoff's *A Community of Writers*, a process-oriented book which encourages students to try many different approaches to generating, revising, and responding to writing with a particular emphasis on reflecting on what happens as they write. The first half of the semester was successful beyond my expectations. The students took risks, tried different techniques, and responded to each other's writing in a variety of ways. Although I commented on their work, primarily by asking questions, most of the feedback they received came from their classmates.

I am convinced that my decision not to give my students grades had much to do with my initial success. It encouraged them to regard each other as credible authorities on the effects of their writing. They came to see feedback as important, not because it revealed to them the "right" way to write (as it had when it came from me), but because it provided ways of seeing their work from different points of view. Without me to refer to as an authority, they were forced to act as a community, arguing over and reflecting on the effects of each other's writing and speculating on the reasons for these effects. In short, they were immersed in the issues surrounding how writing works—the issues of process.

Midway through the semester, however, I began to feel uneasy about my eventual obligation to give students a grade for the course. When they submitted papers for a practice run of their portfolios (a program-wide requirement for the course), I handed them back with a grade attached, and at that point, everything changed irrevocably. From then on, students who before were interested in exploring and experimenting with the writing process, were now only interested in one thing: what I wanted them to do to change their writing into "A papers." I was frustrated and dismayed. All the wonderful exploring and risk-taking seemed to be replaced by a cautious, stale, "what the teacher wants" kind of writing. I worried about what would happen to my students when they left my class for others, where larger enrollments and less time devoted to revision would keep them from consulting their professors about how to "fix" their work. How could they succeed on their own if they didn't begin to learn to take control of the writing process themselves? My students, at least the ones who didn't get As, felt as betrayed and disappointed as I did. Why was I wasting their time with things like freewriting and group feedback if I was just waiting to pounce on them with my real evaluation when these activities were over? Since then, the tension between realizing my obligation to the university's requirement that I give grades and my requirement that students take responsibility for gaining control over their own writing processes has resulted in an ongoing struggle in my teaching. I have found myself searching for ways to keep my authority as a grader from undermining my students' choices as learners.

In "Ranking, Evaluating, and Liking: Sorting Out Three Forms of Judgment," Peter Elbow addresses this problem by establishing "evaluation-free zones"—spaces in which students need not worry about grades and are thus more likely to be motivated by their own needs and interests than by pleasing their teacher. Elbow supposes that, free from the fear of negative consequences, students will feel more comfortable exploring and taking risks. The difficulty with evaluation-free zones, however, is their uneasy relationship with evaluation-full zones. I had already seen what happened in my classroom when my nonevaluative responding gave way to the eventuality of grading. Of course, things might have been different if I had told students, at the beginning of the semester, I would withhold any evaluation but that eventually their writing would be graded. This is, in fact, how many teachers who make use of portfolios organize their courses. Subsequent experience, however, has confirmed that such a scheme merely increases students' anxiety about grades ("How do I know what I'm going to get?"). It also encourages them to ignore or merely play along with my obsession about issues of process while always keeping an eye out for the moment at which the grading of papers will "kick in." As attractive as I find Elbow's evaluation-free zones, I suspect we may never be able, even temporarily, to escape our role as graders.

Michael Bernard-Donals expresses a similar skepticism in an earlier chapter in this book, entitled "Peter Elbow and the Cynical Subject." Bernard-Donals asserts that the teacher's authority, the presence of the grade, and the "rules of the game" are always present in the classroom, no matter what grading schemes we adopt, and even if we temporarily suspend grading altogether. He argues that, since we can never escape the authority that comes with our role as graders, we ought to confront our students with that authority and force them to examine the "rules of the game." Bernard-Donals' approach is an increasingly familiar one among poststructuralists who advocate demystification of institutional rules and power-structures.[1] However, I would like to suggest a different course of action, one less dependent upon confrontation and conflict. If there is no way to escape the negative consequences of our authority as graders, perhaps we can refocus that authority in order to encourage the kind of behavior that is more likely to make our students better writers.

This idea lead me, shortly after that frustrating first semester, to experiment with a system I will refer to as "process grading," which shifts the focus of evaluation from the various texts students produce over a semester to the "cover letters" they write to explain, advocate for, and generally reflect on those texts. Cover letters (or "writer's letters" or "reflective letters," as they are variously known) are documents which students attach to individual papers or to entire portfolios in which they provide the reader with information about how the paper was written and what the student thinks is important about the writing. They may address such issues as the student's purpose in writing the piece, the feedback she received from readers, and her appraisal of its effectiveness. They are required in many writing programs that use portfolios to evaluate students' work, including the two colleges where I participated in portfolio evaluation. At both of these schools, however, the cover letters students wrote often consisted of a few brief, superficial paragraphs which, for the most part, did not deal with the writing process at all but rather summarized the content of the papers. This shouldn't be surprising: the students understand it is the papers and not the cover letter which will be graded. In all the portfolio grading sessions I have ever attended, I have never seen an occasion where a cover letter was a crucial factor in determining whether or not the portfolio passed. Although they are required, students seem to regard them more as afterthoughts than serious or sustained examinations of their writing.

My hope was that process grading would upset my students' perception of the relationship between the cover letter and the writing on which it commented. I wanted them to see the issues of process that the cover letter explored, not as afterthoughts, but as primary in importance, and the papers themselves as testing grounds for these issues. So, rather than base their grade on whether or not their papers matched my expectations of what good writing should look like, I based their grade on how well their cover letters explained the different stages of their writing process and how well they persuaded me they were engaged in what I believed to be the crucial issues of that process. If this practice seems vague (what are the "crucial issues?") and arbitrary (to whom are they "crucial?"), it is certainly no less so than traditional grading where criteria are often subjective and hard to define.

What is liberating about process grading is that I feel much freer to be prescriptive in my comments than when I was grading my students on the quality of their papers. We process-oriented teachers tend to be a fairly nondirective bunch, preferring to ask questions or point out possibilities in students' writing rather than prescribe changes. We live in fear of appropriating students' texts. It's something of a relief, then, to tell my students just whether or not their cover letters are acceptable and just what to do to "fix" them—to present myself, not just as another reader, but as the authority on the subject. By grading students' cover letters rather than their papers, I foreground my authority as the classroom grader while at the same time shifting the site at which I exercise this authority and the area of expertise over which I claim it. I am now pretty much the sole authority on cover letters, but I am no longer the authority on their other writing—the papers to which the cover letters refer. It seems reasonable to me that my authority should center around this type of reflective writing rather than on changes students may make to their essays and stories. I may not know the best way for them to write, but as a writing teacher (and as someone whose professional activities demand a great deal of writing), I do have more experience about what it means to reflect on writing, and I do have suggestions about techniques they might use to analyze their own styles or seek out useful feedback—all subjects which I insist they explore in their cover letters.

The prescriptive nature of my comments on their cover letters allows me to be more nondirective about their papers. Since I am not telling them what to do with the writing the cover letters describe, I do not worry that my directions will cause my students to "fix" these papers in order to conform them to my satisfaction. It is true that revising their cover letters often does lead them to consider changing their papers. But these changes are *theirs*. They are a result of their own reflection and decision making rather than the sort of knee-jerk reaction Elbow laments.

I also believe that in emphasizing the importance of cover letters, I am teaching my students a valuable skill. The level of self-reflection such writing requires is crucial to them if they are going to enter into the academic discourse community. Metacognition, or as Ann Berthoff puts it, "knowing our knowledge," is at the heart of all academic endeavors (44). It fosters skepticism, rigor, and control—qualities too often lacking in students' writing, and qualities difficult to address through comments on a student's text.

Pat Belanoff uncovers some interesting connections between good writing and metacognitive awareness in a study entitled "Freewriting: An Aid to Rereading Theorists." In this study, Belanoff examines freewriting done by students in one of her writing classes. Based on an independent assessment of several essays, the students were divided into several different groups according to the reviewers' perception of their skills as writers. The reviewers then read samples of freewriting these same students had done. Belanoff discovered there were characteristics of freewriting done by the "skilled" writers that were absent from the freewriting of the "poorer" writers. One difference was that the freewriting of the "skilled" group included the frequent use of metacognitive commentary. She says:

> . . . the good writers usually produced freewriting that was periodically very much aware of itself as writing and of the physical conditions and environment of the writer; this awareness manifested itself in metalanguage. Good writers often began freewriting with some mention of the writing itself, the purpose of the writing, or the environment in which they were writing. These blocks of metalanguage often appeared between the fluid prose patches characteristic of such freewriting. (18)

Belanoff comments in particular on the use of such metacommentary to record doubts or frustrations about the writing such as "No, that's wrong," "That sounds stupid!" or even "My hand is tired." She says: "That poor writers have such comments we know, but they seem to feel that writing is for recording what is known, not what is uncertain. The latter stops them and probably throws them off whatever trail they are exploring. Skilled writers articulate the doubt . . ." (25).

The students in Belanoff's freewriting samples articulated doubt in order to incorporate it into their writing—in order to keep it from derailing them. But articulating doubt is useful for other reasons as well, and we ought to devise grading systems which value it. One characteristic of much unsophisticated student writing is its rush to closure. How often have we received student essays in which the overriding purpose seems to be to reach a tidy conclusion with its assumptions unchallenged? Students—particularly students who are new to the college environment—tend to think of doubt as a weakness. They believe the purpose of writing is to transmit knowledge; and thus, if there is no certainty, then there is nothing to transmit and, therefore, no point to writing. Yet, the academy is based on doubt. It thrives on questions and rewards skepticism and the reexamination of easy answers. Encouraging students to articulate their doubt by exploring it in their cover letters keeps them from this premature closure. Grading their cover letters instead of their papers validates their doubts by encouraging students to see them as an inevitable part of their writing process.

I frequently give my students writing prompts which ask them to explore the troubling parts of their writing process: the places they get stuck, the difficulties they have interpreting feedback, the things about their writing (both product and process) they don't like. Interestingly, they often choose to cut these sections from their cover letters when they are submitting them to outside readers as part of their portfolio. Many have expressed the fear that by pointing out their weaknesses, they are giving the reviewers additional reasons to fail their portfolios. Although I personally doubt this actually happens, it does confirm my belief that traditional grading, and even portfolio assessment, tends to drive certain process issues underground. Since students are willing to share problems with me they refuse to reveal to portfolio readers, it seems likely that process grading allows and may even encourage these issues to surface. Because they know the writing I am asking about will not be graded, they feel no need to hide or explain away its weaknesses. By not penalizing them for facing the problems and difficulties of the writing process, I can encourage them to see these occurrences, not as obstacles between them and a good grade, but rather as experiences from which they can learn. Their doubts and frustrations can be incorporated into their writing process rather than stopping it short in much the same way Belanoff's skilled writers incorporated their doubts into their freewriting.

Process grading is also a great help for students who think they are poorer writers than their classmates. Many students who perceive themselves as poor writers (often with a history of negative feedback to validate this perception) are convinced they will never overcome their disadvantage and cannot compete with other writers in the class whom they believe are more naturally gifted. But in a process-graded classroom these students are not required to become better writers. All they are required to do is to write about their writing—not necessarily to make it better. (In many cases, it is precisely this behavior which they need to learn in order to be better writers, but I realize it does not always produce immediate results.) Process grading removes a tremendous burden—and an excuse not to succeed.

They do, of course, need to improve one kind of writing: their cover letters. For all my talk of grading process, I am not unaware that cover letters are themselves a written product. However, cover letters are much easier to improve than other kinds of writing, in part, because students' cover letters usually start out more or less equal—that is to say, equally wretched. Students' cover letters are often, like those in the portfolio programs I mentioned earlier, brief and superficial. I suspect this is partly because early in the semester they don't quite take my requirements seriously and partly because this kind of writing is unfamiliar and difficult. Most of my comments on these initial attempts and some of the writing activities early in the semester are aimed at getting students to write more and at helping them find more things to say about their writing processes. And since everyone in the class tends to have the same sorts of problems with their cover letters, it is fairly easy to develop strategies to help everyone at the same time. How different this is from the usual dilemma of trying to teach a class of widely divergent abilities with diverse individual problems!

Whether or not process grading improves all of students' writing and not just their cover letters is a difficult matter to determine. Clearly, their papers do get better. In courses where students are evaluated through outside portfolio review, my classes consistently show an improvement in the pass rate between the midsemester practice run and the end-of-semester review—just as all my colleagues' classes do. Some of this improvement may be related to my evaluation of their cover letters. Although students know they will be graded, not on their papers, but on the cover letters which describe them, my comments and my evaluations force them to return to their papers and reconsider the decisions they have made in writing them. I do not insist they improve on their original drafts; however, I do require them to select several papers for revision, and I expect them to comment on this process in their cover letters. In other words, process grading forces them to think seriously about the decisions involved in writing and revising their work. The end result is often, though certainly not always, a better paper. When it is not, it may be because without my directions about what and how to revise, students do not always make wise choices. Actually, I find this failure somewhat reassuring. Real learning is seldom a straightforward process, and so it is not surprising to find students' progress, like their writing, is often halting and messy.

We also need to remember that the writing that students produce does not always reflect their growth as writers. At the very least, we need to read students' texts carefully for what they can tell us about their writers' progress. In "Inventing the University," David Bartholomae points out how students who have begun to hear and to imitate the rhythm and syntax of academic discourse, often produce writing that is more awkward than the "seamless" prose of students who remain completely outside of this discourse community. To interpret these students' fumbling attempts at approximating our discourse as a weakness of their writing, Bartholomae says, is to "misunderstand "the degree to which error is not a constant feature but a marker in the development of a writer" (18). Students whose awkward and "error-filled" papers indicate a struggle with academic language do not so much need help untangling their sentences as they need guidance in understanding how their discourse "codes" differ from those of academics. Penalizing students when their writing shows signs of struggle is a mistake, since often their writing not only fails to reflect their progress as writers but actually masks it. This is one of the dangers of grading their writing product rather than their writing process.

Like many other poststructuralists (most notably Pat Bizzell—see "Cognition, Convention, and Certainty" and other pieces), Bartholomae advocates making the conventions of academic writing more explicit and encouraging students to mimic academic discourse even before "at least in terms of our disciplines, they have anything to say" (17–20). I share Bartholomae's conceptualization of what happens when students try to enter our discourse; however, I am skeptical that teaching them to reproduce its textual features before they have internalized them is the most productive (or humane) way to teach them. If what we value about students' writing is their struggle with what is unfamiliar, then we need to provide students with a space where it is safe to acknowledge this struggle. Requiring them to reproduce the self-assured, even aggressive tone of much academic writing, while at the same time admitting such gestures are a fiction, is to put them in the hopeless position of being evaluated on how well they assume an authority they don't have. Such a practice is surely more likely to elicit silence than discourse. Process grading provides students with a space in which to acknowledge their struggles with academic discourse and to examine its conventions *without having to write within them*. Moreover, this system of grading also communicates to students that it is precisely these struggles with language that we value and will reward.

Although I find students' uneven performance reassuring because it seems real rather than contrived, others may be less likely to take comfort from this evidence of the ephemeral nature of learning. In this era of "accountability," any system of evaluation not tightly bound to demonstrable short-term results is likely to create anxieties and encounter resistance. Teachers and administrators will worry that process grading might allow students to slip through without demonstrating they are capable of producing competent writing. Students, especially those who have fared well under traditional grading schemes, may resent not being rewarded for demonstrating the writing skills they already possess.

Currently, many underprepared students *do* slip through, but for students to grow as writers, they must move beyond the safety of what they know. Most teachers who have advocated for a process pedagogy have probably met with these attitudes before. To a large degree, dealing with them successfully is a matter of the skills and resources of the individual teacher. Tying process pedagogy into a grading system, however, is likely to heighten anxieties because it raises the stakes.

Making process grading work requires addressing these anxieties and reassuring administrators, teachers, and students that product still matters. One way of acquiring the benefits of process grading, while still addressing concerns about students' competence as writers, is to couple the classroom teacher's evaluation with an outside portfolio review. Knowing their work will have to pass this review lets students know they must improve at least some of their work to an acceptable level while at the same time removing such a judgment from the classroom teacher's hands and therefore avoiding the "what do you want it to look like?" problem. As for students' desire to be praised for their writing, means other than grades can and should be found. Praise can be given without a grade attached, and public readings and publications, both inside and outside the classroom, are also excellent ways to value student writing without the use of grades.

Any system of grading writing involves an imposition of a teacher's authority and a privileging of our agendas over those of our students. The kind of grading system that best supports a process-based pedagogy does not require us to escape from these realities. If we cannot create sites in our classrooms that are free from contamination by grading, then perhaps what we can do is define separate "spheres of influence"—different (though overlapping) spaces in which either we or our students are in control. This is one great advantage of process grading: it limits teachers' authority to one particular area of the writing process—students' cover letters. By restricting grading to this site, and by making explicit the criteria that are evaluated and the values that support this criteria, process grading allows students more freedom to take risks in the rest of their writing and to establish and test their own authority as writers.

In advocating process grading, I am not suggesting such judgments about quality of texts are not an important part of the job of a writing teacher. I propose they are so important to the grasp and control of good writing that they ought not to be left entirely to teachers. We ought to insist such judgments be a part of the writing process of our students, and process grading is one way to make sure they are.

Note

1. For another example of the poststructuralist approach of confronting students with the way authority is institutionally constructed, see Pauline Uchmanowicz's chapter, "The Politics of Cross-Institutional Grading: An Adjunct's Dilemma," (ch. 9).

12

Irene Papoulis

Gender and Grading

"Immanence" as a Path to "Transcendence"?

In exploring the issue of gender and its role in the process of grading, we can follow many different avenues. We can consider the gender of the student, and notice its effect on teachers' responses, or we can study the gender of the grader. Such studies are subject to much debate, since the moment one makes an assertion about male or female behavior one is faced with a multitude of exceptions. As an alternative, I am interested here in exploring gender and grading not in terms of the grader or the graded, but in terms of the method. My premise is that traditional grading methods are based on principles that have historically been associated with men, and I would like to explore some methods of grading that incorporate womens' traditional roles.

To describe some differences between traditional gender roles, I turn first to Simone de Beauvoir, who pointed out decades ago that western society tends to associate women with "immanence" and men with "transcendence." Women traditionally stayed put in the home: they thought about feelings, nurtured others, and otherwise attended to the present moment; men, of course, moved forth from home, acted in the world, and pointed themselves toward the future. De Beauvoir's purpose in describing immanence and transcendence, when she wrote *The Second Sex* in the years after the second world war, was to rail against the system that perpetuated those categories. Her interest was in enabling women to achieve the transcendence they deserved, and so her view of immanence was that it was deeply stifling:

> The domestic labors that fell to [woman's] lot because they were reconcilable with the cares of maternity imprisoned her in repetition and immanence; they were repeated from day to day in an identical form, which was perpetuated almost without change from century to century; they produced nothing new. (71)

> In no domain whatever did [woman] create; she maintained the life of the tribe by giving it children and bread, nothing more. She remained doomed to immanence, incarnating only the static aspect of society, closed in upon itself. Whereas man went on monopolizing the functions which threw open that society toward nature and toward the rest of humanity. . . . (83)

To de Beauvoir, immanence is a deeply undesirable state, one which must be overcome if women are to have any power in the world. If only they could be transcendent, de Beauvoir said, women could burst upon the world, influence it for the better, and thereby be free of the stifling bonds of immanence.

Given this attitude, it might seem odd at best to attempt—as I am about to do—to resurrect immanence as a useful concept in a discussion about grading. However, I think we will do well to reclaim some of the qualities that de Beauvoir was so eager to dismiss, because those qualities have the potential to help us nurture our students' writing. Unlike de Beauvoir, I am interested in thinking about how, in some ways, immanence can in fact be a very desirable position, particularly when one chooses it freely. As I will explain, if we read student papers in an "immanent" way, we might become increasingly effective in helping students "transcend" their own limitations.

Traditional grading, in which a teacher assigns a letter grade to each piece of writing the student gives her, is "transcendent": connected with the historically male activity of moving outward. The purpose of assigning a fixed letter grade is to thrust the paper into the world—to place it, to determine its value, to move it out from the subjective realm of the student and into the social world of academia. The grade tells the student about her status in that world, thereby helping her leave the "home" of her writing process. Ideally, a good grade rewards her and encourages her to carry on in the same vein; a bad grade chastens her and invites better performance next time, or, at least, awakens her to the reality of her limitations.

Traditional grading's confidence that it will supply the student with a realistic assessment of her abilities, however, is often unfounded. The often premature closure of submitting a paper for a grade tends to create undue worry and pressure in students, who might stifle their most creative insights in the name of needing to please or conform. Another unfortunate consequence is that students who receive good grades become complacent and do not improve. Poor students, on the other hand, can experience a sense of futility in the face of a disappointing grade, and stop trying.

While I realize that grades are usually a necessity in college writing courses, I would like to propose "immanent" grading, a process of delaying grading until the end of the course in order to "stay home" in the present moment with the student and her work before evaluation. Immanent grading's primary interest is in helping the student become a better writer, even while her teacher is obliged to give her a letter grade. Furthermore, a teacher engaged in "immanent grading" pays attention to her own health as a grader. Community with her peers is crucial to her.

I will discuss "immanent grading" here in terms of how it can ultimately yield a more effective transcendence than that of "transcendent grading," and I will focus on three overall categories: teacher collaboration, portfolio grading, and the role of emotions in grading.

Teacher Collaboration

Patricia Carini works at the Prospect School for grades K–8 in Vermont, and she has designed a program of teacher collaboration that could be described as "immanent" grading. One of her basic principles is that teachers need many different pieces of a given student's work in order to evaluate fairly; a single piece is never enough in itself. With this in mind, she has devised a method for collaboration among teachers that has influenced writing teachers at Syracuse University, New York University's Expository Writing Program, and elsewhere. To arrive at a more complete evaluation of a student than he possibly could make on his own, a teacher in the Prospect School will bring a collection of the student's work to a group of fellow teachers. After reading it, his colleagues sit around a table and take turns naming qualities—"style, tone, rhythm, form" (Himley 37–38)—that strike them. To Carini:

> all children define space, explore history, tell a story, or enact life experiences in importantly particular ways. By reflectively, concretely, and often communally *describing* a child's work . . . teachers and researchers can come to understand more fully . . . that child's expressive choices, interests, images, positionings, key words, and ways of learning and thinking, and then use that understanding to support the child's learning." (Himley 19) [emphasis mine]

The key word here for me is "describing," and its vast difference from "evaluating." Carini's colleagues are relatively objective in their comments. They look at the work in terms of what it is and does, not in terms of how good or bad it might be. I would call this form of response to students' work "immanent" because of its focus on the present moment and its willingness to let the student and his work be more significant than the larger social culture in which the work will eventually take its place. Thus, the student and the teacher, in a sense, "stay home" for a while; executed well, immanent responding lovingly nurtures the student's work by sitting back and allowing it to be what it is. Furthermore, the method of bringing one's students' work to a group of colleagues is in itself an element of immanent grading; by postponing evaluation, the teacher makes more space for her students.

In Margaret Himley's book about this method, Carini describes her thoughts as follows:

> Fundamental to this focus on works is a notion of person as the bearer of a unique value and perspective, uniquely situated in the world and in life, and enjoying an individuality and being not interchangeable with that of others. The person cannot, except at a price, be translated or defined in the abstract terms supplied by specialized fields of study. The price of the psychologists or sociologist's classifications is the sacrifice of the intensity, vividness, unevenness and wholeness of an individual existence. (29)

A grade is an ultimate "abstract term," and the purpose of "staying home" and being immanent is to allow the uniqueness of the student to find a place in the classroom and in the teacher's mind. Without such a sense of the student's "unevenness and wholeness," teachers can easily misread and thus unfairly evaluate students, thereby making it much more difficult for those students to know themselves and ultimately move effectively out into the world.

Margaret Himley discusses the way Carini's ideas have been applied to the college writing classroom at Syracuse University. She does not write explicitly about grading, but about what she calls "deep talk" among teachers. In her example, a teacher brings a problematic student essay to a group of teachers:

> . . . because she was having trouble knowing what to say to this student when he came to conferences. Somehow she felt she didn't have the right words to help him see what the problems in the essay really were, or to help him imagine the different kinds of choices he would make as a writer. (Himley 58)

The teachers begin responding to the student paper by going around the table and each paraphrasing brief sections of the text, just as the teachers at the Prospect School do. They then, without any other discussion, also begin "descriptive rounds," in which one at a time they make "low-inferential observations" (58), like "the first three paragraphs are very short, no more than two sentences long. . . ." When they have gone around the table at least once, the chair uses their words to define "clusters of ideas or themes." They then go around the table again, making more "inferential claims and evaluative conclusions" (59), but avoiding any cross-discussion, and the immanence of the process—a group of teachers speaking in turn about a paper—works well for the teacher. After listening to the sum of her colleagues' observations about the text, ". . . the teacher who has asked for the deep talk recognized that the textual patterns that had been described in this essay characterized much of this writer's work in the course so far, and she felt confident about what to talk about in their next conference" (Himley 59). By stepping back for a time from her own observation of the essay, and by pausing to listen to her colleagues, the teacher is able to evaluate her student more fairly than she would if she had simply struggled on her own to arrive at an immediate grade. The grade she gives the student at the end of the semester will grow out of her now-more-complex insight into the student.

At the Syracuse writing program, Himley tells us, teachers meet regularly to describe student texts in this way, and they learn "to hold off quick or habituated understanding and intellectual closure" (60)—which, of course, could manifest itself as an unexamined grade—thereby developing "a shared (if not common) discourse" (60). That sharing is characteristic of immanence, a state in which there is no need to compete or impose one's will, and each paper is accepted as it is. Teachers who have met in the kind of teacher groups Himley describes tend to become more compassionate, more able to meet the student where she actually is, as opposed to where the teacher too-hastily might otherwise judge her to be.

An overworked teacher might well read the above and shudder not necessarily because of its premises but because of the extra work it seems to invite. Let me offer some brief practical suggestions. First of all, a group of teachers can benefit from discussing only one student paper. This could take less than an hour, and yield good insights. Second, I have a brief anecdote from my experience: When I taught writing at the University of California, Santa Barbara in the late 1980s, I was involved with a group of four teachers who decided, during one quarter, to grade one class worth of each others' students' papers. We read our own students' papers as well, but without commenting, and then each student got complete readings from two other teachers. We imagined at first that this would take far more time than our usual isolated grading procedures, and that we would therefore have not even an ounce of free time that quarter. However, one of the first things I noticed was that, oddly enough, as my grading became more public it became (after my initial nervousness and embarrassment wore off a bit) better and less time-consuming. The process of collaborating with other teachers enabled me to question my own too-detailed comments on student papers. When I read other teachers' versions of the same sort of comments I realized that students would be overwhelmed by them and not listen well to them. My colleagues and I decided that good responding involves fewer, better-chosen responses, and the process of figuring out which kinds of responses were most effective became fun for us; the fact that we were immanent with our own grading allowed us to save time and to become more effective with students' writing.

Portfolio Grading

Immanent grading breaks out of the pattern of expectations that most students have when they come to college: they tend to expect each piece of their writing to be evaluated and fit into a clearly defined hierarchy. Of course, as teachers we know how subjective grading is, but students often seem to have an odd faith that the letter their teacher affixes to their paper represents some sort of universal standard. The betrayal that students can feel from a teacher who will not tell them at every instance how they are doing, as manifested in a letter grade, is the result of socialization in a school system where transcendence is the operative principle: the goal is always seen as being to transcend oneself, one's peers, and eventually one's teachers. The practice of portfolio grading seeks to resist that goal, at least temporarily.

There are various kinds of portfolio grading at the college level (see Belanoff and Dickson), but one thing they all have in common is a refusal to assign a quantitative evaluation to a single paper. Some schools have students gather a portfolio of their work in order to pass a proficiency requirement, for example; some teachers require students to select a portfolio of their work over the semester in order to present it for a course grade. Such methods allow for immanence as the student creates her portfolio—she need not "leave the house" until she has produced enough to reflect her best effort.

My own experience with portfolio grading includes collaborative work with teachers. In the three-week summer program that is required for all incoming first year students at Bard College (sponsored by the Institute for Writing and Thinking), faculty are organized into "portfolio groups." Each week, students hand in portfolios, which include their selection of the following from the multitude of writing they have done: a work that has been revised extensively, a work they would like to revise further, and an unrevised work they would like to share. After reading our students' portfolios and writing comments, we meet in groups of three or four to share our evaluation process. We usually bring our most problematic portfolio to the group's attention, sharing the comments we either have written or are considering writing to the student. Members of the group discuss the student and the comments, sometimes causing the teacher to change his mind. I have found these groups to be extremely enlightening, both for the insight they yield into the mysterious world of what other teachers write on student papers, and for my own self-awareness as an evaluator. Like the collaborative group I described in Santa Barbara, they have made me realize how private I used to feel about my written comments to students, and to see that embarrassment about one's comments is quite common among practitioners of the very inexact science of assessment.

In addition to being a resource for good teacher collaboration, portfolios are also a means for students to remain immanent with their writing, as they do not have to thrust anything out into the world until it supposedly is ready at the end of the semester. But what happens then? If we delay grading are we only postponing the inevitable plunge into transcendence, the inevitable slap in the face of "you are a C+ student?" Yes, in a way we are. Some students will be damaged by a grade no matter when they get it, and I would prefer to teach in a system in which there are no letter grades at all.

However, the fact is that most of us need to assign grades, and I am exploring ways to facilitate the transition for students from the immanence of written responses to the transcendence of getting a single course grade. When I first used portfolios in semester-long courses I kept a record for myself of a letter grade for each paper; students received only written comments. To deal with the anxiety that some students felt about not knowing what their grade was so far, I announced that they could consult me whenever they wanted for an in-progress grade. I was surprised that only a few students took advantage of this option; when they did I would glance surreptitiously at my private gradebook and then ask how they would assess themselves. Interestingly, most were within a plus or minus of my quickly averaged assessment of them. In meeting the few students whose self-assessments diverged widely from my grade (they thought, almost inevitably, that they deserved a higher grade then I would give) I was always uncomfortable, because I felt trapped in a painstaking attempt to explain what was "wrong" with the writing of a student who thought he had done well.

The method of posing myself as the secretive authority now seems grandiose and unfair to me, and I have stopped it. I now work in a way that, while still not at all perfect, seems truer to the idea of immanent grading: Early in the semester, and again on the day I collect the portfolios, I spend time in class going over the general criteria for each grade. I have students write a self-assessment to include with their portfolio, containing the letter grades they think they deserve, and using narrative descriptions of their writing experience throughout the semester to explain why. When I give them their final grades I include a note in response to their self-assessments, and I have found for the most part that my grades corresponds surprisingly frequently with their own expectations. Students are usually satisfied, if not always happy, with the grade I give them. Of course, there are sometimes complaints, but fewer than I received with the traditional grading I once did.

Emotions in Grading

In addition to solving some problems, immanent grading's invitation to self-revelation can pose others. For example, it invites "difficult" emotions to enter the picture. Letting a student be where she is, say, can be irritating to a teacher who is eager to move on and to see students move on. Allowing himself to slow down to the student's pace can be emotionally difficult, and hiding his annoyance from the student can be a challenging, and crucial, task. Furthermore, if the teacher feels he has a poor writer on his hands, and other teachers in a peer group point to wonderfully astute things that writer is doing, the teacher might have to take responsibility for his own prejudices against the writer. He might be disinclined to share his feelings with his peers, yet find them difficult to conceal.

Such problems rarely occur when the teacher simply judges with a letter grade and moves on to the next paper. The sticky emotions that immanence causes to erupt, then, can seem—looked at through the lens of transcendent grading—to be embarrassingly unnecessary and messy, emotions that would do better to be circumscribed, relegated to the world of women, and kept safely inside the house.

Yet, the emotions sparked by grading are inevitable and deserve to be attended to. Women have moved into the realm of transcendence since de Beauvoir wrote, but perhaps in allowing us to do so our culture continues to repress the things—seemingly illogical emotions, for example—that we were supposed to be stuck in the house with. Immanent grading recognizes that exposing the emotions that occur in the house is enlightening and useful, even though it can be painful. An effective way to deal with that pain is to allow it to be where it is. When students get emotional about grades it helps to listen calmly and without judgment. Teachers, too, need to accept their own emotions around grading. If a teacher can get an opportunity to express her annoyance to other teachers, she does not need to take it out subtly on the students. For her to feel safe enough, though, other teachers must find ways to respond nonjudgmentally, at least at first, to her emotions. And of course, the more thoughtful teachers become about their own feelings around grading, the more students will benefit from the resulting clarity.

Peter Elbow touches on the emotional aspect of grading in his essay "Ranking, Evaluating and Liking: Sorting out Three Forms of Judgment"; I would say that the kind of grading he advocates is, in some ways, immanent, and could help with a group of teachers, too. Elbow argues that writing improves when the author and her readers like it: ". . . the way writers *learn* to like their writing is by the grace of having a reader or two who likes it—even though it's not good. Having at least a few appreciative readers is probably indispensable to getting better" (200). There is little explicit room for liking in traditional grading, because, as Elbow says, ". . . it's hard to like something if we know we have to give it a D" (202). Sometimes liking is easy, because we do genuinely and immediately like some students' writing, whether or not we think of it as "good." At other times, though, if our initial reaction is dislike, liking can seem impossible, since "It feels as if we have no choice—as though liking and not liking just happen to us" (Elbow 201). In a group of teachers, too, it can seem impossible at first to like one's colleagues and their methods and ideas. I connect liking with immanence, with seeing the open-endedness of the person one is dealing with.

Elbow continues by saying the following: "I sense [liking is] some kind of putting oneself out—or holding oneself open—but I can't see it clearly. I have a hunch, however, that we're not so helpless about liking as we tend to feel" (201). He goes on to give practical suggestions for encouraging liking on the teacher's part, like assigning private writing and writing that the teacher does not comment on, having students share writing so the teacher is not the only judge, and learning to praise the parts that are potentially good in student work (201–2). These are ways to begin "holding oneself open," and they all would do well to be incorporated into immanent grading. In addition, I would say, the more we can become emotionally open to our own, and our students' and colleagues' experience, the easier liking can become. The essence of immanent grading, perhaps, is its insistence on holding oneself open as a grader. Carini's work with noticing, letting the paper be what it is, serves as a way of being open, and so does portfolio grading. Also, when teachers get together to assess student work by holding back from judgment, they are holding themselves open to the student.

On the subject of openness, Carini says the following: "To me, what's so interesting about us is our open-endedness. What I can with confidence predict or explain about a person is so limited" (Himley 28). The key, then, is being open to the open-endedness of others, being curious about it. When a responder is genuinely curious about a paper, her comments will be much more likely to help the writer improve. Immanent grading allows the open-endedness of students and teachers to be a more integral part of the grading process than it could possibly be with traditional grading, and in so doing requires and welcomes emotional response.

In discussing Carini herself and the fact that she is not a well-known figure on the current pedagogical scene, seemingly preferring to stay at her own school influencing other teachers than to lecture and publish widely, Himley says:

> . . . Carini fears that a written text (or a public lecture) may too readily lend itself to formula, recipe, unthinking imitation, quick adoption, and facile use. Although many educators have encouraged her to disseminate her ideas on education and development more widely, Carini has hesitated to do so, because that means talking to large groups and/or writing for large audiences. In both situations, there is a risk of no real dialoguing, no real thinking, no real contextualizing of ideas . (66–67)

I would call this reluctance on Carini's part a resistance to premature transcendence. Without a necessary period of real immanence and interaction with those who receive them, ideas can get too simplified and risk not being understood. Teachers can attend a summer institute at the Prospect School in order to experience Carini's ideas in a more immanent, and also immediate, way.

However, Himley goes on to say:

> But I hypothesize that ultimately this apparent resistance to writing comes out of a much deeper intellectual resistance to the limits of monologue, to stasis, to decontextualization, and to linearity, with its implications of causality and closure—intellectual and epistemological choices typically (though not necessarily) associated with formal written essays or public lectures. (67)

If Himley is correct here in her sense of Carini's reasons for avoiding public writing and speaking, Carini, paradoxically, is resisting those seemingly transcendent modes because of their immanence. In other words, she is saying that to give a public lecture—which we would usually consider a transcendent activity—one is in fact freezing one's words and ideas unnaturally. Hence they seem overly immanent—too static and removed from personal interaction.

In the same way, the quick, seemingly transcendent assigning of a letter grade is often subject to a state of being too immanent. By binding the student prematurely—"you are a 'C' student"—it makes the student stuck. In contrast, the immanence that I am championing here does not stay home too long—it honors staying home so that it is in a better position to go out later; it is fluid, and insists on fluidity. In fact, what I am calling "immanent grading" is grading that allows itself to move as needed back and forth between immanence and transcendence, to incorporate as much flux as possible. Perhaps as a result of our continuing denigration of the stance historically associated with women, transcendent grading—or, in particular, a writing class in which each piece of writing is given a letter grade—locks us and our students into too much rigidity. And it was the rigidity of staying home that made de Beauvoir disparage immanence.

Delaying grading until the end of the semester, or abandoning it altogether in a writing class, then, can be a useful way for teachers to encourage students to take more responsibility for their writing. Saying "this is what your paper is" can be much more powerful than "this is what your paper should be," because the former gives the student the opportunity to look in the mirror as a writer and make his own decisions about how to change. To enable our students—and also our colleagues in teacher peer groups—to look clearly and well at themselves we have to let ourselves become open to the experience of the other, to hold back, if temporarily, our "teacherly" instinct to judge and rank instantly. Women have learned to do this throughout history; immanent grading, perhaps, can help us reclaim the skill.

13

Cherryl Smith
Angus Dunstan

Grade the Learning, Not the Writing

In the writing courses we both teach, our focus is on trying to create an environment in which a student takes on all the difficulty and struggle and joy of being a writer: learning to think, on paper where one can see one's thoughts, about something that matters; learning to push oneself to discover the implications of ideas or the reach of one's language; turning initial thoughts into a text that others can understand; moving beyond generalities to close examination of ideas; creating meaning from one's reading and experience. When we prepare for a new semester, grading enters our thinking only in terms of how best to keep it from interfering with the courses themselves, for in no way can grading be said to be an integral part of the process of writing. Grading is something we must participate in because it is the currency of schools. And it seems to be a currency that is particularly alien to the discipline of writing.

What we know from composition research and our own experience as writers can guide our pedagogy for all the other parts of a writing curriculum. Yet, there is no model for grading that is similarly authentic. Indeed, where would we find one? What author would put up his story, novel, or editorial to be graded? That is not to say, of course, that evaluations are not made on professional writing all the time. Manuscripts are accepted and rejected, editorials supported and rebutted, books praised and criticized. But only in school do we grade writing. Only in school are evaluations of writing quantified.

The purpose of a writing course is not to teach information about writing but to help students become better writers. The writing student is not asked simply to learn about writing but to create it. Writing courses, therefore, can be considered to be much like other courses in the creative or performance arts, music or drawing or dance, in which the student's entire assignment consists of producing original work rather than mastering a particular body of knowledge. The content of a persuasive essay, the organization of its paragraphs and the phrasing of its sentences come from the student's store of ideas and language, and though we can teach the student to manipulate ideas and language with greater skill and control, we are still, like the art teacher, working with original student creations. Like art students, writing students learn their discipline though the process of inventing and revising and receiving feedback on their own work.

Traditional grading is not appropriate for a creative activity and the result of this mismatch is that we have adopted in individual classrooms and as school-wide and statewide assessments, evaluation tools that are ultimately in conflict with our own pedagogical goals. Even holistic scoring, which allows for writing rather than usage to be the subject of evaluation is a way of rating pieces of writing against each other, not a way of measuring individual pieces of writing. The usefulness of holistic assessment for placing students in appropriate writing courses or for conducting research should not distract us, in this discussion, from noticing that "real" writing is never treated this way. Whether one piece of writing is better than another, whether a piece of writing matches a description of the qualities of "good" writing found on a scoring rubric, is a judgment made by evaluators rather than readers, a judgment that is valuable to program planners or researchers, rather than to developing writers.

Some shifts in grading practices have accompanied the changes in composition curriculum over the past twenty years. Teachers have experimented with giving no grades at all, using Pass/No Pass grades, and using portfolios. But for many teachers and in many writing programs, no radical shift has come about. Traditionally, teachers have simply assigned a score or grade to each writing task and then added or averaged these numbers for a final grade. Even if that score or letter is based on some approved program rubric, the model remains essentially unchanged. Whatever other commentary a piece of writing might receive, the grade appears to let the student know how well she has done and is even regarded as a way to motivate students to improve.

In *Punished By Rewards*, Alfie Kohn challenges the myth that grades are necessary to motivate students, urging teachers to stop focusing on grading systems, and to get on with the business of helping students perform better. He notes the "huge amount of research that demonstrates the more you get students to focus on HOW they're doing, the less they're interested in *what* they're doing" (Jago 95). He concedes that sometimes students will not work as hard without grades, that if there's no A to strive for, they will not put in the extra effort, but he argues that this is "an indictment of what grades have done to motivation," rather than a rationale for continuing a bad practice. What we need to do is to rethink the motivation we provide for our students rather than to give in to their habitual need for extrinsic rewards.

Charles Hargis (1990) summarizes some of the more common myths that surround grading and exposes their fallacious logic. Grades are supposed to be motivating, but they actually only motivate the students receiving good grades. There is no evidence to suggest that poor grades motivate the student who is doing poorly; they are more likely to contribute to a condition called "learned helplessness." Grades are supposed to provide goals to reach for, but that myth only confuses grades with real learning. Grades are supposed to be part of an evaluation process, but they tell us nothing specific about a student's strengths and weaknesses and cannot help us to prepare remedial instruction. Teachers' grading practices and standards vary considerably even when they're using the same grading system.

Hargis goes on to point out that although "grades have become a student's responsibility," they should rightly be considered the teacher's responsibility. Teachers who are sympathetic to students may be generous in their grading; other teachers, worried about accusations that they are lowering standards, will try to be tough. But "if grades are evidence of how much is learned, then the evidence of good teaching and learning must be good grades" (25). Furthermore "a normal distribution of grades is primary evidence that a teacher who is assigning the grades is not attending instructionally to the individual differences of his or her students" (25).

Peter Elbow distinguishes between ranking, which he argues is unreliable, uncommunicative, and oversimplified—but which is what we do every time we give a grade—and evaluation, which involves "looking carefully enough at the performance or person to make distinctions between parts or features or criteria" (188), a process he approves. He is sympathetic to some aspects of students' anxiety about grades, however, and suggests giving a ballpark grade on a midterm portfolio or using an analytic grid to provide feedback to students. In a similar fashion, Irvin Peckham recognizes that we have to grade students at the end of a course but also notes that "we do not . . . have to grade their essays. Nor should we" (16). He reviews some of the reasons students give for wanting grades, and notes the resistance many teachers have encountered when they have not graded student essays. He reminds us that Sarah Freedman's study shows that ninth graders valued grades much more than their teachers did; he also notes some of the results of the study by Connors and Lunsford, such as that most teachers thought grades did more harm than good, and those who did grade essays wrote significantly shorter comments than teachers who only commented (30).

The major innovation in the evaluation of writing, both for individual classrooms and for writing programs, has been portfolio assessment, which allows teachers to give an overall assessment to a collection of student work rather than grading individual pieces of writing. The outpouring of books, conferences, and program changes that portfolios have generated demonstrates not only the value of portfolios but the enormous need for change in grading practices that has been felt by writing teachers. Both holistic assessment (White) and portfolio grading (Belanoff and Elbow) were developed in order to replace assessments that seemed inconsistent with current composition pedagogy.

But, perhaps precisely because we have been successful in developing assessment tools that seem to be more and more like what we do in writing classes, we have not addressed the inherent incompatibility of quantitative evaluation with the teaching of writing. Although a collection of writing in a portfolio can give a teacher a useful sample on which to evaluate a student's work, to reduce that work to a single grade or score is to use an information-based model for "assessing" what is not information but creative work. The fact that we *can* rank order pieces or portfolios of writing does not mean that it is pedagogically useful to do so. Indeed, such ranking obstructs writing ability, misleads students and the public about the nature of our discipline, and perverts our best intentions for a method of evaluation that is consistent with process pedagogy.

Sitting down with students and going over portfolios to see what has been accomplished and what still needs to be worked on makes good pedagogical sense, but we are not aware of any such justification for assigning a letter grade or a pass/fail designation to that portfolio. Nowhere else in our curriculum do we seem to forget what we know as writers and researchers and say things to students we could not possibly say to real writers. Elsewhere, we try to respond to their writing not as evaluators but as informed readers; we assume that they are trying to make sense and we show them where we are having difficulty understanding them. We do this based on what we have learned about the way writing works in the world outside the classroom. The poem you submit to the *Iowa Review* is not given a score of 5. Your letter to Aunt Sarah is not rated B–. We do not give a good college application essay an A. The grade or score seems inappropriate in these cases because it fits neither the transaction nor the author's purpose.

We are not suggesting that we can or should refuse to give grades or to conduct writing assessments, or that a description of the qualities of good writing may not be useful information for students to have. What we do want to propose is that we step out from our reactive position vis-à-vis the evaluation of writing. Rather than trying to fit writing into an information model, giving grades and scores, treating creative work like a test question, we need to conduct evaluation on our own terms.

In our courses, we have been experimenting with grading systems that are not tied to the quality of a student's writing. Rather than evaluate how well a student writes, we want to evaluate how well a student has accomplished the goals of the course, to what extent a student has learned what we have asked him to learn. By grading writing itself, we not only interfere with the writing process by making ourselves evaluators rather than readers, we create the false sense that quality of writing can be addressed with grades, that there is such a thing as a B paper or an A writer.

The alternatives to traditional grading we have worked out so far, take portfolios as a starting point, and view portfolios as especially valuable for their efficacy in allowing us to collect and respond to writing without the interference of evaluation (Smith 280–81). In the rush to use the portfolio as a whole group assessment tool, its origin as a way for an artist to collect and display her best work is sometimes forgotten. The viewer does not reduce the artist's work to a single score or letter, but responds to what he sees. So, whether we ask students to turn in a full portfolio of all the work they have completed, or to turn in a selected portfolio of their best writing, they are not graded on the quality of their writing. We simply respond to the overall portfolio in a more general, holistic way than we would respond to an individual piece of writing. The grading handout we give to students looks like this:

GRADING CRITERIA

To get a passing grade (C) in the course you must meet the following requirements:

1. Complete *writing assignments* in class and out of class on time.
2. Complete *reading assignments* on time.
3. *Attend class* no less than 90% of the time.
4. Meet minimum standard for *formal papers and exams.*

For a better than passing grade, you will need to exceed one or more of the requirements.

Writing Assignments

The writing for the course is designed as an aid to learning rather than as a way of testing you. I will be looking for:

- evidence that you are engaged with the text or task
- evidence that you're pushing yourself
- evidence that you've spent time

- evidence that you're making connections
- evidence that you're being more than superficial
- evidence that you've pursued ideas
- evidence that you're experimenting or thinking independently

Reading Assignments and Attendance

Being prepared for class and making it to class counts. Since this is not a lecture course, it will be impossible to "get the notes" if you are not here. If you haven't done the reading, you may be unable to do the in-class writing or activity that day. You get credit for being involved.

Final Versions of Formal Papers and Exams

Here I'll be looking for the familiar qualities: clarity, insight, connections, conclusions, detailed explanation and analysis, readable prose, etc.

This was actually written for a literature course, but we then found we could use the same criteria for literature, composition, and, with slight modifications, for poetry writing and teacher education courses. We are moving here toward separating the work a student puts into a course, for which we want to award a grade, from the judgment of quality we or other readers might give individual pieces of writing. Nevertheless, we resist the notion that we're simply trying to reward effort or participation in the course. There is a correlation between the effort a student puts in, the degree to which the student participates, and her success in a course, whether we're grading traditionally or by other methods. But we're trying here to read the portfolio for evidence of the writerly behaviors we've tried to emphasize in the course. We are counting attendance but not how much a student contributes to class discussions or even how many revisions appear in the portfolio.

The idea is that students, themselves, can review their work in the course, can read the portfolio as a history of what they have accomplished so far. To increase student involvement in this process, we ask students to assign themselves a midterm course grade. The midterm portfolio then becomes an opportunity, not so much for us to tell students where they stand, as for the students to try to do this for themselves:

MID-TERM PORTFOLIOS

The midterm portfolios should include all the work you've done so far, arranged in some easy-to-follow fashion.

Please write an annotation to the portfolio that helps me read the work you have done. Your annotation should point to evidence in your portfolio that you are meeting the course requirements. It should identify

> evidence, in your writing, of the various criteria listed in the grading handout. If it's appropriate, you might also indicate any changes you have in mind for yourself for the second half of the term.
>
> The grade at midterm is a marker, only. It will not be computed as an average for the final grade, but indicates where you stand now. You will turn in a final portfolio at the end of the semester for your final grade.
>
> Along with your annotation, please indicate what grade you feel your portfolio should get at this time. If our assessments are the same, I'll simply indicate that when I write back to you. If our assessments differ but not by much, I'll let you know that, too, along with what I think is lacking or present in your portfolio that accounts for the difference. If there is a big difference between our assessments (and my experience has been that most students evaluate themselves pretty close to the way I evaluate them) I'll meet with you to go over the course requirements and grading criteria.

There are a number of advantages to asking students to grade themselves and to write these kinds of assessments. Perhaps the major one, for our purposes, is that the student is required to view the portfolio the way we do. Rather than trying to measure how good the writing is, students need to evaluate the whole body of material they have produced so far in order to discuss their work in the course. The point is not whether the finished papers meet specific criteria but how to describe what has been accomplished, and how to plan for the rest of the semester.

The major disadvantage is that the line between the invisible qualities of thought and attention described in the grading criteria and the visible features of good writing may not be entirely distinct. We are closer to "information" with this kind of grading system but, while even information is not objective, this grading system does depend on subjective analysis of texts.

This year we intend to try out a more objective way of grading that is used by some colleagues in creative writing: contract grading. With the stipulation that the instructor may return material as incomplete, grades depend simply on the number of pages written. Besides needing to determine what will be an appropriate number of pages for each grade, we will need to devise a way of counting revisions that neither discourages revising nor encourages a student to try to appear to revise. Contract grading is promising because it seems to allow for a complete separation of grading from the issue of writing quality. The contract can stand apart from the instructor's interaction with the student and his work.

The "minimum standard," or an instructor's decision to return work as incomplete, does appear to leave in place a connection between grading and writing quality that is disturbing. However, in actual practice when we use the grading criteria and self-assessments described above, we never tell students that a piece of writing does not meet a minimum standard; in fact, we never think of writing in these terms. We simply respond to any paper as a work-in-progress until the end of the semester. Perhaps when we become more confident in this new way of grading, we will likely delete references to "minimum standards" which, at this point, we feel obliged to include in public statements on grading policy.

In conclusion, what we are proposing is a slight change of emphasis which we believe can have a profound effect on teaching writing. Whenever we give grades in writing courses, we are grading the work a student has done *in our course.* That work appearing in any non-school context would not be graded at all, and in another course or at another school would likely be graded differently. Although we are required to account for a student's performance by assigning a grade, this accounting system need not interfere with our roles as readers and teachers. If we assign grades to a student's performance without the misleading practice of assigning grades to pieces of writing, we believe grading will recede into a minor, bookkeeping status like taking attendance, at the same time that grades will become more predictable for both students and teachers.

14

Peter Elbow

Changing Grading while Working with Grades

Discussions about grading are often tangled and unproductive, partly, I think, because of the complex, ambivalent, and sometimes painful experiences most of us have had with grading, first as receivers of grades and then as graders. In order to think more strategically and pragmatically about grading—for example, to try to figure out what goals are served by grading and then figure out better ways to serve them—I find it helpful simply to notice and remember that grading is not inevitable. We can step outside of grading; it's not "natural"; it's not like gravity.

I taught for nine years at the Evergreen State College where, since it started in 1971, faculty have given narrative evaluations instead of grades. The system works fine on all counts—including its success in placing students in high quality professional and graduate schools. Institutions can prosper without grades. For example, while Evergreen is a nonelite state college in Washington, Hampshire College is an elite private institution here in Amherst, Massachusetts that also has a solid history of success with no grades.

It's probably even more important to notice that, no matter where we teach, we can still step outside of grading for certain periods of time. Freewriting gives us a ten-minute time-out. Many teachers use whole assignments that are required but ungraded. Others of us sometimes start off a course with two or three weeks of extensive writing that is required but not graded.

Every time we get students to do nongraded writing, we are inviting students to notice that the link between writing and grading can be broken: it is possible to write and not worry about how the teacher will evaluate it; it is possible to write in pursuit of one's own goals and standards and not just someone else's. When teachers assign journal writing and don't grade it, this too is an important time-out from grading.

Portfolios, too, can be a way to refrain from putting grades on individual papers: for a while we can just write comments and students can revise. Grading can wait until we have more pieces of writing in hand—more data to judge. And grading contracts can permit us to step outside of most grading while still working within a regular grading system.

But can we ever step outside of the *mentality of evaluation*? After all, humans inevitably judge. Yet again it is helpful simply to notice that on some occasions some humans do not. We sometimes like or love someone and gradually realize that we are not judging them at all (and if we start judging, we may even realize that we judge them negatively). We can like a text and notice (or not notice) that in fact it's not very good. Liking and loving *can* operate on a different plane from evaluating.

But we sometimes step outside of evaluation even on a more intellectual, academic, or cognitive plane. We can ask of a paper, "What does it say? What does it imply or entail or what are the consequences?" and answer in a nonevaluative way. Not always, of course, since our answers to such summary or interpretive questions often have an evaluative edge or even a judgmental thrust—especially when the text is written by a student rather than by a respected author. But it is *possible* to answer in a nonjudgmental way. A careful summary of a bad paper need not reveal anything of its badness.

Remarkably enough, the same thing can happen when we are asked, "Where do you agree or disagree with this paper?" Even if we disagree completely with everything a paper says, it does not follow that we consider the paper bad. We often disagree with excellent writing. Even more frequently, we agree with terrible writing. (For more on these matters, see my "Time Outs From Grading and Evaluating While Working in a Conventional System.")

As I get ready then, to try to think more clearly and strategically about grading, it helps me simply to notice that it is possible and not inhuman to spend some time outside of grading and even outside the mentality of evaluation.

I want to work on grading because I find it a problem. It seems to me that grades:

- Aren't trustworthy.
- Don't have clear meaning.

- Don't give students feedback about *what* they did well or badly.
- They undermine the teaching-and-learning situation in these ways:
    - By leading many students to work more for the sake of the grade than for learning.
    - By leading to an adversarial relationship between students and teachers (since some students quarrel with our grades and many feel resentful at the grades they get).
    - By leading to a competitive atmosphere.
    - Finally, figuring out grades is difficult and anxious—making work for us.

The essential fact about conventional grading is that it is one dimensional. We can visualize this literally as a vertical line with no element of the horizontal. Grades are simply numbers and, of course, numbers are defined entirely by the austere minimality of numbers: n is entirely defined as "greater than $n - 1$ and less than $n + 1$." B has no other meaning than, "worse than A and better than C." Conventional grades demarcate eleven levels of "*pure quality*"—wholly undefined and unarticulated.

This pure, numerical, one dimensional verticality—no words or concepts attached—is the main reason why conventional grades are untrustworthy descriptors for complex human performances, and why they lead to such difficulty and dispute. We see even steeper verticality when faculty members grade essays on a scale of 1 to 100—as some law school faculty do.

In this essay, I suggest two ways to deal with this unrelenting verticality: (1) reduce it somewhat by using fewer grades—what I call "minimal grading"; (2) add a bit of the horizontal dimension by using criteria.

Minimal Grading

We can reduce the verticality of conventional grades by simply using fewer levels. Most of us use minimal grades when we make low stakes assignments and grade them pass/fail or */*+/*–. But we tend to assume that if an assignment is important and we want students to take it more seriously and work harder on it, we should use conventional grades with the eleven or so levels of quality.

But this assumption gets in our way; it rests on a failure to distinguish between *stakes* and *levels*. Every act of grading involves two very different questions: "How much credit is at stake in this performance?" "How many levels of quality shall I use on my evaluation scale?" When students take an assignment more seriously and work harder, it usually has little to do with our having added levels to our grading scale, and much more to do with our having raised the stakes and made the assignment *count* for more of the final grade. Few students will struggle hard for an A that doesn't much help their final grade. (Of those few who do struggle for a low stakes A, most are doing it because they care about the topic or the task—not because of the reward of an A. Only the most *obsessively* grade-dependent will struggle hard for an A that won't help them much in the end.)

Thus the most reliable way to use grades to make students work harder is to raise the stakes—as long as we make the passing level high enough. And we need only increase the number of levels to three or four to get those students working hard who are motivated by the desire to distinguish their work as superior. Even a two-level scale can be very demanding if we put the bar at a high level. At MIT for the last twenty years or so, faculty have given nothing but Pass and Fail as final grades to all first year students in all courses. The stakes are very high indeed and so are the standards, but only two levels are used. If we use three levels we have even more scope for making strategic decisions about where to place the bars.

But there *is* something that raising the number of grading levels will reliably achieve: *it will make us work harder*! Think of the difference between reading a stack of papers in order to give them conventional grades, versus reading them only in order to pick out those that stand out as *notably weak* or *notably strong*. (Most faculty find it easier to give grades for graduate seminars because on most campuses, the custom is to use only two or three levels: A, A–, and B+.)

I'm suggesting, then, that we can get what we need from the grading of important or high stakes assignments if we use just three, or at most four, levels and make *pass* hard enough to get. Most of our difficulties with grading come from having too many levels, that is, too much verticality:

- The more levels we use, the more untrustworthy and unfair the results. We know that the history of literary criticism has shown (along with informal research by students who turn in the same paper to multiple teachers) that good readers cannot agree in their rankings of quality. Your A paper is liable to become a B in my hands—or vice versa. (Diederich provides the classic research on this matter.)
- The more levels we use, the more chances students have to resent or even dispute those fine-grained distinctions we struggled so hard to make in the first place. ("That wasn't a B–, that was a B!") Thus the more levels we have, the more the slide towards an adversarial student/teacher relationship and consequently the more damage to the teaching/learning climate. Yes, as long as there are *any* distinctions or levels at all, *some* students will be disappointed or resentful at not getting the higher level they were hoping for; but fewer levels means fewer borderline performances.

- The more levels we use, the more we establish a competitive atmosphere among students and a pecking order culture.
- The more levels we use, the more work for us. It's hard making all those fine distinctions—say between A and A– or B+ and B. If we use just three levels, all we need to do is pick out papers that stand out as notably strong and notably weak.

In short, boundary decisions are always the most untrustworthy and arguable. Fewer boundaries means fewer boundary decisions.

Objections to Minimal Grading.

"But how can we compute a final grade for the semester using eleven levels, if our constituent grades use only three levels?"

This is truly a problem if we have produced only a couple of constituent grades—if we've assigned only a couple of papers. But if we have a good number of papers or assignments on a three-level scale, we can simply use a mathematical formula and just count up points for the final grade: 3 for Strong, 2 for Satisfactory, and 1 for Weak. Alternatively, if there are a lot of low stakes assignments graded Satisfactory/Unsatisfactory, we can decide that students with Satisfactory on all their low stakes assignments start off with a foundation of B. Then their final grade is pulled up or down by Strongs or Weaks on their high stakes assignments; or vice versa, we can average the high stakes pieces, and if the result is some kind of "satisfactory" or "2"—let low stakes pieces decide the gradations between C and B. A multitude of scoring systems are possible—and I haven't even mentioned other factors which many teachers count in their final grading such as attendance, participation, effort, and improvement.

"We already use minimal grading: most faculty already give nothing but As and Bs."

It is exactly this restricted use of the grading scale that has exacerbated two intertwined problems: grade inflation and grade meaninglessness. When some faculty members give a full range of grades and others give mostly As and Bs, we have a situation of semantic chaos. The grade of B has become particularly ambiguous: readers of a transcript have no way of knowing whether it denotes good strong competent work (many college catalogues define it as an "honors grade") or disappointing, second rate work. C might mean genuinely satisfactory work or virtually failing work.[1] Critics of "grade inflation" charge that even "A" has lost its meaning of genuine excellence (though some research undercuts that charge, see U.S. Department of Education). If instead of using symbols like A, B, and C, teachers used meaningful words like "excellent," "honors," "outstanding," "strong," "satisfactory," "weak," "poor," "unsatisfactory," all parties to grading would have a better understanding of the message.

"Some teachers will probably still give mostly Excellent or Strong."

Inevitably so. But the point here is to have teachers sign their names to words rather that completely ambiguous letter grades. For surely it can happen that most of the performances on a paper or even in a course are in truth genuinely excellent or strong, and therefore we want to sign our name honestly to that assertion. But with conventional grading, when a teacher gives mostly As and B+s, no one knows whether she is saying, "This was a remarkable outcome" or just, "I don't want to make it too hard to get a good grade in my course."

I actually have some hope that we'd see a bit less grade inflation in a three-level scale where teachers use a word like "excellent" or "honors" for the top grade rather than just A– or A. If a group took as their highest priority to get rid of too many high grades, they could even insist on a term like "top 10%" or "top quarter" for the top grade.

And surely the *worst* grade inflation is at the lower level, not the upper level. Most teachers give passing grades and even Cs to performances that they consider completely unsatisfactory. Grades would communicate much more clearly if we had to decide between the categories of "satisfactory" vs. "unsatisfactory" or "unacceptable."

"But minimal grading doesn't really solve the problem of meaninglessness. Grades are just as ambiguous if most students get Satisfactory."

Not really. That is, even though minimal grading with words will probably give most students the grade of Satisfactory, we will have *clearly communicated* to readers, by the fact of our three-level scale and the use of this word "satisfactory," that this single grade is being used for a wide range of performances. This result is *not* so ambiguous as with conventional grading where no one knows whether B is being used for a wide range or a restricted range of performances.

"But you're still evading the main problem of all.
Sure, sure, it may be technically 'unambiguous' to give most of the
class a grade like Satisfactory, but the term still remains empty.
It doesn't tell us enough. It's too unsatisfying to leave
so many students in one undifferentiated lump."

Yes, "unsatisfying" is exactly the right word here. For it's a crucial fact about minimal grades that they carry *less information*: conventional grades record more distinctions. By sorting students into more groups that are thus more finely differentiated, conventional grades give students a sense of seeing themselves as better and worse in relation to more of their peers. Conventional grades *feel* more precise than minimal grades at the job of telling students exactly how well or how badly they did.

Thus students will tend, at first anyway, to experience minimal grading as *taking something away from them*, and they will be correct—even though what is being taken away from them is bad information. Information itself feels precious; distinctions themselves feel valuable; even spurious precision is missed. When students (or colleagues) contemplate moving to minimal grading, they often put out of their minds what most of them actually do know in some corner of their minds: that this information was bad and this precision was spurious. People are easily seduced into a mindset of wanting to see themselves sorted into levels—*even* people who have a pretty good idea that they will find the information painful. "Doctor, I need you to tell me if I have cancer." "Teacher/examiner, I need you to tell me *exactly* how bad my paper is." There may be trustworthy knowledge about the cancer, but there can be no trustworthy *one-dimensional, numerical* knowledge about how bad a paper is. (Consider further that there often is *not* trustworthy knowledge even about the cancer. Thus, if we *really* want accuracy and precision in grading, perhaps we should make grades more analogous to the outcomes of much medical evaluation: "Based on my long training in composition and my extensive experience in teaching writing and my careful examination of your paper, I feel quite confident in saying that there is a 60% likelihood that it is a C+.")

Supposing the additional information and precision of conventional grades were entirely trustworthy and accurate. Two things would nevertheless be true. First, neither the students nor any other readers of the grades would get the benefit unless they saw all the grades for the whole class. That is, a student can't feel the "information" or "precision" carried by her B– unless she sees what grade everyone else got. Second, that precise, accurate, and trustworthy grade would tell the students nothing at all about *what it is* they did well or badly at.

This is the place to signal a turn toward my second suggestion. In arguing all along for minimal grading, I seem to be arguing for less information. No. I am arguing for less *bad* information: if the only grades we can give are purely one-dimensional or vertical, the only honest thing would be to cut back on information and go for minimal grades. But minimal grading is not my only proposal. My larger purpose is not to reduce information but increase it. In the next section I want to show that when we take away *bad information* from students by moving to minimal grading, we can give them *better information* or meaning in return. We can make minimal grades more meaningful than conventional grades if we find a way to tell students what they are actually weak, satisfactory, or excellent *at*. To do so, we need to work out the *criteria* for our minimal grades.

Using Explicit Criteria in Grading

So far I've argued only for reducing the unrelieved verticality of conventional grades. But using criteria permits us to add a crucial *horizontal* dimension. By spelling out the various features of writing that we are looking for when we grade, we are saying that "quality in writing" is not a single, monolithic, one-dimensional entity. And of course we are giving more information and meaning to our grades and making them less mysterious.

How do we name criteria? The simplest criteria are the traditional and commonly used pair, *form* and *content*. The distinction is definitely useful in grading. Despite some criticism of the distinction as old fashioned or even theoretically suspect, students obviously benefit from knowing our different judgments about these two general areas: meaning-and-thinking versus clarity-organization-mechanics. Almost as commonly used in evaluating is a more elaborated set of criteria with elements like these: *ideas*, *organization*, *syntax/wording*, *mechanics*. Many teachers like to articulate in their evaluation the intellectual operation that is most central to a particular assignment by using criteria like these: *detail*, *analysis*, *persuasion*, *research*, *documentation*. All those criteria are textually oriented; some teachers like to use more rhetorically oriented or process oriented criteria like these: *connecting with the subject*, *connecting to an audience*, *voice*, *substantive revision*. The important principle here is that we do well to *name* and *acknowledge* and *communicate* the features of writing that influence our judgments. Scholars and critics have not been able to agree on what "good writing" really is, so we get to decide what we are actually looking for and admit it openly to our students.

If we have a large number of papers to grade and we are assigning lots of papers—or if we are teaching a large class that doesn't center on writing and we have little or no help in grading—we probably need to resort to the simplest, least time consuming way to use criteria: just give one overall grade (or perhaps form/content grades), yet nevertheless spell out explicitly for students the other features or characteristics of writing that we are looking for when we grade. Thus we might announce, "In grading this set of papers I will try to count these four criteria equally: . . ." Or "I will grade most on the strength of your argument, but I'll also take some account of these other three criteria: . . ." If our criteria are at all complicated, we can explain and describe them in a handout. And in order to help students do the best job of *meeting* our criteria in their writing, we need to announce the criteria *with* the assignment—before students write—and not wait till afterwards when we hand back the graded papers.

The point is that even if we give nothing but a single minimal grade, we can make that grade carry much more information and meaning if we spell out our criteria in public. And using criteria even in this minimal way helps us grade more fairly. For the process of figuring out the criteria and announcing them publicly renders us less likely to be unduly swayed if one particular feature of the writing is terrible or wonderful. For example, teachers often get annoyed by papers that are full of grammar and spelling mistakes and nonstandard dialect, and consequently overlook virtues in information, ideas, or reasoning in such papers—ultimately giving them unreasonably low grades. We are less likely to slip into this unfairness if we have specifically announced our criteria.

However, we get the most benefit from criteria if we can actually give a grade on each one. We tell each student how well we think he did on each of the features of writing we are looking for. In doing this we are making *multiple vertical judgments* of quality.

Objections to Explicit Criteria

"But this will make grading too much work!"

The principle of minimal grading comes to our rescue here. For just as it isn't so hard to read through a set of papers and merely pick out ones that stand out for being weak or strong, so it isn't so much harder merely to notice if an essay seems notably weak or notably strong on the criteria we have named as important. We just hold the criteria in mind for a moment and see if that feature of the paper stands out for being strong or weak. In my efforts not to make it too onerous to use criteria, I even announce to students that Satisfactory is the "default" grade and so I will make a notation *only* if I find something notably strong or weak. If we use criteria in this more complete fashion, we have a kind of grid, and our "grade" on a paper might look something like this:

Weak	*Satisf*	*Strong*	
			Genuine revision, substantive changes, not just editing
		✓	Ideas, insights, thinking
✓			Organization, structure, guiding the reader
			Language, sentences, wording
✓			Mechanics: spelling, grammar, punctuation, proofreading
			Overall

This is the form a grid might take when I photocopy a set of blank ones and make check marks. I often write a comment in addition: something more "readerly" and less evaluative—some comment about the thoughts and feelings and reactions I had at various points in reading. I think these discursive comments actually do more good in the long run than carefully evaluative ones. Indeed I came to use grids when I gradually realized that my readerly comments were leaving students too dissatisfied, but I didn't want to give a regular grade. Grids were a way to give a bit of quantified evaluation but not just on one dimension.

When I write comments on a computer—as I now prefer to do—I put the grid on a little file that I bring in to every comment that I write. This way I can write in little comments about a criterion, or a comment at the end about the whole paper. If I were using my computer on the same paper as above, my grid response might look more like the following:

Genuine Revision, Substantive Changes, Not Just Editing:
Ideas, Insights, Thinking: *Strong. I liked the way you complicated things by exploring points that conflict with your main point.*
Organization, Structure, Guiding the Reader: *Weak. I kept feeling confused about where you were going—though also sensing that my confusion came from your process of complicating your thinking. This confusion would be GOOD if it weren't a final draft.*
Language, Sentences, Wording:
Mechanics: Spelling, Grammar, Punctuation, Proofreading: *Weak. Because of all the mistakes, this paper doesn't fulfill the contract and is not acceptable. I'll call it acceptable this first time IF you give me a fully cleaned up version by next class.*
Overall: *Unsatisfactory for now.**

*Unfortunately, the visual lay out of a grid works at right angles to my metaphor of the "vertical and horizontal" dimensions of grading. That is, we tend to represent and visualize judgments of quality in vertical dimension from "low" quality to "high" quality (see Lakoff and Johnson on the metaphors embedded in allegedly literal language). But if we want to create a simple usable grid that uses words, it's much easier to represent quality as moving horizontally from left to right. That way, we can continue on the left-right dimension to spell out the criteria in words.

When we use criteria in this fuller way and make *multiple judgments*, we finally make our grades carry the most explicit meaning—rather than letting them remain mysterious or magical. And we finally give students some valuable feedback on the particular strengths and weaknesses in their writing—feedback that they don't get from conventional grades.

Indeed mere check-marks on a grid (perhaps with a few short comments) are sometimes clearer and more useful to students than the longer comments we write in our late-at-night, unrevised prose.

Of course, my emphasis on criteria is nothing new. As teachers responding to writing, we continually articulate criteria. But we too seldom invite our sophistication about criteria to enrich our official grading—leaving our grades themselves crudely one-dimensional.

Grids are particularly useful for responding to a revised final version when we have already given lots of feedback to a draft. After all, extended commenting makes more sense at the draft stage: we can give encouragement ("Here's what you need to work on to make it better") instead of just giving an autopsy ("Here's what didn't work"). A mere summary "verdict" can be more justifiable on the final draft. We can just read through the paper and check off criteria on the grid and give no comments. Surely we are helping students more if we assign six papers and give full feedback only on a draft and just use a grid on the final version, than if we assign only four papers and give full feedback on the draft and the revision.

Let me say a word about the process of figuring out one's criteria. When students ask me, "What are you looking for?" I sometimes feel some annoyance (though I don't think my reaction is quite fair). But I enjoy it when *I* ask the question of myself: "What actually *are* the features in a piece of writing that make me value it?" If I try to answer this question in an insecure, normative way, I tie myself in knots: "What *ought* I to value in student essays?" But we are professionals in our fields and so we get to ask the question in an *empirical* way: "What *do* I value in the writing in my field?" For there *is* no correct answer to the question, "What is good writing?"

This process of empirical self-examination can be intellectually fascinating. We learn to notice more clearly how we read—and this can even prompt some change in how we read. For example some faculty members discover that they are judging on fewer criteria than they realized (for example, mostly on the basis of correct restatement of textbook and lecture material and correct mechanics)—and this realization leads them to attend to other criteria. Or they discover that they use different criteria for student writing than for professional writing (for example, in student writing they disapprove of the use of first person writing or personal anecdote, but in published professional writing in their field they value it).

The use of criteria has a powerful added benefit because it enhances the possibilities of productive *self-evaluation*. When we ask students to give or suggest a conventional grade for themselves, we are putting them in an unhelpfully difficult spot. They have to make a subtle choice among too many levels; and because the grade is one dimensional, they can scarcely help translating the question into almost moral terms: "Am I an A person or a B person?"

When, however, I use criteria and minimal grades and ask students to decide whether they see themselves as strong, satisfactory, or weak in a wide range of skills or abilities, they find the questions eminently answerable. Their answers are remarkably honest and accurate. I ask these questions at the beginning of the semester ("How would you rate yourself on these criteria, strong, OK, or weak, now as we are beginning the course?"). This helps them set goals. I ask the question again at midsemester. Most important, I ask them at the end ("Do you think your performance has been strong, satisfactory, or weak on these criteria this semester?"). Also, I find it very productive to ask students to generate the criteria that they think are important—again at the beginning, middle, and end of the semester.

The Institutional Dimension

I've suggested two procedures we can use in grading papers while still working within a conventional grading system: minimal grades as a way to diminish the verticality; articulated criteria as a way to add the horizontal dimension.

But minimal grading and criteria are not just useful *within* a conventional grading system. They could vastly improve institutional grading itself. At present, a transcript consists of a myriad of single letter grades that no reader can trust since faculty members have different standards. When a student gets a B, it can mean anything from good honors work to disappointing work. Nor can readers translate those grades into meaningful or useful information. Even when a student gets an A, we don't have any idea what skills or kinds of writing the student is good at and not so good at.

Transcripts would be much more useful if they represented a different deployment of energy and ambition. On the one hand we should be *less* ambitious and stop pretending that students can be reliably sorted into eleven vertical levels of quality—or that the sortings would mean the same thing in different teachers' hands and in different readers' minds. Transcripts would be more honest, accurate, and trustworthy if they settled for recording only three levels, say, Honors, Satisfactory, Unsatisfactory (or at most four: Honors, Strong, Fair, Unsatisfactory).

On the other hand, we can afford to be far *more* ambitious where it counts and give grades on *criteria* for each course. Thus, at the end of a course we would provide the registrar and the transcript with a small grid of grades for each student. We would give a grade for the student's overall performance—using three, or at most four, levels. But we would also list the three to six criteria that we think are most important, and for each we would tick off whether we thought this student's work was satisfactory or notably weak or notably strong.

It would help us in our teaching if we could say to students at the start of the course what criteria we would be ranking them on for final transcript grade. But faculty members would not all be forced to use the same criteria. There could be a large list of criteria to choose from. (Textual criteria like clarity, organization; process criteria like generating lots of ideas, revising, working collaboratively; rhetorical criteria like awareness of audience and voice; genre-related criteria like informal personal writing; analysis, argument.) Teachers could even create their own criteria. Indeed, there's no reason why teachers should be obliged to use the same criteria for every student in a course. After all we might want to bring in certain criteria only occasionally in order to note certain students as particularly creative or diligent—or unable to meet deadlines—yet not want to speak about these criteria for all students.

This sounds complicated, but given computers, this system would not be hard to manage—both for giving course grades and in producing a transcript. (Elementary school report cards have long used criteria in this way; and many high school teachers have recently been given a list of fifty or more criteria they can add to the grades they give on report cards.) Readers of the transcript would finally get useful information about substance and be spared the untrustworthy and harmful alleged information about levels of quality.

Final Comment

I have been implying a visual metaphor in my suggestions: less of the vertical (minimal grading); more of the horizontal (using criteria). But I would point out that my suggestions also imply a move away from the tradition of *measuring* or *norm-based* assessment toward the tradition of *mastery* or *criteria-based* assessment. Measuring or norm-based assessment involves making a single complex master all-determining decision about each student so as to place him or her at one spot along a tall one-dimensional line. All are strung out along a single vertical line—each at an exact distance above or below every other student. Mastery or criteria-based assessment, on the other hand, implies multiple simpler decisions about each student so that all are placed in a complicated multidimensional intersecting space—each student being strong in certain abilities, okay in others, and weak in yet more—with different students having different constellations of strengths and weaknesses. (See D. C. McClelland for the classic formulating essay in the criteria-based tradition. This tradition is also represented in the "New Standards Project"—see Myers and Pearson.)

I end with a rhetorical question. Which kind of assessment gives us a more accurate picture of humans and their abilities? And which kind of grading will lead to the healthier climate for teaching and learning?

Note

1. For a more detailed discussion of this ambiguity, see Carbone and Daisley's "Grading as a Rhetorical Construct" (ch. 7).

15

The Conversation Continues

A Dialogue on Grade Inflation

> I feel that grades are important so long as As aren't given out like candy to eager kids. — *Jesse P. Boudreau (first-year writing student)*

As a number of our chapters touch on the issue of grade inflation. Maureen Neal suggests a potential conflict between teachers who use portfolios to raise the level of students' writing (and thus their grades), and administrators who view a preponderance of high grades as evidence of low standards. Pauline Uchmanowicz notes that grade inflation may result from the economic status of students at differing institutions and from the role which these institutions serve in a market economy. And Steven VanderStaay points out that even teachers who encourage grade inflation by guaranteeing high grades may find that their students are more comfortable with the same ranking and sorting that reformers oppose.

We set up a web forum on the Internet, and asked our contributors to respond to these ideas and to discuss their views of grade inflation. Is it a problem which writing teachers ought to address? And have any of them ever sensed pressure from students or administrators to adjust their grades, either upward or downward? – EDS.

Kathleen Blake Yancey

Our department opened the academic year two years ago with a discussion about grade inflation and about how our grades were too high (and, therefore, about how we needed to be concerned about this because the dean certainly was). Since then, candidates for tenure and promotion have their grade distributions sent up with their packages so that our grades construct us in key ways. One of the interesting things about this "she says euphemistically" is that we are not asked to review our grades, to analyze them, to situate them according to some philosophy. Our grades over/determine us as they do our students.

Michael Bernard-Donals

We have a raging grade inflation "problem" where I work. Every year a representative from the Dean's office comes during the orientation workshop we hold for new graduate teaching assistants before the beginning of the semester, and she wags her finger at us and complains that if students aren't writing well, their grade should reflect it. (And writing well generally means, for the Dean, correctness.) And for years, the director of the lower division would worry along with the Dean, but not do much about the "problem."

Grade inflation isn't a problem so much as it's a symptom of far too much "coaching" and far too little frank talk about grades, institutional power, and students' real experience with school. If we spend a great deal of time coaching our students, having them do draft after draft, and allowing them lots of freedom to "write what they want," then sure, their grades will get better. No doubt about it, and no problem. But this approach to writing lets students "go with the flow," and in effect, lets teachers go with it too: everyone's experiences are valuable for themselves alone ("and don't you teachers go messing with the logic of my experiences"), and the teacher's job is to make the language and form clear without any hard looking at the structure of the experience (not just the language used to convey that experience). Tough assignments, ones that include discussions about fairness and unfairness, ones that include teachers' (often mostly non-tenure track teachers with little job security) sense of ideological "place," ones that include analyses of why some interpretations are judged better than others, may go some of the way toward alleviating our sense of the problem of grade inflation because it acknowledges students' sense of the game, and it, in effect, has us say, as teachers, "yeah, we know that you know that it's not quite fair, but we also know you're pretty damn smart," and allows us to push students.

My experience over the last three years has been that, as I've become a much better writer of assignments and a much more adept teacher, I've also become a tougher grader. But because my authority as a teacher has risen (and not fallen to the level of "more well-informed peer" or some such), my student evaluations are much better. Students say I'm really tough, and a really hard grader, but that they learn more that way than they have in courses where they got easy As or Bs. I'm OK with that.

Margaret Daisley

Although I had one bad semester when I definitely felt that my department pressured me into allowing several students to redo papers and readjust grades, usually I don't feel any specific department pressure. I always tell first year students that writing classes are not graded "on the curve." And when I get to the point of assigning grades, I don't look at the grades as a total collection until I'm done. But then, when I'm done I can't help totaling up all the As, Bs, Cs, etc. and wondering how it might look to my department. I guess I feel the presence of my department as audience for that collection of grades, but still they are a silent audience.

Students, on the other hand—ha! I feel that I am constantly pressured by students to adjust grades, on an individual basis, but I feel that this is a normal, natural part of the process. What bothers me, though, (and in fact is the reason I became interested in these issues) is when a student will try to negotiate a better grade, but not using any argument that has to do with writing—or even other issues such as attendance, meeting deadlines, etc. The first semester I taught, one student told me (very angrily) that because I had "given" him a low grade, now his grade point average was below a 2.0—as if I was responsible for that! There have been a number of times, however, where students plainly were just having a "bad semester"—for instance, some vague personal problems that plainly affected their overall performance during the semester, where I have encouraged them to take an "incomplete" and work with me another semester to make it right. Only one time was I sorry I did this—it was kind of a con job on the student's part. But another time, it turned out that the student had a learning disability, which was not diagnosed until later. It was rather rewarding to see her self-confidence zoom when she found that she could succeed in college, after all.

Maureen Neal

One unlikely source of pressure is from colleagues, especially those who may be more traditional in approach or outlook. Even then, this is something more *felt* than spoken. Sometimes criticism over grade inflation is disguised as something else—"concern" for the methodology, for example, which allows students to "correct all their mistakes" (i.e., revise) before grading. I also think—and I'm out on a limb here—that some of the felt pressure over grade inflation is internal rather than external. In my undergraduate education courses, the bell curve was preached to us as gospel, even though our grades in that education course didn't reflect it. But I think part of the pressure to conform to some recognizable pattern of grade distribution is internal. I also think that we may begin to doubt our own abilities to be accurate and consistent when grades are lopsided one way or another. Sometimes, too, I feel as if I'm cheating students out of a feeling of special satisfaction when there is an especially high number of As and Bs. I can't explain this—I wish someone could.

I also feel that we need a good working definition of grade inflation—in my chapter I say that it's an *unwarranted* preponderance of high grades—but that leaves a lot of room for debate. It's when high grades are not earned, but given, but then, who's to say what's necessary for that A or B to be "earned" rather than "given"? All of which makes me sort of want to throw up my hands and wonder why we worry so much about a grade at all and what, exactly, a given grade really means. The ironic thing is that I know over the last several years my standards and expectations for freshman comp students have risen tremendously—what would have been an A portfolio three years ago would not merit that grade this semester—yet, I still feel somehow negligent when I work up semester grades and have fourteen As and Bs in a group of thirty students. As Margaret suggests, too, students also contribute to the situation when they fall out of their chairs or spit in disgust at any grade lower than a B. In one class, I had a student I really liked who cried for ten minutes over a B+ rather than an A. It's situations like that which make me wonder why we put a grade on a paper or portfolio.

Steven VanderStaay

I found the previous comments about basing grades on effort and improvement interesting. While I once taught "composition," my new job defines my writing courses as "Creative Nonfiction." The actual work we do in the classroom is the same, but I am strictly instructed to grade "performance" and not improvement or effort.

There are other differences. My colleagues attend the AWP [Association of Writing Programs] conference, and not the 4 Cs, etc. Yet, what goes on in their courses looks rather like advanced comp—except for this attention to "performance." No one other than myself uses portfolios that I know of, for example. And some simply grade writing as "publishable" or not.

These, and other experiences, have led me to think that what is "judged" and graded in a composition class may be unique within academia. That is, assuming that all disciplines grade what they value, and that the discipline of composition values effort, engagement, improvement—even personal "growth" and contributions to a classroom "community," as well as "performance"—perhaps its grading mechanisms and traditions should be specific to its needs and necessarily unlike those in other fields and disciplines.

Nick Carbone
(A response to Steven VanderStaay)

Steven, the AWP models you referred to, where the judgment is based on whether a piece is publishable indicates a product—finished prose—that is judged. Whereas in composition courses teachers are often as concerned, or perhaps more concerned, with teaching skills—how to peer review, how to work in groups, how to do research and ask critical questions, how to shape an argument—which are addressed with recursive strategies (Hairston's term from that essay where she cited Kuhn and described the paradigm shift) that emphasize the ways rather than the ends of writing. In other words, we grade what we value. We set standards for what we value and think should be taught, and grades, however we use them, ultimately reflect those values (much the way the NCTE [National Council of Teachers of English] standards reflect a set of values about what literacy is).

It seems to me you're suggesting then that our values differ from the academy's at some level. This is not to say we don't value well-wrought prose—we delight in it, fairly dancing out into the hall to show colleagues wonderful student writing, even if it's just one diamond of a sentence in a rough draft—but we do give a very different emphasis. I think this sometimes confuses students. We often talk about pursuing this recursive work by calling attention to it. "This course will be a lot of work," I say, "you have to write and rewrite and rerewrite, and write some more; you have to do a lot of work, but if you do it, you'll learn something and do well." So we emphasize effort, and sometimes in our comments we downplay shortcomings in a piece to build on strengths, to encourage a reluctant student to do another draft. It's easy to see, now, that students would think effort was worth an A, to take an A for effort as the course's M.O. for grading.

And this is in spite of also making clear—either by contracts, or syllabi, or other comments, or discussion, or class consensus—that other criteria are at stake. But it's also easy to see why others would see such a course—and this is one of the criticisms leveled at process-based courses—as bankrupt of standards. Because the standards are different and difficult to explain sometimes, and because many teachers design courses where students are meant to succeed, not wash out, and because many teachers work extra hard at helping students do well, who regard students lack of success as sometimes a teaching failure on their part, it's easy to see where the charges come from about grade inflation and low standards.

In the model above teachers try to "own" grades, redefine their purpose, if only for the course or for the semester. But ultimately, when grades are recorded and sent to the registrar, that ownership is lost and people will make of them what they will, which usually means a whole different set of assumptions about how to read them, what they mean, and what they are for. Unfortunately for students, they live more with those other assumptions than they do with our pedagogy.

Brian Huot

I like what Kathi says about our grades overdetermining us. It's like we all know what an A or B is, and in truth, as Kathi says in an earlier post, it depends upon the context, the assignment. Margaret said earlier that she might give students higher or lower grades, depending on the circumstances. This is in keeping with the literature that has demonstrated that graders give higher grades when papers come from honor students. Melanie Sperling in a 1994 *RTE* [*Research in the Teaching of English*] piece reports that the teacher in her study gave different kinds of responses to students depending upon a number of factors. It's interesting to note that the two students in her study who got the most collegial responses were the perceived best student in the class and a student who needed "kid glove" treatment. It seems to me we might think about grades in term of response.

In that light, it makes sense that a certain student would receive a higher grade in some circumstances because the goal of that grade-giving, as with all response, would be to teach and motivate that student. Of course, this construction of grades as pedagogical response conflicts with their function as some kind of normative/objective scale that we supposedly all know the value of. I advocate the use of grades as a response mechanism (although in my own classes it's the lack of grades as a response mechanism because I give only a course grade to a portfolio), as a way of taking control of assessment and response for the teaching of writing.

Kathleen Blake Yancey

But a quick anecdote. This month I was in a workshop for faculty who teach in our honors program. The scientists in the program raised the issue of grades: was it OK, they wanted to know, if their grades were high? OK from the point of view of the program, that is, and OK for them, that is. They weren't sure; what they knew, as they said, was that it was much more difficult to give a low grade to a student they saw as a person than to a student whose face looked a lot like the other 250 faces in the crowd. It seems to me that when we start educating people (rather than delivering curriculum, as though there were no recipient of the delivery) we change the grading game, too.

Works Cited

Aisenberg, Nadya, and Mona Harrington. 1988. *Women of Academe: Outsiders in the Sacred Grove*. Amherst: University of Massachusetts Press.

Agnew, Eleanor. 1993. "Departmental Grade Quotas: The Silent Saboteur." ERIC, ED 358 478.

Anson, Chris M., ed. 1989. *Writing and Response: Theory, Practice, and Research*. Urbana, Ill.: National Council of Teachers of English.

Appleman, Deborah, and Douglas E. Green. 1993. "Mapping the Elusive Boundary between High School and College Writing." *College Composition and Communication* 44: 191–99.

Backscheider, Paula. 1973. "Turn on the Power: Marking and Grading in Remedial Composition." *Illinois English Bulletin* 61(2): 13–20.

Bakhtin, Mikail. 1990. "The Problem of Speech Genres." In *The Rhetorical Tradition*, ed. Patricia Bizzell and Bruce Herzberg. Boston: Bedford.

Bartholomae, David. 1986. "Inventing the University." *Journal of Basic Writing* 5: 4–23.

———. 1995. "Writing With Teachers: A Conversation with Peter Elbow." *College Composition and Communication* 46(1): 62–71.

Bartolome, Lilia I. 1994. "Beyond the Methods Fetish: Toward a Humanizing Pedagogy." *Harvard Educational Review* 64: 173–94.

Bazerman, Charles. 1989. "Reading Student Texts: Proteus Grabbing Proteus." In *Encountering Student Texts: Interpretive Issues in Reading Student Writing*, ed. Bruce Lawson, Susan Sterr Ryan, and W. Ross Winterowd. Urbana, Ill.: National Council of Teachers of English.

Beale, Walter H., and Don W. King. 1981. "A Grading Contract that Works." *Exercise Exchange* 26(1): 17–20.

Belanoff, Pat. 1991. "Freewriting: An Aid To Rereading Theorists." In *Nothing Begins With N*, ed. Pat Belanoff, Peter Elbow, Sheryl Fontaine. Carbondale: Southern Illinois University Press.

———. 1991. "Myths of Assessment." *Journal of Basic Writing* 10: 54–66.

———. 1994. *Portfolios.* Blair Resources for Teaching Writing. Englewood Cliffs, N.J.: Prentice Hall-Blair Press.

Belanoff, Pat, and Marcia Dickson, eds. 1991. *Portfolios: Process and Product.* Portsmouth, N.H.: Boynton-Cook.

Belanoff, Pat, and Peter Elbow. 1991. "State University of New York and Stony Brook Portfolio-based Evaluation Program." In *Portfolios: Process and Product,* ed. Pat Belanoff and Marcia Dickson. Portsmouth, N.H.: Boynton/Cook Heinemann.

Berkey, Richard. 1996. Personal interview (10 May).

Berlin, James. 1987. *Rhetoric and Reality.* Carbondale: Southern Illinois University Press.

———. 1988. "Rhetoric and Ideology in the Writing Class." *College English* 50: 477–94.

———. 1993. "Composition Studies and Cultural Studies: Collapsing Boundaries." In *Into the Field: Sites of Composition Studies,* ed. Anne Ruggles Gere, 99–116. New York: Modern Language Association.

Bernard-Donals, Michael. 1991. "Answering and Authoring in the Classroom: Some Bakhtinian Suggestions for the Teaching of Writing Through Literature." *Works and Days* 17 (Spring): 37–46.

———. 1994. "Reading 'Reading My Readers': An Oppositional Response." *College Literature* 21.3 (October): 47–51.

Berthoff, Ann. 1981. *The Making of Meaning: Metaphors, Model and Maxims for Writing Teachers.* Upper Montclair, N.J.: Boynton/Cook.

Bialostosky, Don H. 1991. "Liberal Education, Writing, and the Dialogic Self." In *Contending with Words: Composition and Rhetoric in a Postmodern Age,* ed. Patricia Harkin and John Schilb. New York: Modern Language Association.

Bishop, Wendy. 1989. "Revising the Technical Writing Class: Peer Critiques, Self-Evaluation, and Portfolio Grading." *Technical Writing Teacher* 16(1): 13–25.

Bizzell, Patricia. 1982. "Cognition, Convention and Certainty: What We Need to Know About Writing." *Pre/Text* 3: 213–43.

———. 1986. "Foundationalism and Anti-Foundationalism in Composition Studies." *Pre/Text* 7(1–2): 37–56.

Black, Laurel, Donald Daiker, Jeffrey Sommers, and Gail Stygall, eds. 1994. *New Directions in Portfolio Assessment: Reflective Practice, Critical Theory, and Large-Scale Scoring.* Portsmouth, N.H.: Boynton/Cook Heinemann.

Bloom, Benjamin, ed. 1974. *Taxonomy of Educational Objectives, Handbook I: The Cognitive Domain*. New York: David McKay.

Blumenthal, Sharon. 1994. Personal email (November).

Bogart, Quentin J., and Kathleen M. Kistler. 1987. "California Community College and California State University English Faculty Grading Practices: An Assessment." *Community/Junior College Quarterly* 11(1): 39–45.

Borja, Francisco, and Peter H. Spader. 1985. "AWK: Codes in Grading Essays: Making Essays More 'Objective.'" *College Teaching* 33(3): 113–16.

Bowles, Samuel, and Herbert Gintis. 1976. *Schooling in Capitalist America: Educational Reform and the Conditions of Economic Life*. New York: Basic Books.

Bowman, Joel P., Bernadine P. Branchaw, and Thomas J. Welsh. 1989. "The Application of Behavioral Techniques to Business Communication Instruction." *Journal of Business Communication* 26(4): 323–46.

Brannon, Lil, and C. H. Knoblauch. 1982. "On Students' Rights to Their Own Texts: A Model of Teacher Response." *College Composition and Communication* 33: 157–66.

Branthwaite, Alan, Mark Trueman, and Terry Berrisford. 1981. "Unreliability of Marking: Further Evidence and a Possible Explanation." *Education Review* 33(1): 41–46.

Brodie, James Michael. 1995. "Whatever Happened to the Job Boom?" *Academe* (January–February): 12–15.

Brooke, Robert. 1988. "Underlife and Writing Instruction." *College Composition and Communication* 39: 23–41.

Bruffee, Kenneth A. 1984. "Collaborative Learning and the 'Conversation of Mankind.'" *College English* 46: 635–53.

Buchholz, William J. 1979. "Behavioral Evaluation: The Checkmark Grading System." *College Composition and Communication* 30: 302–5.

Bullock, Richard. 1991. "Autonomy and Community in the Evaluation of Writing." In *The Politics of Writing Instruction: Postsecondary*, ed. Richard Bullock and John Trimbur, 189–202. Portsmouth, N.H.: Boynton/Cook.

Burke, Kenneth. 1969. *A Rhetoric of Motives*. Berkeley: University of California Press.

Burnette, Paul E. 1980. "Staff Grading as an Alternative to Schizophrenia in Composition Class." *English Journal* 69(8): 32–36.

Carini, Patricia. 1994. "Dear Sister Bess. An Essay on Standards, Judgment, and Writing." *Assessing Writing* 1(1): 29–67.

Carini, Patricia F. 1979. *The Art of Seeing and the Visibility of the Person*. Grand Forks: North Dakota Study Group on Evaluation.

Carson, David L., and John B. McTasney. "Grading Technical Reports with the Cassette Tape Recorder: The Results of a Test Program at the United States Air Force Academy." *Journal of Technical Writing and Communication* 3(2): 131–44.

Cazden, Courtney B. 1988. *Classroom Discourse: The Language of Teaching and Learning*. Portsmouth, N.H.: Heinemann.

Cazort, Douglas. 1982. "Advice from a Recent Has-Been to a TA Starting Cold." *Freshman English* News 10(3): 1–4.

CCCC Committee on Assessment. 1995. "Writing Assessment: A Position Statement." *College Composition and Communication* 46(3): 430–37.

Ceccio, Joseph F. 1976. "Checkmark Grading and the Quarter System." *ABCA Bulletin* 39(3): 7–9.

Christenbury, Leila. 1979. "Three Techniques of Student Evaluation." In *How to Handle the Paper Load*, ed. Gene Stanford, 113–18. Urbana, Ill.: National Council of Teachers of English.

Clark, Thomas David. 1981. "Cassette Tapes: An Answer to the Grading Dilemma." *ABCA College* 7(2): 113–18.

———. 1981. "Cassette Tapes: An Answer to the Grading Dilemma." *ABCA Bulletin* 44(2): 40–41.

Collins, Randall. 1971. "Functional and Conflict Theories of Educational Stratification." *American Sociological Review* 36: 1002–19.

Connors, Robert J., and Andrea A. Lunsford. 1993. "Teachers' Rhetorical Comments on Student Papers. *College Composition and Communication* 44: 200–33.

Connors, Robert. 1985. "Mechanical Correctness as a Focus in Composition Instruction." *College Composition and Communication* 36: 61–72.

Cooper, Marilyn M., and Michael Holzman. 1989. *Writing as Social Action*. Portsmouth, N.H.: Boynton/Cook.

Copeland, C. T., and H. M. Rideout. 1901. *Freshman English and Theme-Correcting in Harvard College*. New York: Silver, Burdett.

Courts, Patrick L. and Kathleen McInerney. 1993. *Assessment in Higher Education: Politics, Pedagogy, and Portfolios*. Westport, Conn.: Praeger.

Crystal, Mary Cage. 1996. "Winter Pickets." *The Chronicle of Higher Education* 26 (January): A15.

Daiker, Donald. 1989. "Learning to Praise." In *Writing and Response: Theory, Practice, and Research*, ed. Chris Anson. Urbana, Ill.: National Council of Teachers of English.

de Beauvoir, Simone. 1974. *The Second Sex.* New York: Random House.

Dickson, Marcia. 1991. "The WPA, the Portfolio System, and Academic Freedom." In *Portfolios: Process and Product*, ed. Pat Belanoff and Marcia Dickson, 270–78. Portsmouth, N.H.: Boynton/Cook.

Diederich, Paul. 1965. "Grading and Measuring." In *Improving English Composition*, ed. Arno Jewett, and Charles E. Bish, 81–91. Washington, D.C.: National Education Association.

———. 1974. *Measuring Growth in English.* Urbana, Ill.: National Council of Teachers of English.

Dragga, Sam. 1985. "Praiseworthy Grading." *Journal of Teaching Writing* 4(2): 264–68.

Duke, Charles B. 1980. "An Approach to Revision and Evaluation of Student Writing." Paper presented at the annual meeting of the Conference on College Composition and Communication, Washington, D.C. (March). ERIC, ED 188 167.

Edwards, D. 1982. "Project Marking: Some Problems and Issues." *Teaching at a Distance* 21: 28–34.

Ehrenreich, Barbara. *Fear of Falling: The Inner Life of the Middle Class.* New York: Pantheon.

Elbow, Peter. 1990. *What Is English?* New York: Modern Language Association.

———. 1993. "Ranking, Evaluating, and Liking: Sorting Out Three Forms of Judgment." *College English* 55(2): 187–206.

———. 1993. "Reflections on Academic Discourse: How it Relates to Freshmen and Colleagues." *College English* 53(2): 135–55.

———. 1994. "Will the Virtues of Portfolios Blind Us to Their Potential Dangers?" In *New Directions in Portfolio Assessment: Reflective Practice, Critical Theory, and Large-Scale Scoring*, ed. Laurel Black, Donald Daiker, Jeffrey Sommers, Gail Stygall, 40–55. Portsmouth, N.H.: Boynton/Cook Heinemann.

———. 1995. "Being a Writer vs. Being an Academic: A Conflict in Goals." *College Composition and Communication* 46(1): 72–83.

———. 1997. "Time Outs From Grading and Evaluating While Working in a Conventional System." *Assessing Writing* 4(1): 1–12.

Elbow, Peter, and Pat Belanoff. 1994. *A Community of Writers: A Workshop Course in Writing*, 2nd ed. New York: McGraw-Hill.

Eliot, Charles W. 1930. "President Eliot's Inaugural Address." In *The Development of Harvard University Since the Inauguration of President Eliot, 1869–1929*, ed. Samuel Eliot Morison, lix–lxxxvii. Cambridge, Mass.: Harvard University Press.

Ellman, Neil. 1975. "Peer Evaluation and Peer Grading." *English Journal* 64 (March): 79–80.

———. 1979. "Structuring Peer Evaluation for Greater Student Independence." In *How to Handle the Paper Load*, ed. Gene Stanford, 130–32. Urbana, Ill.: National Council of Teachers of English.

Erenberg, Lewis A. 1981. *Steppin' Out: New York Nightlife and the Transformation of American Culture, 1890–1930*. Westport, Conn.: Greenwood Press.

Evans, Tricia. 1982. "English and Assessment." In *Teaching English*, ed. Tricia Evans. London: Croom Helm.

Faigley, Lester. 1992. *Fragments of Rationality: Postmodernity and the Subject of Composition*. Pittsburgh, Pa.: University of Pittsburgh Press.

Foucault, Michel. 1990. "The Archeology of Knowledge." In *The Rhetorical Tradition*, ed. Patricia Bizzell and Bruce Herzberg. Boston: Bedford.

———. 1979. *Discipline and Punish: The Birth of the Prison*. Trans. Alan Sheridan. New York: Vintage.

Freeman, Caryl P., and Richard A. Hatch. 1975. "A Behavioral Grading System That Works." *ABCA Bulletin* 38(2): 1–9.

Freire, Paulo. 1970. *Pedagogy of the Oppressed*. New York: Seabury Press.

Gage, John T. 1984. "An Adequate Epistemology for Composition: Classical and Modern Perspectives." In *Essays on Classical Rhetoric and Modern Discourse*, ed. Robert J. Connors, Lisa S. Ede, and Andrea A. Lunsford. Carbondale: Southern Illinois University Press.

Gappa, Judith, and David Leslie. 1994. "Education's New Academic Work Force." *Planning for Higher Education* 22: 1–6.

Gardiner, Ellen. 1997. "Peter Elbow and Anti-Foundationalism." In *The Role of Rhetoric in an Anti-Foundationalist World*, ed. Michael Bernard-Donals. New Haven: Yale University Press, forthcoming.

Gentile, Ronald J., and Laura Cox Wainwright. 1994. "The Case for Criterion-Referenced Grading in College-Level Courses for Students with Learning Disabilities." *Research and Teaching in Developmental Education* 11: 63–74.

Giroux, Henry. 1983. *Theory and Resistance in Education: A Pedagogy for the Opposition*. South Hadley, Mass.: Bergin & Garvey.

———. 1992. "The Discourse of Critical Pedagogy." *Cultural Studies*, ed. L. Grossberg, C. Nelson, and P. A. Treichler, 199–212. New York: Routledge.

———. 1994. "Doing Cultural Studies: Youth and the Challenge of Pedagogy." *Harvard Educational Review* 64: 278–307.

Gleason, Barbara. 1994. "Self-Reflection as a Way of Knowing: Phenomenological Investigations in Composition." In *Into the Field*, ed. Ann Ruggles Gere, 60–71. New York: Modern Language Association.

Graff, Gerald. 1992. *Beyond the Culture Wars: How Teaching the Conflicts Can Revitalize American Education*. New York: Norton.

Girard, Rene. 1991. *A Theater of Envy*. New York: Oxford University Press.

Grandgent, Charles H. 1930. "The Modern Languages, 1869–1929." In *The Development of Harvard University Since the Inauguration of President Eliot, 1869–1929*, ed. Samuel Eliot Morison, 65–105. Cambridge, Mass.: Harvard University Press.

Griffin, C. W. 1982. "Theory of Responding to Student Writing: The State of the Art." *College Composition and Communication* 33: 296–301.

Grogan, Nedra, and Donald A. Daiker. 1989. "Team-Grading in College Composition." *Writing Program Administration* 13(1–2): 25–33.

Hairston, Maxine. 1981. "Not All Errors are Created Equal: Nonacademic Readers in the Professions Respond to Lapses in Usage." *College English* 43: 794–806.

Hake, Rosemary L. 1986. "How Do We Judge What They Write?" In *Writing Assessment: Issues and Strategies*, ed. Karen L. Greenberg, Harvey S. Wiener, and R. A. Donovan, 153–67. New York: Longman.

Hake, Rosemary L., and Joseph M. Williams. 1981. "Style and Its Consequences: Do as I Do, Not as I Say." *College English* 43: 433–51.

Hallinan, Maureen T., and Ruy A. Teixeira. 1987. "Opportunities and Constraints: Black-White Differences in the Formation of Interracial Friendships." *Child Development* 58: 1358–71.

Hamp-Lyons, Liz. 1995. "Uncovering Possibilities for a Constructivist Paradigm for Writing Assessment." *College Composition and Communication* 46(3): 446–55.

Hamp-Lyons, Liz, and William Condon. 1993. "Questioning Assumptions about Portfolio-Based Assessment." *College Composition and Communication* 44(2): 176–90.

Hanson, F. Allen. 1993. *Testing Testing: The Social Consequences of the Examined Life*. Berkeley: University of California Press.

Hargis, Charles. 1990. *Grades and Grading Practices*. Springfield, Mass.: Charles C. Thomas.

Harris, Joseph. 1994. "The CCC Review Process." *College Composition and Communication* 45: 303–6.

Harris, Winifred Hall. 1977. "Teacher Response to Student Writing: A Study of the Response Patterns of High School English Teachers to Determine the Basis for

Teacher Judgment of Student Writing." *Research in the Teaching of English* 11: 175–85.

Hartwell, Patrick. 1987. "Creating a Literate Environment in Freshmen English: Why and How." *Rhetoric Review* 6: 4–17.

Haswell, Richard H. 1983. "Minimal Marking." *College English* 45: 600–4.

Haswell, Richard, and Susan Wyche-Smith. 1994. "Adventuring in Writing Assessment." *College Composition and Communication* 45(2): 220–36.

Hays, Janice. 1978. "Play It Again, Sandra: The Use of Tape Cassettes to Evaluate Student Compositions." Paper presented at the annual meeting of the Conference on College Composition and Communication, Denver, Colo. (March–April). ERIC, ED 162 332.

Heath, Shirley Brice. 1983. *Ways With Words: Language, Life, and Work in Communities and Classrooms*. New York: Cambridge University Press.

Herzberg, Bruce. 1991. "Michel Foucault's Rhetorical Theory." In *Contending with Words: Composition and Rhetoric in a Postmodern Age*, ed. Patricia Harkin and John Schilb. New York: Modern Language Association.

Hiatt, Mary P. 1975. "Students at Bay: The Myth of the Conference." *College Composition and Communication* 26: 38–41.

Hill, Adams Sherman. 1892. *The Foundations of Rhetoric*. New York: American Book.

———. 1895. *Principles of Rhetoric*. New York: Harper.

Hillocks, George, Jr. 1986. *Research on Written Composition: New Directions for Teaching*. Urbana, Ill.: ERIC.

Himley, Margaret. 1991. *Shared Territory: Understanding Childrens' Writing as Works*. New York: Oxford University Press.

hooks, bell. 1994. *Teaching to Transgress: Education as the Practice of Freedom*. New York and London: Routledge.

Huot, Brian. 1973. "Reliability, Validity, and Holistic Scoring: What We Know and What We Need." *Illinois English Bulletin* 61(2): 13–20.

———. 1989. "Involving Students in Evaluation." *English Journal* 78(7): 75–77.

———. 1994. "Beyond the Classroom: Using Portfolios to Assess Writing." In *New Directions in Portfolio Assessment: Reflective Practice, Critical Theory, and Large-Scale Scoring*, ed. Laurel Black, Donald Daiker, Jeffrey Sommers, and Gail Stygall 325–33. Portsmouth, N.H.: Boynton/Cook Heinemann.

Hurlbert, C. Mark, and Michal Blitz, ed. 1991. *Composition and Resistance*. Portsmouth, N.H.: Boynton/Cook.

Jago, Carol. 1995. "An Interview with Alfie Kohn." *California English* (Winter): 26–27.

Jobst, Jack. 1984. "Computer-Assisted Grading: The Electronic Handbook." *Journal of Teaching Writing* 3(2): 225–35.

Kean, Patricia. 1994. "Temps Perdus: The Woes of the Part-Time Professoriate." *Lingua Franca* (March/April): 49–53.

Kearns, Edward. 1993. "On the Running Board of the Portfolio Bandwagon." *Writing Program Administrators* 16(3): 50–58.

Kirby, Susan C. 1987. "Self-Evaluation: A Way to Improve Teaching and Learning." *Teaching English in the Two-Year College* 14 (February): 41–46.

Klammer, Enno. 1973. "Cassettes in the Classroom." *College English* 35: 179–80, 189.

Knoblauch, C. H., and Lil Brannon. 1981. "Teacher Commentary on Student Writing: The State of the Art." *Freshman English News* 10(2): 1–4.

———. 1990. "Teacher Commentary on Student Writing: The State of the Know." *College Composition and Communication* 41(2): 201–13.

Kohn, Alfie. 1993. *Punished By Rewards*. New York: Houghton Mifflin.

Kutz, Eleanor, and Hephzibah Roskelly. 1991. *An Unquiet Pedagogy: Transforming Practice in the English Classroom*. Portsmouth, N.H.: Boynton/Cook.

Lakoff, George, and Mark Johnson. 1980. *Metaphors We Live By*. Chicago: University of Chicago Press.

Lamberg, Walter. 1980. "Self-provided and Peer-provided Feedback." *College Composition and Communication* 31: 63–69.

Larson, Richard L. 1986. "Making Assignments, Judging Writing, and Annotating Papers: Some Suggestions." In *Training the New Teacher of College Composition*, ed. Charles W. Bridges, 109–16. Urbana, Ill.: National Council of Teachers of English.

Lees, Elaine O. 1979. "Evaluating Student Writing." *College Composition and Communication* 30: 370–74.

Lotto, Edward, and Bruce Smith. 1979. "Making Grading Work." *College English* 41: 423–31.

Lounsbury, Thomas R. 1911. "Compulsory Composition in Colleges." *Harper's* 123: 866–80.

Lucas, Catharine. 1992. "Introduction: Writing Portfolios—Changes and Challenges." In *Portfolios in the Writing Classroom: An Introduction*, ed. Kathleen Blake Yancey, 1–11. Urbana, Ill.: National Council of Teachers of English.

Lynch, Denise. 1982. "Easing the Process: A Strategy for Evaluating Compositions." *College Composition and Communication* 33(3): 310–14.

Mack, Nancy, and James Thomas Zebroski. 1991. "Transforming Composition: A Question of Privilege." In *Composition and Resistance*, ed. Michael Blitz and C. Mark Hurlbert, 154–64. Portsmouth, N.H.: Boynton/Cook.

MacLeod, Jay. 1987. *Ain't No Makin' It: Leveled Aspirations in a Low-Income Neighborhood*. Boulder, Colo.: Westview Press.

Marling, William. 1984. "Grading Essays on a Microcomputer." *College English* 46: 797–810.

Maylath, Bruce A. R. 1994. "Words Make a Difference: Effects of Greco-Latinate and Anglo-Saxon Lexical Variation on Post-secondary-level Writing Assessment in English" Ph.D. diss., University of Minnesota, 1994. Abstract in *Dissertation Abstracts International* 55: 2807.

———. 1996. "Words Make a Difference: The Effects of Greco-Latinate and Anglo-Saxon Lexical Variation on College Writing Instructors." *Research in the Teaching of English* 30: 220–47.

McClelland, D. C. 1973. "Testing for Competence Rather than for Intelligence." *American Psychologist* 28: 1–14.

McColly, William. 1970. "What Does Educational Research Say about the Judging of Writing Ability? *Journal of Educational Research* 64(4): 148–56.

McDonald, W. U., Jr. 1975. "Grading Student Writing: A Plea for Change." *College Composition and Communication* 26: 154–58.

Merriam, Melinda. 1996. "Implementing Portfolios: Why Grades Can Go Up." Unpublished essay.

Milton, Ohmer. 1972. *Alternatives to the Traditional: How Professors Teach and How Students Learn*. San Francisco: Jossey-Bass.

Milton, Ohmer, Howard R. Pollio, and James A. Eison. 1986. *Making Sense of College Grades*. San Francisco: Jossey-Bass.

Myers, Greg. 1986. "Reality, Consensus, and Reform in the Rhetoric of Composition Teaching." *College English* 48(2): 154–73.

Myers, Miles, and P. David Pearson. 1996. "Performance Assessment and the Literacy Unit of the New Standards Project." *Assessing Writing* 3(1): 5–29.

Miller, Susan. 1991. *Textual Carnivals*. Carbondale: Southern Illinois University Press.

Nash, Charles C. 1981. "The Cottey Grade and Comment Sheet." *Teaching English in the Two-Year College* 7(2): 113–18.

Nieto, Sonia. 1994. "Lessons from Students on Creating a Chance to Dream," Harvard Educational Review 64: 392–426.

Nystrand, M., and D. Brandt. 1989. "Response to Writing as a Context for Learning to Write." In *Writing and Response: Theory, Practice, and Research*, ed. Chris M. Anson. Urbana, Ill.: National Council of Teachers of English.

Odell, Lee, and Charles R. Cooper. 1980. "Procedures for Evaluating Writing: Assumptions and Needed Research." *College English* 42: 35–43.

Orwell, George. 1950. *Shooting an Elephant and Other Essays*. London: Seckler and Warburg.

Pasternack, Steve R. 1981. "Properly Motivated, Students Become Good Peer Graders." *Journalism Educator* 36(3): 17–18.

Peckham, Irvin. n.d. "Beyond Grades." *Composition Studies/Freshman English News* 21(2): 16–31.

Peek, George S. 1982. "Grading by Jury: Accurate and Consistent." *Improving College and University Teaching* 30(2): 75–79.

Phelps, Louise Wetherbee. 1989. "Images of Student Writing: The Deep Structure of Teacher Response." In *Writing and Response: Theory, Practice, and Research*, ed. Chris M. Anson, 37–67. Urbana, Ill.: National Council of Teachers of English.

Proffitt, Edward. 1977. "Grading and Student Choice." *Freshman English News* 6(2): 1–2.

Purves, Alan C. 1992. "Reflections on Research and Assessment in Written Composition." *Research in the Teaching of English* 26: 108–22.

Raymond, James C. 1976. "Cross-Grading: An Experiment in Evaluating Compositions." *College Composition and Communication* 27: 52–55.

Rentz, Kathryn C. 1985. "Some Discouraging Words about Checkmark Grading." *Bulletin of the Association for Business Communication* 48(2): 20–23.

Rigsby, Leo C. 1987. "Changes in Students' Writing and Their Significance." Atlanta, Ga.: Conference on College Composition and Communication.

Rorty, Richard. 1979. *Philosophy and the Mirror of Nature*. Princeton, N.J.: Princeton University Press.

Rose, Mike. 1989. *Lives on the Boundary: The Struggles and Achievement of America's Underprepared*. New York: Free Press.

Rubens, Philip M. 1982. "Oral Grading Techniques: An Interactive System for the Technical Writing Classroom." *Technical Writing Teacher* 10(1): 41–44.

Rudolph, Frederick. 1981. *Curriculum: A History of the American Undergraduate Course of Study Since 1636*. San Francisco: Jossey-Bass.

Rushing, S. Kittrell. 1987. "Grading on Disk Works Well for Teacher and Class." *Journalism Educator* 42(3): 37–39.

Rycik, Jim. 1994. "Guidelines and Cautions About the Use of Portfolios." *Ohio Reading Teacher* 29(1): 25–28.

Sadler, Myra, and David Sadler. 1995. *Failing at Fairness: How Our Schools Cheat Girls*. New York: Touchstone (Simon and Schuster).

Sawyer, Thomas M. 1975. "Accountability: Or Let Others Grade Your Students." *College Composition and Communication* 26: 335–40.

Scannell, Dale P., and Jon C. Marshall. 1966. "The Effect of Selected Composition Errors on Grades Assigned to Essay Examinations." *American Educational Research Journal* 3: 125–30.

Schuster, Charles I. 1994. "Climbing the Slippery Slope of Assessment: The Programmatic Use of Writing Portfolios." In *New Directions in Portfolio Assessment: Reflective Practice, Critical Theory, and Large-Scale Scoring*, ed. Laural Black, Donald Daiker, Jeffrey Sommers, and Gail Stygall, 314–23. Portsmouth, N.H.: Boynton/Cook Heinemann.

Schwegler, Robert A. 1991. "The Politics of Reading Student Papers." In *The Politics of Writing Instruction: Postsecondary*, ed. Richard Bullock and John Trimbur, 203–25. Portsmouth, N.H.: Boynton/Cook.

Selfe, Cynthia L. n.d. "Using Groups to Pre-Evaluate Papers in the Technical Writing Classroom." ERIC, ED 226 369.

Shanker, Albert. 1995. "Where We Stand: Raising the Bar" (advertisement). *The New Republic* 5 (June): 17.

Shor, Ira. 1992. *Empowering Education: Critical Thinking for Social Change*. Chicago: University of Chicago Press.

Shotter, John. 1993. *The Cultural Politics of Everyday Life*. Toronto: University of Toronto Press.

Sims, Gerald K. 1989. "Student Peer Review in the Classroom: A Teaching and Grading Tool." *Journal of Agronomic Education* 18(2): 105–8.

Sirc, Geoffrey. 1989. "Response in the Electronic Medium." In *Writing and Response: Theory, Practice, and Research*, ed. Chris Anson, 187–205. Urbana, Ill.: National Council of Teachers of English.

Slater, John Rothwell. 1913/1922 repr. *Freshman Rhetoric*. Boston: D. C. Heath.

Smallwood, Mary Lovett. 1935. *An Historical Study of Examinations and Grading Systems in Early American Universities*. Cambridge, Mass.: Harvard University Press.

Smit, David W. 1994. "A WPA's Nightmare: Reflections on Using Portfolios as a Course Exit Exam." In *New Directions in Portfolio Assessment: Reflective Prac-*

tice, Critical Theory, and Large-Scale Scoring, ed. Laurel Black, Donald Daiker, Jeffrey Sommers, and Gail Stygall, 303–13. Portsmouth, N.H.: Boynton/Cook Heinemann.

Smith, Cherryl Armstrong. 1991. "Writing Without Testing." In *Portfolios: Process and Product*, ed. Pat Belanoff and Marcia Dickson. Portsmouth, N.H.: Boynton/Cook Heinemann.

Sommer, Barbara. 1994. "Recognizing Academe's Other Faculty." *Planning for Higher Education* 22: 7–10.

Sommers, Jeffrey. 1991. "Bringing Practice in Line with Theory: Using Portfolio Grading in the Composition Classroom." In *Portfolios: Process and Product*, ed. Pat Belanoff and Marcia Dickson, 153–64. Portsmouth, N.H.: Boynton/Cook Heinemann.

———. 1995. Personal correspondence (15 September).

Sorenson, Ritch L., Grant T. Savage, and Larry D. Hartman. 1993. "Motivating Students to Improve Business Writing: A Comparison between Goal-Based and Punishment-Based Grading Systems." *Journal of Business Communication* 30(2): 113–32.

Sperling, Melanie. 1994. "Constructing the Perspective of Teacher-as-Reader: A Framework for Studying Response to Student Writing." *Research in the Teaching of English* 28: 175–207.

Stewart, Donald C. 1984. "The Continuing Relevance of Plato's Phaedrus." In *Essays on Classical Rhetoric and Modern Discourse*, ed. Robert J. Connors, Lisa S. Ede, and Andrea A. Lunsford. Carbondale: Southern Illinois University Press.

Strunk, William, Jr., and E. B. White. 1979. *The Elements of Style*. 3rd ed. New York: Macmillan.

Taylor, Denny. 1990. "Teaching without Testing: Assessing the Complexity of Children's Literacy Learning." *English Education* 22: 4–74.

Throop, David P., and Daphne A. Jameson. 1976. "Behavioral Grading: An Approach Worth Trying." *ABCA Bulletin* 39(3): 3–5.

Tieje, R. E., E. G. Sutcliffe, H. N. Hillebrand, and W. Buchen. 1915. "Systematizing Grading in Freshman Composition at the Large University." *English Journal* (4): 586–97.

Tobin, Lad. 1993. *Writing Relationships: What Really Happens in the Composition Class*. Portsmouth, N.H.: Boynton/Cook Heinemann.

Trimbur, John. 1991. "Literacy and the Discourse of Crisis." In *The Politics of Writing Instruction: Postsecondary*, ed. Richard Bullock and John Trimbur, 277–95. Portsmouth, N.H.: Boynton/Cook.

Tritt, Michael. 1983. "Exchange Grading with a Workshop Approach to the Teaching of Writing." *English Quarterly* 16(1): 16–19.

Uchmanowicz, Pauline. 1995. "The $5,000–$25,000 Exchange." *College English* 57(4): 426–47.

University of California, Academic Senate. 1938. "A Plan for the Co-operation of the Departments of the University in Securing Correct and Effective English Expression in Oral and Written Exercises." 1916. Lois Whitfield Johnson. "Evolution of the Examination in Subject A at the University of California." Diss. University of California: 342–45.

U.S. Department of Education. 1996. *The New College Course Map and Transcript Files: Changes in Course-Taking and Achievement, 1972–1993*. Washington, D.C.: U.S. Department of Education, Office of Educational Research and Improvement.

Veysey. Laurence R. 1965. *The Emergence of the American University*. Chicago: University of Chicago Press.

Weaver, R. H., and H. W. Cotrell. 1987. "Lecturing: Essential Communication Strategies." In *Teaching Large Classes Well*, ed. Maryellen Gleason Weimer, pp. 57–70. San Fransisco: Jossey-Bass.

Weeks, Francis W. 1978. "The Meaning of Grades." In *The Teaching of Business Communication*, ed. George H. Douglas, 163–66. Champaign, Ill.: American Business Communication Association.

West, Cornel. 1993. "The New Cultural Politics of Difference." In *The Cultural Studies Reader*, ed. Simon During, 203–17. London and New York: Routledge.

White, Edward M. 1988. *Teaching and Assessing Writing*. San Francisco: Jossey-Bass.

———. 1992. *Assigning, Responding, Evaluating*. 2nd ed. New York: St. Martin's Press.

Wiebe, Robert. 1967. *The Search for Order, 1877–1920*. New York: Hill & Wang.

Weiser, Irwin. 1992. "Portfolio Practice and Assessment for Collegiate Basic Writers." In *Portfolios in the Writing Classroom: An Introduction*, ed. Kathleen Blake Yancey, 89–101. Urbana, Ill.: National Council of Teachers of English.

Why Man Creates. 1968. Saul Bass and Associates. Pyramid Films (25 min.).

Wiggins, Grant. 1993. *Assessing Student Performance: Exploring the Purpose and Limits of Testing*. San Francisco: Jossey-Bass.

Willis, Paul. 1977. *Learning to Labour: How Working Class Kids Get Working Class Jobs*. New York: Columbia University Press.

Yarbro, Richard, and Betty Angevine. 1982. "A Comparison of Traditional and Cassette Tape English Composition Grading Methods." *Research in the Teaching of English* 16(4): 394–96.

Younglove, William. 1983. "A Look at Behavioristic Measurement of English Composition in the United States Public Schools, 1901–1941." ERIC.

Zak, Frances. 1990. "Exclusively Positive Responses to Student Writing." *Journal of Basic Writing* 9: 40–53.

Zavarzadeh, Mas'ud. 1994. "The Pedagogy of Pleasure 2: The Me-in-Crisis" and "Reading My Readers." *College Literature* 21 (3): 6–14, 19–33.

———. 1992. "Theory as Resistance." In *Pedagogy Is Politics: Literary Theory and Critical Teaching*, ed. Maria-Regina Kecht, 25–47. Urbana and Chicago: University of Illinois Press.

Zavarzadeh, Mas'ud, and Donald Morton. 1991. "Theory Pedagogy Politics: The Crisis of 'The Subject' in the Humanities." In *Theory / Pedagogy / Politics: Texts for Change*, ed. Mas'ud Zavarzadeh and Donald Morton, 1–32. Urbana: University of Illinois Press.

Zimbler, Linda J. 1994. "Faculty and Instructional Staff: Who Are They and What Do They Do?" *National Center for Education Statistics Survey Report*. U.S. Department of Education, Office of Educational Research and Improvement (October). ERIC, ED 375792.

Ziv, Nina D. 1984. "The Effect of Teacher Comments on the Writing of Four College Freshmen." In *New Directions in Composition Research*, ed. Richard Beach and Lillian S. Bridwell, 362–80. New York: Guilford.

Zizek, Slavoj. 1989. *The Sublime Object of Ideology*. London: Verso.

About the Contributors

PAT BELANOFF, director of the writing programs at the State University of New York, Stony Brook, is coauthor (with Peter Elbow) of *A Community of Writers* and (with Betsy Rorschach and Mia Rakijas) of *The Right Handbook*. Belanoff, who is president of the State University of New York Writing Council, has also published studies of the women of Old English literature. She is currently chair of the Conference on College Composition and Communication (CCCC) Assessment Committee.

MICHAEL BERNARD-DONALS teaches rhetorical and critical theory at the University of Missouri, Columbia. He is the author of *Mikhail Bakhtin: Between Phenomenology and Marxism* and articles on rhetoric, the teaching of writing and theory, and contemporary culture. His article, "Mikhail Bakhtin: Between Phenomenology and Marxism," appeared in the February 1994 edition of *College English*.

RICHARD BOYD teaches at San Diego State University, Department of Rhetoric and Writing Studies. He has published essays in *Rhetoric Review* and *Journal of Advanced Composition* and has recently completed a manuscript tracing the operation of mimetic desire in the current traditional classroom.

NICK CARBONE is completing his Ph.D. in composition and rhetoric at the University of Massachusetts at Amherst, and is currently teaching at Marlboro College in Vermont. He has previously published in *Computers and Composition*.

MARGARET DAISLEY is a Ph.D. candidate in composition and rhetoric in the English Department at the University of Massachusetts, Amherst. She has taught composition in the University of Massachusetts' Writing Program and at Springfield College. In addition, she has been co-presenter in several writing workshops on her own campus, as well as at the University of New

Hampshire, Bard College, and the CCCC. She has published three articles in *Computers and Composition* and presented papers at the CCCC, National Council of Teachers of English, and computers-and-writing conferences.

ANGUS DUNSTAN is associate professor of English at California State University, Sacramento, where he teaches courses in children's literature, language acquisition, and composition.

PETER ELBOW is professor of English and director of the writing program at the University of Massachusetts, Amherst. He is author of *Writing Without Teachers*, *Writing With Power*, *Embracing Contraries*, and *What is English?* With Pat Belanoff, he is author of the writing textbooks, *A Community of Writers* and *Sharing and Responding*. He edited *Voice and Writing*.

BRIAN HUOT is an associate professor of English at the University of Louisville, where he teaches graduate and undergraduate courses in composition theory and practice. He has published essays on assessing student writing in *College Composition and Communication*, *Review of Educational Research*, and other journals devoted to writing and education. He has also contributed to various anthologies on assessment, including the recent *New Directions in Portfolio Assessment* and co-edits, with Kathleen Blake Yancey, *Assessing Writing*, the only journal devoted solely to writing assessment.

TAMMY R. JONES is an instructor in the Department of English at the University of Memphis. She is director of undergraduate advising in English.

BRUCE MAYLATH is an assistant professor of English at the University of Memphis, where he teaches technical communication. Much of his research focuses on language history, lexical patterns, assessment, and translation issues. His scholarly work includes chapters in *Language in Science and Humanities*, *Academic Literacies in Multicultural Higher Education* and, with Chris Anson, *Teacher as Writer*, as well as articles in professional journals.

MAUREEN NEAL is an assistant professor of English at Mesa State College in Grand Junction, Colorado, where she teachers composition and literature. She has presented papers at the CCCC, the Miami Conference on the Teaching of Writing, and the Penn State Conference on Composition and Rhetoric. She has published articles on composition theory and English education and is pursuing research interests in discourse analysis, sociolinguistic approaches to composition studies and hyperfluency.

IRENE PAPOULIS teaches at Trinity College in Hartford, Connecticut, and is an associate of the Institute for Writing and Thinking at Bard College in

New York. She is the author of chapters in *Into the Field: Sites of Composition Studies* and in *Writing Ourselves in the Story: Unheard Voices From Composition Studies.* She has published articles in *English Education* (with Cherryl Smith), *Freshman English News*, and other journals.

CHERRYL SMITH is associate professor of English at California State University, Sacramento. She publishes poetry as well as work in composition, and teaches courses in both fields. She is author (with Sheryl I. Fontaine) of *A College Writer's Choice: Using Your Creative and Cultural Resources for Academic Writing* (Harcourt Brace, forthcoming).

BRUCE W. SPECK is acting director of the Center for Academic Excellence at the University of Memphis. His publications include three annotated bibliographies: *Editing*, *Peer Review*, and *Managing* and *Publication Process*, all published by Greenwood Press. In addition, he has published chapters in *Rhetorical Designs for Professional* and *Technical Writers*, *The Politics and Processes of Scholarly Publishing*, and *Approaches to Teaching Non-Native English Speakers Across the Curriculum.* His annotated bibliography on the grading of writing was expected to be published by Greenwood Press in 1997.

PAULINE UCHMANOWICZ, after working for over a decade in a series of part-time and temporary positions, is currently a tenure track assistant professor at the State University of New York, New Paltz, where she teaches cultural studies. She has delivered papers addressing the interconnectness of rhetoric, composition, and cultural studies at national conferences, including the Modern Language Association and the CCCC. Her article on the politics of part-time college teaching recently appeared in *College English*. She has published poetry in several literary journals, including *The Massachusetts Review*, *New American Writing*, *Ohio Review*, and *Mudfish* and she is currently co-editing, with Richard Marback, *Personal, Professional, Public: Faces of Composition Studies*, a collection of essays on identity politics within English studies.

STEVEN VANDERSTAAY has taught in an inner-city high school and a small, rural school district on the Iowa prairie. His publications include *Street Lives: An Oral History of Homeless Americans*, as well as essays and articles on teaching, literacy, and social theory. An assistant professor of English at Western Washington University, he teaches courses in English methods, language, and creative nonfiction.

CHRISTOPHER C. WEAVER is an assistant professor of English at the University of Alaska Southeast, Juneau. His involvement in assessment projects has included coordinating a grant to implement a Writing-Across-the-Curriculum program, involvement in portfolio assessment committees on both the department and university-wide levels, and participation in PORTNET, an ongoing study on outside evaluation of portfolios.

KATHLEEN BLAKE YANCEY is an assistant professor of English at the University of North Carolina, Charlotte. She has edited two collections of essays: *Portfolios in the Classroom: An Introduction* and *Voices on Voice: Perspectives, Definitions, Inquiry*. With Brian Huot, she cofounded and coedits the journal, *Assessing Writing*.

FRANCES ZAK is associate director of the writing programs at the State University of New York, Stony Brook, where she has served on the writing faculty since 1984 and teaches undergraduate and graduate courses. She has conducted workshops in response for faculty and graduate students, and has presented numerous conference papers on her research in response and the relationship between response, evaluation, and grading. Her article, "Exclusively Positive Responding to Student Writing," was published in the *Journal of Basic Writing*.

Index